Paul Brighton is Executive Principal Lecturer and Head of the Department of Media and Film at the University of Wolverhampton. He was previously a journalist and worked for BBC Radio 4 and BBC News 24.

'A lively and engaging read…comprehensive and thorough.'

Angus Hawkins, Professor of Modern British History,
University of Oxford and author of *Victorian Political Culture*

ORIGINAL
SPIN

DOWNING STREET
AND THE PRESS IN
VICTORIAN BRITAIN

PAUL BRIGHTON

I.B. TAURIS
LONDON · NEW YORK

Published in 2016 by
I.B.Tauris & Co. Ltd
London • New York
www.ibtauris.com

ISBN: 978 1 78076 059 9
eISBN: 978 0 85772 887 6

A full CIP record for this book is available from the British Library
A full CIP record is available from the Library of Congress

Library of Congress Catalog Card Number: available

Typeset in Perpetua by 4word Ltd, Bristol
Printed and bound by CPI Group (UK) Ltd, Croydon, CR0 4YY

MIX
Paper from
responsible sources
FSC
www.fsc.org   FSC® C013604

TABLE OF CONTENTS

TO MY MOTHER AND IN MEMORY OF MY FATHER

In the writing of this book I am indebted to many people. In thanking the few I would especially like to thank Stephen Jacobs, Emma Edwards, Aidan Byrne and Frances Pheasant-Kelly. Their efforts enhanced the book and without them it would not have been possible for it to be produced in the short-time scale. In no particular order, I would also like to thank Eleanor Andrews, Dorothy Hobson, Lee and Sara Kenny, Sally Parker, Pat Wood, Paul Henderson and Carol Foster. A special 'THANK YOU' to my family and two very special cousins, Derek Thom and Janice Williams, not forgetting my best friend, my mother, always there when needed. Finally may I express my warmest and grateful thanks to my publishers, in particular Joanna Godfrey.

ILLUSTRATIONS

1. William Pitt, studio of John Hoppner, c.1805.
2. Robert Jenkinson, 2nd Earl of Liverpool, by Sir George Hayter, 1823. © National Portrait Gallery, London.
3. Arthur Wellesley, 1st Duke of Wellington, by William Salter, 1839. © National Portrait Gallery, London.
4. Charles Grey, 2nd Earl Grey, after Sir Thomas Lawrence, c.1828. © National Portrait Gallery, London.
5. William Lamb, 2nd Viscount Melbourne, by Sir Edwin Henry Landseer, 1836. © National Portrait Gallery, London.
6. Sir Robert Peel, 2nd Bt, by John Linnell, 1838. © National Portrait Gallery, London.
7. John Russell, 1st Earl Russell, by Sir Francis Grant, 1853. © National Portrait Gallery, London.
8. Edward Stanley, 14th Earl of Derby, by Frederick Richard Say, 1844. © National Portrait Gallery, London.
9. George Hamilton Gordon, 4th Earl of Aberdeen, by John Partridge, c.1847. © National Portrait Gallery, London.
10. Henry John Temple, 3rd Viscount Palmerston, by Francis Cruikshank, c.1855–59. © National Portrait Gallery, London.
11. Benjamin Disraeli, Earl of Beaconsfield, by Sir John Everett Millais, 1st Bt, 1881. © National Portrait Gallery, London.
12. William Ewart Gladstone, by Sir John Everett Millais, 1st Bt, 1879. © National Portrait Gallery, London.
13. Robert Arthur Talbot Gascoyne-Cecil, 3rd Marquess of Salisbury, by Sir John Everett Millais, 1st Bt, 1883. © National Portrait Gallery, London.
14. Archibald Philip Primrose, 5th Earl of Rosebery, by Elliott & Fry. © National Portrait Gallery, London.

INTRODUCTION

O N 20 NOVEMBER 1911, the newly elected Conservative leader Andrew Bonar Law wrote to the influential editor of *The Observer*, J.L. Garvin, to thank him for recent comments. Bonar Law mentioned, however, that he was writing '... for the last time I am afraid for I shall not be able to do so in the future'.[1] The implication – the commonplace nature of which can be seen in the fact that it did not need to be made explicit to be understood by Garvin – was that close and regular contacts between politicians and journalists, while acceptable in some circumstances, were not to be thought of once that politician became a party leader and Leader of the Opposition, still less if he actually reached Number 10 itself.

However, Garvin had spent much of the previous few years in very close and regular contact with the private secretary of Bonar Law's predecessor, the former Prime Minister Arthur Balfour; and, indeed, had corresponded directly, often at some length and in great policy detail, with Balfour himself on a number of occasions: all this with a politician who professed never to read newspapers and to be entirely indifferent to their views and contents.

Nevertheless, Bonar Law's view seems to have taken something of a hold – at least among the broader media community, if not among professional historians of the period. Existing accounts of prime ministers and the press and media start either after World War II[2] or, at the earliest, with Lloyd George during and after World War I.[3]

However, over half a century earlier, John Lalor, the editor of the *Morning Chronicle,* wrote:

> Lord Palmerston hurried forward to grasp my hand, assured me that he was amazed at the knowledge and insight my articles displayed, was proud to know me, and so forth; BUT there were just two or three points on which he ventured to think I was mistaken... He so overwhelmed me...

with his winning courtesy that I felt myself getting involved. I got away as soon as I could, and vowed in my own mind that I would accept no more invitations to a tete-a-tete with the Secretary of State whose policy I had to review. [4]

This occurred after Palmerston, then Foreign Secretary, had approached the paper's proprietor, John Easthope, asking him to persuade the editor to visit him for a private briefing on his Portugal policy.

On another occasion, Palmerston delivered a speech to two personal friends and three 'sessional' (the nineteenth-century equivalent of freelance) journalists in a hotel room purely for the convenience of the 'sessionals', who had been thwarted in their pursuit of a story in the form of an electioneering speech by Palmerston in his Tiverton constituency.

* * *

But it was not just Palmerston. Almost all major nineteenth-century political figures had dealings with the press – including those who professed utter indifference and contempt towards it. George Canning ran and edited a periodical (the *Anti Jacobin*) before he became Prime Minister. Among his occasional contributors were believed to have been his friend Robert Jenkinson, the future prime minister (as Lord Liverpool); Lord Grenville, another future prime minister; and the current holder of the office, William Pitt the Younger (though his contributions were sometimes delayed by his other responsibilities). Liverpool, as a young foreign secretary, may well have written anonymously for *The Times*. Meanwhile, yet another future prime minister, Lord Melbourne, then a young man called William Lamb, contributed to the *Morning Chronicle* in the opposing cause. A serious Robert Peel and a noisier young Lord Palmerston contributed light-hearted squibs to *The Courier*.

The apparently Olympian Lord Salisbury (Balfour's uncle) was the Victorian equivalent of a freelance journalist in his early years, after his father's disapproval of his marriage left him rather more impecunious than was normal for a marquess's son. In the days before paid MPs, his articles for the *Quarterly Review* were a welcome source of income. Disraeli was involved in running a newspaper, *The Representative*, in the 1820s – a doomed venture, for which he was anxious to disclaim all responsibility when he became a leading politician.

Gladstone, as well as being a prolific contributor to journals and periodicals, was also far more attuned to the demands of the press – both operationally and in terms of public opinion – than his somewhat austere exterior might imply. Indeed, like Palmerston, he was fully alive to the potential for harnessing public opinion and converting it into popular and electoral support by adroit use of the press, harnessed to novel methods of political campaigning.

Prime ministers who are often regarded as uninterested in, or even contemptuous or oblivious of, the press in reality had much more nuanced and pragmatic private views. Lord Derby's earlier relative lack of involvement changed as his career evolved, to the extent that he was happy to seek credit for his hard work in securing press support for reform during his third and final premiership. Indeed, his lack of involvement was always overstated: Derby happily contributed to a political pamphlet promoting the Grey government and his own role in its abolition of slavery in the early 1830s. The Duke of Wellington's numerous disparaging remarks about the press are less often balanced by his later expressions of regret for not recognizing its power and influence, and for not taking sufficient pains to win it over. Lord John Russell, often viewed as completely indifferent or even hostile, eventually realized that, in order to win his internal battles with Palmerston, he too would need to cultivate, and possibly even ally with, sections of the press.

Almost every Victorian prime minister came to be closely associated with individual newspapers. On occasion – as demonstrated by the case of Lord Aberdeen and John Delane, editor of *The Times* – individual journalists and editors became very close allies and occasional co-adjutors of a particular premier. Aberdeen was accused of writing or inspiring articles in Delane's *Times* attacking Palmerston and his foreign policy. Earlier, he was similarly suspected of writing for the pro-government *Courier* when Wellington was prime minister.

Several prime ministers also came into contact with the somewhat murky world of the 'subsidized' press in Ireland. (At this stage, it was common for governments to provide funding for friendly newspapers well-disposed towards them, which might not otherwise be commercially viable). Wellington, Peel, Melbourne and Derby all experienced the moral and political compromises inherent in this strange sphere on the margins of politics, journalism and espionage. Not for the faint-hearted, and rarely referred to in public discourse at the time, it nevertheless remained a part of the uneasy balance between the two islands.

* * *

In the late twentieth and early twenty-first centuries, it would be regarded as at best an eccentricity and at worst an outright lie for a senior political figure to claim that he or she paid no attention to the press and the wider media. It would also be regarded as evidence, in the unlikely event that it was true, of a lamentable failure to address a crucial part of the job.

In earlier times, however, it was almost a necessary rhetorical trope for prime ministers – and, for that matter, aspiring prime ministers – to profess complete indifference to the press and its works. It was simply not part of the code of acceptable political conduct for senior political figures to acknowledge so much as an awareness of the press in their public comments. In just about every case, however, the relationship between government and press was much more complicated than this apparent lofty unawareness suggested.

Various euphemisms for press management were employed. Of course, no one talked of 'spin' in the nineteenth century – at least not in the context of the press. To be accused of 'managing' the press would usually be to be charged with something a little discreditable, despite the almost universal nature of such practices. In the eighteenth century, and into the early nineteenth, direct press subsidies (hardly different from the type employed in Ireland) were almost an official function of government – to ensure at least some press support even when the going was rough. It was often colloquially referred to as 'nobbling' the press. Indeed, by the late nineteenth and early twentieth centuries, even some admirals and generals could teach the politicians a trick or two when it came to mobilizing the press on behalf of themselves and their policies. As Sir Garnet (later Lord) Wolseley put it in a letter to Lord Minto: 'The Press has become a power which a man should try to manage for himself'.[5]

Reading the biographies (and, in a few cases, autobiographies) of the statesmen of this era, it is striking to observe how relatively little there is about their press engagement in books written during or soon after their lives. It is likely that this is not something either they or their surviving relatives wished to see highlighted. In part this was a reflection of the social standing of journalists and journalism. Although the social status of journalists did rise during the nineteenth century, and proprietors started to receive honours, there was still a perceived social gulf between a senior political figure and a newspaper editor – still more between a politician and a working journalist. When Alfred Harmsworth, later Lord Northcliffe, sent a journalist from his paper *Answers* to interview Mr Gladstone, it might have seemed a hopeless errand for the so-called 'Mr Answers' to seek such an illustrious prey were it not for the fact that 'Mr Answers' was in fact a peer of the realm.

Press management – engaging in a relationship with members of the press and seeking to influence one's portrayal and hence public support – was also likely to have been underplayed because it was important to be perceived as a 'statesman' rather than as a politician. Subconsciously, perhaps, there was a feeling that a mere politician might, at a push, be revealed to be involved with the press, but statesmen had their minds on loftier matters.

Yet it is striking how many of the early biographies of these statesmen were written by journalists. Monypenny and Buckle, Disraeli's official biographers, were both senior *Times* journalists and Buckle served as the editor from 1884 to 1912. John Morley, although by then a politician, had edited the *Pall Mall Gazette* and the *Fortnightly Review* before undertaking his *Life of Gladstone*. J.A. Spender, of the *Westminster Gazette*, respectively wrote and co-wrote the official lives of Campbell-Bannerman and Asquith. A.G. Gardiner of the *Daily News* wrote the life of the Liberal leader Sir William Harcourt, himself a journalist in his youth. These were all authorized biographers, acting with the support of the subject's family or estate. Other journalists also wrote unofficial political biographies: T.E. Kebbel of Lord Derby and Disraeli, for example, and Justin McCarthy of Gladstone. However, little is said in these volumes of their subjects' use of, or relations with, the press.

This was not, presumably, from any lack of interest on the authors' part in their own profession. Histories of the press and journalism started appearing as early as the 1850s, and with some regularity thereafter.[6] The omission of any detailed reference to politicians' practices of press management may, instead, have resulted from a feeling that the topic was not seemly in a respectful and largely laudatory 'tombstone' biography. By contrast, many of the lively reminiscences of journalists from the period do give us fascinating anecdotal evidence of direct contacts of the sort we have already seen Lord Palmerston conducting.

The relative social positions of the journalist and the politician throughout the whole of this period and beyond were such, therefore, that one is more likely to find a journalist proudly reciting his close contacts with a Cabinet minister or party leader than vice versa. In the early nineteenth century, as in the eighteenth, editors as well as writing journalists were largely anonymous figures, and the distinction between owners/proprietors and editors much looser than it later became. Even Thomas Barnes, the first editor of *The Times* to stand out as a clear and defined personality in the pages of history, was almost completely unknown to his readers and the rest of the public during his time in the job. There were, of course, many famous names working in journalism of various kinds. Some of the early press histories often read like an account of famous literary figures earning pin money or attempting to start their careers 'at the bottom'. Defoe, Swift, Richard Steele, Addison, Fielding, Johnson, Smollett, Coleridge, Charles Lamb and Dickens are all paraded for us in the pages of these histories, implying what could almost be termed a plea for respectability on the part of the press by indicating that, if such great authors could muddy their hands with newsprint, it was good enough for everyone else. 'If it was good enough for them…' runs the subtext of some of the early accounts of the birth and growth of newspapers.

So, to find out the real extent of the contact between prime ministers and the press, one is always operating – at least to an extent – in an arena and within the rhetoric of concealment. Even Lord Palmerston himself, undoubtedly the most assiduous, and one of the ablest, of the prime ministerial media managers, did not go out of his way to draw attention to his activities in his public statements. However, he also avoided the other extreme – that of regularly expressing public disapproval of and disdain for the press. Other prime ministers, though – as recently as Balfour and Asquith – have certainly expressed an airy disregard for the fourth estate.

One of the challenges, then, is to distinguish between those prime ministers who conducted press relations either because they positively enjoyed it, or because they recognized it as an essential part of the job; and those who actively disliked it, but learned to embrace it. Others professed indifference simply because it was one of the expected tropes of political discourse while, as it were, holding their noses and performing the unwelcome task as invisibly and with as little risk of being detected as possible. Not all the prime ministers previously judged to have been ineffective in this field will turn out to have been so.

As we uncover the press relations of individual prime ministers, we shall also highlight some other common themes and trends which mark the changing relationship between Downing Street and the press throughout the nineteenth century. As the social position of journalism as a profession, and of individual proprietors, editors and journalists solidified, how was the balance of power between politicians and the press affected? If the fundamental dynamic of the relationship remained unchanged – you have information I do not have but want, and I want you to give it to me before anyone else – what were the means by which it was played out, developed and evolved throughout the century.

The press itself was dramatically transformed throughout the nineteenth century. We shall remark, in subsequent chapters, how circulation figures for successful newspapers climbed from the low thousands in the early part of the century through the tens and then the hundreds of thousands, finally heading towards seven figures. We shall see *The Times* establish a position of unique numerical and editorial supremacy in mid-century, only to be threatened by a new generation of mass-circulation papers and an increasingly prevalent regional press after government taxes (the stamp duty, the paper duty and the tax on advertisements) were removed early in the second half of the century.[7] By the 1880s, *The Times* had a circulation in the 60,000s (a fairly small increase on figures which had given it a vastly dominant position in the market in the 1850s), but that of *The Daily Telegraph*, founded as the newspaper duties started to come off in the mid-1850s, was over 300,000. Other papers like the *Daily Chronicle* and the *Daily News* neared 100,000, and the *Standard* reached 250,000 in the 1880s. Meanwhile, the Sunday newspapers reached new circulation heights too. *Lloyd's Weekly* was selling 900,000 by the 1880s, becoming the first million-seller in 1896, just as the new *Daily Mail* was born.[8]

Technology, methods of transport and distribution and advances in mass literacy all drove these changes. At its simplest, however, a mutually advantageous relationship between a politician and a newspaper is founded on the simple transaction: I'll tell you something no-one else (yet) knows if you give me your support and/or report it favourably. There are all sorts of variations and shadings, but if a paper knows something before everybody else finds out, it is more likely to support the source of that information in the hope of receiving more of the same. This model is still applicable to the politician-press relationship today. As circulations rose and papers became less dependent on government subsidies, this model became more established across the period under examination. Newspapers, proprietors, editors and journalists were perceived as becoming more powerful; circulations were rising; journalists' and editors' social positions started to rise too, with the result that newspaper men were often linked to politicians at the family as well as professional level; and the protocols of their relationships with political figures changed accordingly. Our task is to chart how the prime ministers of Victorian Britain, including some of the greatest as well as some of the least-regarded premiers we have ever had, responded to and kept pace with these changes.

CHAPTER ONE

THE AGE OF
PITT THE YOUNGER

N O ONE SHOULD imagine that press management was unheard of before, or that it sprung into being on 19 December 1783: the day William Pitt the Younger became Prime Minister. The date is chosen, rather, because it has always looked like a natural political and prime ministerial turning point. The longevity of the ministry, and the fact that it spanned the eighteenth and nineteenth centuries, are two of the more obvious reasons why this is so.

The art of press management, as an alternative to out-and-out censorship, claimed several notable practitioners in the eighteenth century. It was in 1695 that William III lifted press restrictions, for the first time enabling the existence of a press largely unfettered by government taxes and other obstacles. This heralded what was sometimes referred to as the first golden age of the press, before the Stamp Act was introduced by the Robert Harley-Viscount Bolingbroke ministry under Queen Anne in 1712.[1]

This fairly brief period got its name because it was the era in which the Whigs and Tories strove to harness some of the most glittering literary lights of the age to their cause. The great Duke of Marlborough, with his political partner Sidney Godolphin, sought to protect themselves from journalistic attack by securing the adherence of giants such as Daniel Defoe, while the Tories won the priceless support of Jonathan Swift for one of the most famous of all negative press campaigns, aimed at nothing less than the toppling of England's greatest soldier from his pinnacle.[2]

In an era where periodical and newspaper circulation numbers were only in the low thousands, the influence of these publications was still great. Copies were passed from hand to hand, sent to the provinces and devoured as an alternative to official messages from on high, delivered in churches or by the local worthies.

1. William Pitt, studio of John Hoppner, c.1805.

The Stamp Act of 1712, designed to curb this war of words by pricing the papers out of the hands of all but the wealthiest, was introduced by the Tories, but embraced, and indeed extended, by the Whigs who monopolized power under the first two Georges, from 1714 to 1760. Within a few years of the Hanoverian succession of 1714, Sir Robert Walpole had established himself as Chief or Prime Minister (not yet an official title). Walpole, like Robert Harley, avoided the temptation to counter the many press attacks against him, most notably in *The Craftsman*, with outright censorship. Instead, he paid out vast subsidies to buy press support. He distributed something like £50,000 to writers and papers to ensure that the government's case was heard and read during his two decades of power.[3]

His Whig successors, Pelham and his elder brother Newcastle, though less personally interested in press affairs, were not averse from employing the talents of writers as great as Henry Fielding to buttress their political position journalistically. While Pelham was happy to build personal bridges with Fielding, formerly in decided opposition to Walpole, Newcastle, of an altogether more highly strung disposition than his younger brother, preferred to pay direct subsidies – not to secure better coverage but rather to encourage his opponents to simply shut up shop and go away![4]

By contrast, their fellow Whig but opponent within the party, William Pitt the Elder, father of Pitt the Younger and later Earl of Chatham, adopted a different strategy. He cultivated 'popularity' in a sense specific to the eighteenth century: support from elite, influential but non-Whig sources within the City of London and the provinces, which he was able to convert into press support through the efforts of powerful City merchants like William Beckford. Pitt the Elder defined many of his positions in opposition to the ruling Whig aristocracy – and even to the King – while managing to attract popular support for so doing, by virtue of being seen as a doughty opponent of the old gang who had monopolized power for so many decades. It was a tricky tightrope to walk while in senior office; but, while he shared the leadership with Newcastle during most of the Seven Years War of 1756–63, he pulled it off.[5]

Other eighteenth-century prime ministers had their own press tactics. The unpopular Scottish peer Lord Bute, when elevated by George III from personal tutor and adviser to Prime Minister (for one unhappy year), called on Tobias Smollett to manage his press image with unfortunate results for all concerned. The beleaguered Lord North, who ended up running George's losing fight to preserve the allegiance of America in the late 1770s and early 1780s, enlisted none other than Dr Samuel Johnson to present his cause in the best possible light. Even the great doctor's orotund periods were not enough, however, to save both the war and the Prime Minister from defeat.[6]

North's resignation marked the beginning of a struggle by George III, from March 1782 to the end of 1783, to find a government equally to his taste. Lord Rockingham, who had led what was thought of as pure Whig opposition to North (who would retrospectively be seen as a Tory prime minister, although North himself would not have accepted the term), was certainly not the answer, but, in the event, he died in July 1782. Shelburne looked more palatable; but, by straddling George loyalists and opposition Whigs, he only survived for eight months. After Shelburne's fall, George was horrified by the prospect of a coalition between his old ally North and his arch-enemy Charles James Fox, who both agreed to serve under Rockingham's titular successor as Whig leader, the Duke of Portland. For nine long months, the King tolerated an administration which he detested.[7]

When George III found the occasion and the means to dismiss the coalition, he did so at once; and, shortly before Christmas 1783, he appointed what sceptics termed a 'mince-pie administration' under the 24-year-old Pitt the Younger. In fact, Pitt's Christmas ministry would remain in office for the rest of the eighteenth century.

*　*　*

The reputation of the Younger Pitt, founded like his father's on parliamentary oratory of the highest order, and fostered by reverential political disciples and biographers, makes it especially difficult to picture him as an active press manager. However, there is much more evidence linking the son with press subsidies and other forms of press management than there is of similar activities undertaken by his father. Not only did he contribute occasional pieces for his protégé Canning's *Anti Jacobin* in the 1790s, but he was more directly involved with the minutiae of political management – electioneering as well as press management – than his father. Pitt the Elder had Beckford to act as his proxy in the spheres with which he did not wish to be seen to be associated. In addition, he was able, while in power, to avoid the necessity of spending much time on general elections. The great man left much of the detail of the 1761 poll to Newcastle; while, in 1768, he was *hors de combat* as a result of illness. His son, by contrast, personally oversaw elections in 1784, 1790 and 1796 (in those days of seven-year parliaments); and, as well as having supporters like Canning and George Rose undertake writing or press management on his behalf, was also far from fastidious about continuing the press subsidy traditions of the era.

Newspaper circulations were still low in the 1780s, which can be attributed to several factors. Among them were essentially manual production technologies, slow communications, relatively low literacy levels, levels of taxation (the Stamp, Advertisement and Pamphlet duties: see below for rates, 1712–1815) and the role of the Post Office in making it prohibitively expensive to export or import international newspapers.

The Stamp Duty was levied at the following rates. In 1712, it was a half-penny for a half sheet and a penny a sheet, with additional charges added by Walpole in 1727. In 1757 it was a penny for a sheet or a half sheet. In 1776, it went up to a penny-half-penny a sheet. Pitt put it up to two pence in 1789 and to three pence-half-penny in 1797; and Lord Liverpool and Chancellor Vansittart put it up to four pence in 1815. Meanwhile, the Advertisement Duty was at a shilling each in 1712; two shillings in 1757; two shillings and six pence in 1776; three shillings in 1789 and three shillings and six pence in 1815. The Pamphlet Duty was levied at two shillings a sheet from 1712 to 1815, and three shillings a sheet thereafter. As will be seen, the next major changes were made by Gladstone as Chancellor in the 1850s and early 1860s.

For all of these reasons, a circulation in the hundreds and low thousands remained broadly viable and commercially respectable well into the nineteenth century. Production technologies began to improve towards the end of the eighteenth century by harnessing the power of steam. Indeed, the first John Walter, who started the *Daily Universal Register* in 1785, changing its name to *The Times* in 1788, seemed prouder of his steam printing breakthrough than of his new paper. Further advances followed. Roads improved, and the speed of travel also increased dramatically – again thanks to the power of steam. Literacy levels rose, and the extreme sabbatarianism of earlier days relaxed to the extent that Sunday newspapers were no longer regarded with the same horror by more affluent readers.

However, when Pitt came to office in 1783, and even when Liverpool left it in 1827, much of this remained nascent or entirely in the future. There was something like one newspaper for every 300 British citizens. So what strategy did Pitt propose to adopt in order to maximize the potential influence of the press outlets available to him? The first was to revert to eighteenth-century type and buy support. As early as 1784, when his weak parliamentary position led him to call an early election (the last had only been in 1780), Pitt's government was already making payments to the *Public Ledger*, the *London Evening Post* and the *Morning Herald*, plus the *Whitehall Evening Post* and the *St James's Chronicle*. There are records of secret government payments, often referred to as 'secret service payments' (though that should not be taken to imply anything as formal or structured as the 'secret services' of more recent times) of £100 to each; but that may only have been for part of a year: and the payments would increase in the more troubled years after the French Revolution. Three years after the revolution, 'under the immediate sanction of Mr Pitt', the *True Briton* and *The Sun* were launched simultaneously.[8] Moreover, Pitt, like his immediate predecessors, had his stable of 'Treasury hirelings'. Indeed, some merely continued where they had left off after the fall of Shelburne. If one is to believe one of the few working journalists to have left an account of his work, William Augustus Miles, it was perfectly possible to work for a newspaper at this period without realizing that one's employer was in the pay either of the government of the day or, for that matter, of the opposition.[9]

PITT IN PEACETIME

In Pitt's early years of office, it is continuities with past practice rather than radical departures from it that are most apparent. Pitt was also easily captured in visual caricatures: his extreme youth, slimness and apparent freedom from vice (other than alcohol) contrasted sharply with the physical appearance of his main rival Fox (large, unshaven and portrayed as both debauched and – especially after the episode of his India Bill – corrupt). Although caricatures are not the main focus of this book, it is worth noting at this stage that Pitt and Fox mark a new stage in popular recognition of politicians mediated via the press. Their long rivalry, distinct political personalities and recognizable faces made them easier subjects than some of their predecessors. Even the fact that statesmen no longer wore the full-bottomed wigs of the earlier years of the century made their features sharper and easier to differentiate. Pitt the Elder, with his hawk-like profile, was the obvious earlier exception to this trend towards greater visual impact, as, to a lesser extent, were the ever more exaggeratedly corpulent portrayals of Walpole. However, many of the less distinctive figures of the early eighteenth century bore at least a superficial resemblance to each other under their ample hairpieces – one thinks of Kneller's Kit-Kat Club portraits. From now on, however, Wellington's nose, the straw in Palmerston's mouth, Derby's large whiskers, Russell's diminutive stature and the obvious contrasts between Gladstone and Disraeli would not only assist the caricaturists, but also made the politicians themselves more defined personalities in the minds of readers who would almost certainly never see or meet them in person.

Superficially, Pitt the Younger and Walpole were as unlike as could be imagined – both physically and in terms of personality. However, neither minister was above capitalizing upon whatever press advantages he could claim. Some accounts have pointed to Pitt's use of the helping hand offered by the Post Office distribution network to give preference to pro-government papers throughout the country. The same charge had been levelled at Walpole. Pitt was identified as an early exponent of the stratagem of sending highlighted copies of favourable articles from national (London) papers to the provincial press, so that they could be incorporated in these publications too. Walpole and his Whig contemporaries were accused of doing the same. An article in *New Monthly Magazine* said:

> ... a public officer was instructed to open a communication with the proprietors of [provincial] journals of large circulation, and the result was that, to a vast majority of them, two or three London papers were sent gratuitously, certain articles of which were marked with red ink, and the return made was the insertion of as many of these as the space of the paper would allow. Thus was the whole country agitated and directed by one mind, as it were...[10]

According to the author of the first volume of *The History of The Times*, Henry Dundas was at the head of this operation (in addition to his activities as press manager for Scotland) and, on Pitt's behalf, coordinated the press management activities of George Rose, Charles Long and Thomas Steele, all junior figures in Pitt's administration and his personal followers. The importance of Dundas's diverse functions in Pitt's service is demonstrated by Pitt's reaction when in 1805, late in Pitt's second ministry, Dundas (now Lord Melville) was obliged to resign over corruption charges: the prime minister was seen in the chamber after the crucial vote with his hat pulled low over his head to hide his tears. Not the least of Dundas's services to

Pitt was his leading role in press and propaganda management. His detailed involvement allowed Pitt to maintain the customary public position of a lofty lack of interest in such regrettable necessities. However, this pose did not fool everybody: at the time, the writer David Williams described this pose as 'palpable affectation'.[11]

The reference by the *New Public Magazine* to 'a public officer' might incline one to start wondering about an earlier version, even a prototype, of Bernard Ingham and Alastair Campbell: the first prime ministerial press officer, perhaps. In fact, the work that would now be done by communications departments and press officers was often carried out by a combination of government officials and junior ministers – the likes of George Rose under Pitt the Younger, and J.W. Croker under Liverpool and his immediate successors.

There was also something of a link – both rhetorical and practical – between dealings with the press and so-called secret service activity. There is an interesting link between gathering news and information and disseminating and influencing it: and the two activities, very discrete for us, in the eighteenth century sometimes came very close to merging. In William III's time, and under Harley's Tories and George I's Whigs, Defoe's letters show him as busy both with his propagandist, writing role and with that of travelling around provincial England and Scotland gathering information that would be of use to his political paymasters. Although later journalists may not have carried out these roles to the same extent, some undoubtedly still did. Even more significant, however, was the fact that for much of this period and into the nineteenth century, press management was funded by, and was to some extent a branch of, the secret service. The subsidies described earlier were largely secret service payments. Indeed, this phenomenon is both a consequence of, and more broadly a metaphor for, elite attitudes towards the press and the management of public opinion. Press management and the organization of pro-government propaganda was not regarded as a fit subject for political and public discourse; and it was part of the rhetorical equipment expected of an aspiring statesman to disclaim not merely personal ambition but also a desire for, and interest in, popularity: both in the narrower sense specific to the eighteenth century, and in the broader meaning understood by us. Still less was an active striving to secure popularity, something which could never be acknowledged or even suffered to have attention drawn to it.

PITT AT WAR

The only recorded instance of Pitt's direct and personal press involvement is in relation to his protégé Canning's *Anti Jacobin* periodical. Pitt's early years as prime minister were a time of peace, and his primary focus was domestic. For some years after the French Revolution, it seemed possible to hope that Britain would not have to significantly increase its role in continental politics – let alone become involved in full-scale war. In 1792, there was a campaign for Britain to help in saving Poland from the predatory clutches of Prussia and Russia. Burke, Sheridan, Wilberforce and Josiah Wedgwood were all in favour. In due course, the struggling but grateful King of Poland, Stanislaw Poniatowski, sent 'Merentibus' medals not only to Burke, but to the editors of the supportive *Sun* and *Morning Chronicle*. Stanislaw, in a desperate attempt to ensure the independent survival of his nation, clearly set to one side the snobbery that still operated against press honours in Britain.[12] Pitt himself, however, was responsible for a very forthright prediction of many more years of peace just months before Britain became involved in the war in 1793. For the rest of his time in office, Pitt had to do what few prime ministers have achieved: transform himself from a successful peacetime leader to an acclaimed warlord. Great wartime leaders – Pitt's father, Lloyd George, Churchill – were either less successful, or failed to make a similar impact, in peace. Successful peacetime premiers – Walpole, Asquith – were relative failures in war. Palmerston achieved a measure of success in both areas. But only the Younger Pitt can claim dual eminence; although, as a war leader, he is often ranked a little below his father and Churchill, and perhaps on a par with Lloyd George.

It was in the context of the shift from a peacetime to a war footing that Pitt faced his severest domestic challenges; and these, in turn, prompted the *Anti Jacobin*. Social unrest on various fronts confronted ministers (as it would later do under Liverpool). As well as acting to make it more difficult to spread what they regarded as seditious print propaganda, and raising Stamp Duty, some ministers also tried their own hands as propagandists. George Canning himself was a keen amateur versifier; and it seems likely that some or most of the anonymous contributions he solicited from his political colleagues were also in verse form, while other paid writers provided the rest of the prose. As we have seen, Canning's close university friend Robert Jenkinson (later Lord Hawkesbury, and then Earl of Liverpool) probably contributed;

Grenville was another future prime minister who may have taken a turn; and Pitt himself became an occasional, if somewhat unreliable, contributor. There are stories of deadlines missed, apologies from Number 10 and last-minute arrangements for rushed copy. Canning, Liverpool and Grenville were not the only future prime ministers involved in this round of press warfare. Among the young contributors to Whig papers taking on the *Anti Jacobin* was the young William Lamb, another future prime minister as Lord Melbourne.

The *Anti Jacobin* was also vocal in calling on the government to use its extensive power over advertisement revenue to cause problems for opposition or non-supportive newspapers. For papers to survive in the eighteenth century, two main sources of revenue were available – secret service subsidies and advertising – and access to at least one was essential. The government itself was a major advertiser in newspapers, and the choice to take out or decline government advertising could make or break a paper. The political opposition might be able to match the governing party in payment of subsidies; clearly, it could not do so when it came to government advertising. As with favourable treatment by the government of the day over the distribution of papers via the Post Office, here too was a method of indirect control and influence which ministers were rarely averse to exercising. When the *Anti Jacobin* called on the government to distinguish between papers which maintained 'a fair and ENGLISH' opposition and those which it regarded as outside the patriotic framework of acceptable opinion, implicit in the call was an acknowledgement that such a distinction had already been drawn. Indeed, the *Morning Chronicle*, *Morning Post* and *Courier* were deprived of official advertising only a month later. It is unlikely that a paper under the direct inspiration of the loyal Pitt disciple Canning would nail its colours to the mast with such assurance without knowing the decision to withdraw government advertising from its rivals had either already been taken or was likely to be so immediately.

There is a curious ambivalence about the conventions of anonymity applying to contributions to the *Anti Jacobin* (and to other papers in later decades) by senior political figures. We can assume that it was part of the political and rhetorical culture of the eighteenth and nineteenth centuries that prime ministers and other senior figures would be seen as compromising their dignity by contributing signed articles to daily or weekly papers. Even Palmerston and Disraeli drew the line at the practice decades later – though, as we shall see, they certainly made contributions. In the late twentieth and early twenty-first centuries, conversely, prime ministers and party leaders routinely contribute signed articles to newspapers – except that they do not really do so, since they are almost invariably ghosted by a member of their communications department under their byline. An exact inversion of the proprieties and conventions of earlier ages!

PITT OUT OF OFFICE

Pitt was prime minister twice: from 1783 to 1801, and again from 1804 until his death in January 1806. He fell from office in 1801 not because of the prosecution of the war, but over the issue of Catholic emancipation. Although appointed as the nearest George III could find to a 'King's Friend', in fact their relationship was wary and lacked personal warmth on either side. George, perhaps fearing a repeat of what he would have seen as his abandonment by his previous prime ministerial confidants and not wishing to bestow the almost unlimited trust he had placed in Pitt's father in 1766–7, doubtless viewed the son with a more equivocal eye. Pitt himself recalled the oscillations in his father's relationship with the King (and, indeed, with his grandfather George II), and the King's churlish attitude towards his father's funeral and memorials in 1778. This all made for a cautious marriage of convenience. Pitt's views on parliamentary reform and the slave trade diverged sharply from the King's; and pragmatism, not principle, governed his reluctant decision not to push ahead with either in direct opposition to George. But when Pitt decided once again to side with reformers, over the issue of Catholic rights, he came into sharp collision with the King once again. He had, of course, gained great credit with the King for staunchly upholding his rights during the Regency Crisis of 1788–9; but, ironically, it was a renewed collapse of the King's fragile mental health in 1801, and the connection made between this temporary bout of insanity (now generally seen as the result of porphyria) and Pitt's pressure for Catholic emancipation, which ended Pitt's first ministry. Although Pitt's resignation was postponed for two months during the King's indisposition, he ended by losing his job, his policy and his principles. He abandoned the policy, promised never to raise it again during George's lifetime, and gave way to the rather unlikely figure of Henry Addington as prime minister.

HENRY ADDINGTON

Henry Addington was a Pitt supporter, and had been Speaker of the Commons before his surprising ascent to greatness. If, as in Canning's famous squib, Pitt was to Addington as London was to Paddington, the connection was partly due to the fact that his father had been Pitt the Elder's doctor. The precariousness of Canning's own social origins – he was the son of an actress – made his attribution of the nickname 'The Doctor' to Addington dangerous ground for both of them. Addington, however, had a solemnity and ponderousness which made all the more memorable a notorious episode in the Commons. During a lull in parliamentary proceedings, one of the early parliamentary reporters in the gallery famously shouted: 'a song from Mr Speaker!' Not only was the gallery convulsed, but the shoulders of Pitt himself, still Prime Minister and a man of notably controlled demeanour in public, were seen to heave with barely suppressed laughter.

Addington, however, seemed determined to surprise. Not only did he drastically revise the conduct of the war, pursuing a determined attempt to end, or at least suspend, hostilities (now, of course, against Napoleon rather than Robespierre, Danton and the earlier revolutionaries), but he was also a very assiduous cultivator of the press. Perhaps because of an awareness of the somewhat patronizing – occasionally sneering – tone of elite attitudes towards him, and also because of the fragility of his base of support after over 17 years of Pitt's administration, he must have felt the need to tap into all possible sources of strength. Because of his later role in the passage of the 'Six Acts', including one instituting governmental control of the press, as Home Secretary in Liverpool's government, he has never been a favourite of journalists with an interest in the history of their profession, but his earlier involvement as Prime Minister makes him more varied and interesting than the repressive and fearful figure often seen in popular histories. William Cobbett, the great radical journalist, was an early supporter of Addington – though he later recanted. Indeed, in the politics of the time, Addington was more likely to appeal politically (if not personally) to the opposition than Pitt. It was Pitt, along with Grenville, who was more closely identified with a vigorous and seemingly indefinite opposition to France. It was Pitt, too, who had introduced the first round of enactments aimed at cutting down the activities of the radical press.

One of the most important aspects of Addington's press management activities was to cultivate *The Times*. When Addington came to office in 1801, the paper – even allowing for its first three years under a different name – was only 16 years old. It had yet to acquire the 'Thunderer' nomenclature or reputation it would enjoy during the later part of the nineteenth century; and the first John Walter, its inaugural proprietor, was far less fastidious about accepting press subsidies than his descendants. Walter's initial experience with this form of engagement with the political establishment was, however, unfortunate. Thomas Steele, one of Pitt's junior ministers, offered him £300 a year to support Pitt, after what was seen as the supportive role played by Walter's paper during the Regency Crisis of 1788–9. However, subsequent criticisms of the King's elder sons resulted in losses in the form of libel damages arising from the pursuit of this theme. The subsidy was stopped in 1799 after a disagreement; and, while it may not have been formally renewed by Addington, there was a decided thaw in relations once he took over in 1801. Addington's key policy, as we have seen, was the attempt to negotiate peace with France. At the forefront of this was the Foreign Secretary Lord Hawkesbury (the future Prime Minister Lord Liverpool); and relations between the Foreign Office and *The Times* were particularly close. Indeed, Cobbett, long after his recantation, accused *The Times* of having been 'enlisted by the Foreign Office',[13] and was certain that Hawkesbury himself, as well as Addington's brother Hiley, contributed articles to the paper; if this was indeed the case, they would have anticipated Palmerston in doing so by several decades.

The arrangement between Addington's government and *The Times* is believed to have been the promise (and delivery) of 'exclusive' official news in return for publishing articles direct from the Treasury (possibly by Addington himself) as well as from Hawkesbury and the Foreign Office. The paper also became a yardstick for changes in ministerial thinking before any public expression of change was desirable. It was probably inevitable that the amicable political relationship between Pitt and Addington would break down. Ostensibly on the same side of the political divide, the policy divergences were too obvious, and the zeal of their followers too insistent, for harmony to prevail. If one recalls the gradual political estrangement between Margaret Thatcher and John Major and their respective followers in the 1990s, one gets a sense of what was happening 190 years earlier. Something similar happened in the 1960s between friends and family of John

Kennedy, and allies and supporters of Lyndon Johnson. Significantly, *The Times* started attacking Pitt and his friends some time before verbal hostilities were begun (over the Amiens peace, and eventually over other issues as well) in parliament itself, let alone between the protagonists. Even the primary causes of the disputes – relations with Europe – were the same in the 1800s as in the 1990s! The reference to the family dimension of the Kennedy-Johnson tensions is also particularly appropriate, given the evidence that some of the articles most hostile to Pitt in *The Times* seem to have been penned personally by Hiley Addington.

William Cobbett also alleged that, in addition to its close relationship with *The Times*, which later soured, the Addington ministry also set up *The Pilot* and the *Royal Standard*. (Cobbett saw the founding of these publications as a direct attempt to do down his own *Political Register*). His further allegation, that the ministry spent £12,200 buying Daniel Stuart's *Morning Post*, however, appears to have been inaccurate. The ministry clearly felt the need for as much external support as possible. An anonymous memorandum was composed for them comparing their position with that of the Shelburne ministry in 1782–3, and making recommendations for a vigorous press strategy based on that precedent. The rather speculative conclusion was that, had such advice been offered to and adopted by Shelburne, his administration might still be in office to that day (some 20 years later): 'If Lord Shelburne had comprehended in one system every species of political literature, abominable as some of it appeared, he might have been Minister to this day'.[14] This may have been a highly hypothetical conclusion; but the memorandum's clear implication was that an energetic and strategic press campaign, in and of itself, would be sufficient to ensure political survival and success. Even in the twenty-first century, it may be wondered whether spin doctors would advance such an audacious claim. In some respects, Addington's proactive press policy more closely echoes that of another unexpected prime minister of a few decades before: Lord Bute.

The memorandum was entitled 'On the Press', and was circulated to the Addington ministry in 1803; it may even have been written by Thomas Steele or Charles Long, who (like Hawkesbury and others) had served under Pitt and remained in office under his successor. There are echoes of earlier periods of public dissension over policy. The ministry knew that its peace policy was far from universally supported in parliament: the Pittites were poised to pounce on what they saw as backsliding; and, as with the contentious peace negotiations after the wars of Marlborough and the Elder Pitt, winning support for the Peace of Amiens would be just as crucial and as difficult as it had been to rally support for the Treaties of Utrecht and Paris in the previous century. If the press was not brought on to Addington's side, the memorandum predicted a dire future in which '... literary talents, the instruments of incalculable Good or Evil, are left to the disposal of the vilest factions, or to avoid starvation by hiring themselves to the enemy and abusing the Government of their country'.[15]

PITT'S FINAL BOW

Addington lasted three years as Prime Minister. When the peace failed, so, in due course, did he. Pitt returned for a second and final ministry, lasting a little over a year and a half, and ending with his own death in January 1806. Despite the perceived failure of his predecessor's main policy, the peace treaty, Pitt's own position was weaker than might have been expected. He wished to form a sort of grand coalition with Fox and the opposition Whigs: but that was too much for George III. Addington and his supporters were initially hostile, though some of his ministers resumed office under Pitt – again including Hawkesbury, the future Lord Liverpool. Pitt had also been strengthened, during the 1790s, by some of Fox's less fiercely anti-war supporters, including the former (and future) prime minister, the Duke of Portland. Pitt also retained the support of papers who, like *The Sun* and *The Courier*, had been his most loyal supporters in office and out. However, Hiley Addington's continuing articles for *The Times* ensured that Pitt would only secure its support when he had agreed terms with the Addington faction, which did not occur until January 1805. Addington, ennobled as Lord Sidmouth, came into the cabinet as Lord President of the Council, replacing the already elderly and ailing Duke of Portland. However, six months later he was out again, and the Pitt ministry reeled under the twin blows of Melville's impeachment and resignation and the loss of Austerlitz, tempered, of course, by the glory of Trafalgar. Political hostility remained just under the surface – with, for instance, Hiley Addington voting against Pitt over the Melville charges. *The Times*, however, having been brought back into the Pittite fold, did not abandon him when the Addingtons did; and it was Pitt's own failing health and premature death which ended the ministry.

LORD GRENVILLE AND ALL THE TALENTS

Lord Grenville had been Pitt's Foreign Secretary for ten years, up to 1801, but in the next five years their relations soured. Grenville was amongst the hardest of hardliners on the prosecution of the war: moreover, personal disdain made him unlikely to wish to follow Addington. On the face of it, that should have entailed a speedy return to government with Pitt. Paradoxically, however, Grenville and his followers had found some common ground with Fox while in opposition to Addington. This common ground did not encompass the war; Fox remained a dove to Grenville's hawk. But on other grounds – notably the need for an inclusive, all-embracing ministry – they shared objectives. For this reason, after Hawkesbury turned down the chance to try to prolong Pitt's ministry, the King was left with little option but to turn to Grenville and Fox. Well might the King exclaim to Fox, after an absence lasting over 22 years, how little he had expected to see him in his room again.

The Grenville ministry was dubbed 'The Ministry of All the Talents'; but it failed to include those of Pitt's remaining supporters. Fox became Foreign Secretary, but was dead within eight months, to be succeeded by the future Prime Minister Lord Grey. The Chancellor was Lord Henry Petty, later Lord Lansdowne, beginning a Cabinet career that spanned half a century. The administration itself lasted only 14 months, during which the slave trade was abolished. However, it was Catholic Emancipation which did for Grenville, just as it had once done for Pitt. The outcome was inevitable as long as George III reigned; and a wit observed that, while he could understand a man running into a brick wall, he could not understand a man building a wall with the express purpose of running into it.

Grenville showed relatively little interest in, and aptitude for, press management while Prime Minister; but redressed the balance in the years of opposition that followed. After his ministry fell, in March 1807, Grenville remained in alliance with Grey, Holland (Fox's nephew), Brougham and the other opposition Whigs. He was certainly involved in much of their correspondence and thinking on how to use the press to maintain or gain support during the long years of Pittite (or, as it was increasingly referred to, Tory) domination after 1807. Peel, a future Chief Secretary for Ireland, claimed that Grenville's ministry spent just as much on Irish press subsidies as its predecessors and successors (and more than was publicly voted for in

Parliament) despite subsequent Whig criticism of the practice. The Grenville ministry also continued to receive the support of the increasingly influential *Times*; but there is little or no evidence of the close contact between the paper and the government that had been maintained under Pitt and especially Addington. Fox, whose Libel Act of 1792 had enhanced the role of juries in libel trials – a major boon to the press – was not especially interested or active in press management. Grey, as we shall see, was to be one of the prime ministers most vocal in lofty disdain for it, and Grenville's interest, such as it was, came later.

Holland, however, had some interest in the press as a tool, and the young barrister Henry Brougham harboured what can fairly be described as an obsession with it – contemporaries might have described it as an 'itch to meddle'. These were the two Grenville ministry supporters most involved in press campaigning for the 1807 election – held just after the ministry had fallen. Brougham and his colleagues started a collection of funds and opened what was, in effect, a press bureau under Brougham's management ahead of the election. Grenville's own grouping had also secured the support of the *Morning Star* in 1805, while Pitt was still in office. Other papers were sympathetic, or were given pro-Whig material: the *Morning Chronicle*, *The Globe*, the *British Press* and *The Pilot*, while *The Statesman* had been established as a pro-government paper in 1806.[16] However, this all looks rather like too little too late; having disdained the press during his time in office, it was difficult to imagine that the newspapers could then restore Grenville to the premiership. It was almost impossible to dislodge even a brand-new incumbent ministry directly through the ballot box before the Reform Act of 1832; and, crucially, it was the new administration which had called the election, not the old.

THE DUKE OF PORTLAND

In March 1807, George reprised his action of late 1783 and secured the removal of a ministry he had never liked from the start. Fox's death almost certainly augmented the King's dislike for the administration this time round, whereas, in 1783, for all his feeling of betrayal at the hands of North, it was Fox who was the focus of his most intense disapproval. There was, from the King's perspective, an appealing range of talents on the Pittite, or as we shall now call them, the Tory side. Hawkesbury would have his turn as Prime Minister another day – and it would prove a long one, too. The lawyer-politician Spencer Perceval was another eligible man. Canning and Castlereagh, rivals and talents both, would spend time at the centre of power. But it was to the unlikely figure of the Duke of Portland that the King now turned. The same man whom George could not wait to remove as Prime Minister when he headed the Fox-North coalition in 1783 was, ironically enough, his first choice in 1807. Nearing 70, like his royal master, in frailer health and with little or no inclination ever to open his mouth in the House of Lords, he was nevertheless a figure to whom younger, more ambitious men could rally without loss of pride or self-esteem.

Portland had always been an unusual politician. In an age of oratory, it was not merely in his final years that he was reluctant to speak in parliament: it was a feature of his entire career. He was not entirely oblivious to the importance of the press and public opinion. However he appeared to have exerted a moderating influence on at least one of Fox's entries into pamphleteering controversy, and had a rather equivocal attitude to the radical journalist and activist John Wilkes and all his works, despite the enthusiasm of some of his then Whig colleagues.[17] He was not above writing to the papers when he felt the need – notably on the occasion of a grain crisis. But there is little evidence of his personal hand at work in relation to press management during his second spell as Prime Minister. In a curious episode, his administration was accused by Lord Sidmouth (the former Addington) of backing a rather raucous publication called *Yorke's Weekly Political Review*. In 1808, the middle year of the Portland government, it advocated the massacre of French prisoners taken in Spain during the Peninsular War (itself, of course, part of the broader war against Napoleon). Sidmouth, currently out of office again, said anyone in power that encouraged the paper '… will deserve to be hanged'. Oddly, the paper does appear to have received Treasury support. Even more oddly, that support may have originated within the Addington ministry itself![18]

Portland's own ministry, run throughout on the loosest of reins from the centre, lasted for two and a half years. Hawkesbury, who succeeded his father as Lord Liverpool in 1808, was a quiet and effective Home Secretary (reprising his role during the final Pitt years). Perceval continued to grow in parliamentary confidence. However, the other two outstanding figures of the period, Castlereagh and Canning, took their burgeoning rivalry to the point of violence: fighting a duel in 1809 which triggered, in its wake, the fall of the administration. Portland's own health was declining rapidly. He finally resigned in autumn 1809, staying on as a nominal Cabinet member for a few more weeks before his death. Perhaps because his resolute silence resulted in the desire for an active Commons performer, it was Perceval rather than Liverpool who got the call this time (Liverpool, though also an excellent speaker, was now in the Lords). He was to be the last prime minister personally appointed by George III, now himself almost blind and only a year short of his final descent into incapacity; though he was not, of course, the last of his reign. Liverpool, when his turn came unexpectedly, was appointed by the Prince Regent, the future George IV.

SPENCER PERCEVAL

Perceval, who remained Prime Minister until his assassination in May 1812, earns a distinct place in this account not so much for his skill at press management, but because he found himself caught in the crossfire of more than one of the early nineteenth-century scandals – conducted, for the first time, in the press as well as in courtrooms. The need to manage the press as well as the events themselves during these tumultuous developments formed a new dimension to the office of prime minister. Among these testing developments were the so-called 'Delicate Investigation' into the personal and sexual conduct of the Prince's estranged wife Princess Caroline. Just before Perceval succeeded Portland, the Mary-Anne Clarke affair took place, in which the erstwhile mistress of the Prince's brother the Duke of York, the Commander-in-Chief of the army, was accused of procuring commissions and other favours in return for payment. The choice of this politician to confront these scandals seems particularly ironic given Perceval's own personal piety and evangelical religious zeal.

While Perceval's role in the Mary-Anne Clarke/Duke of York affair was primarily parliamentary, the investigation of Princess Caroline's personal conduct and alleged sexual dalliances after her estrangement from the Prince of Wales became a party matter, and had implications for press relations too. Initially, many Tories, notably Perceval, supported the Princess partly because she had the qualified backing of the King, with the Prince in traditional Hanoverian opposition to his father. The Delicate Investigation, ostensibly secret, soon became public: indeed, some of the Princess's supporters, including Perceval, initially wanted to publish the findings, as part of an appeal to public opinion on Caroline's behalf. However, when it was decided by Portland among others that this would not be wise or desirable, the hunt was on to track down and burn all surviving copies of what became known simply as 'The Book'. Naturally, the press had other ideas, and wanted to get hold of it as quickly as possible. Francis Blagdon, previously in the employ of *The Sun*, and once convicted of libel at the hands of Perceval, started a new paper called *The Phoenix*, with the intention of publishing 'The Book' in instalments. Eventually, he was prevailed upon not to; and, by the time Perceval had become Prime Minister, he was producing *Blagdon's Political Register*, with the express purpose of combating Cobbett's similarly named radical title. Unhappily for Perceval, Blagdon proved an unreliable political supporter. His *Register* was described as 'wavering' in its support by 1810; and, along with *The Phoenix*, it closed in 1812, the year of Perceval's own assassination.[19]

Arthur Wellesley, the future Duke of Wellington, had already told Castlereagh during 1808 that the press had come to 'rule everything in this country'. (As we shall see, Wellington, often seen as displaying nothing but lofty, aloof contempt for the press throughout his military and political careers, had a much more nuanced view, which developed as his experience of non-military affairs grew). At the time of Portland and Perceval, the strongest pro-government paper was *The Courier*. Under Portland, there is evidence of backsliding by the paper: but Perceval's ministry (according to Canning) solidified its loyalty with a subsidy of £2,000 as soon as it came into office in 1809.[20] *The Times* was not systematically opposed to Perceval, although it was highly critical of his original appointment and of his offer of positions to Grey and Grenville. It retained much closer links with Sidmouth's group and the Addington viewpoint. The Whig opposition relied principally on the *Morning Chronicle*; and, by this time, probably had more of the London press in its corner than the administration. Circulations remained small. According to a Stamp Office audit of 1811, *The Courier* had a figure of about 5,800, *The Times* about 5,000 and the *Morning Chronicle* 3,500. There were many more papers than there were for most of the eighteenth century, but their lifespans often remained very short, and the reliance upon government advertisements, subsidies and/or favourable distribution arrangements through the Post Office remained substantially unchanged. One of the other pro-ministry papers, *The Sun*, although still reliably loyal on the whole, had a circulation so small that it was not even included in the Stamp Office survey. The most powerful thrice-weekly was probably the *Evening Mail*, with its circulation of 3,000 and its wavering political affiliations. Of the journals, Leigh Hunt's *Examiner* and Cobbett's *Political Register* probably made the most waves, while the more moderate *Edinburgh Review* was on its march to real influence later in the century.

To help him negotiate this shifting media landscape, Perceval had two advisers who were both interested in and knowledgeable about the press. J.C. Herries, a future Chancellor and briefly joint Commons leader of Derby's Tories in uneasy alliance with Disraeli and Lord Granby several decades hence, had written pro-government pieces for the press, as well as pamphlets, as far back as Pitt's time. He was Perceval's private secretary as well as a Treasury official. Charles Arbuthnot, a regular throughout the coming Liverpool years, and friend of Wellington, was the Treasury man responsible for patronage. An unsigned Treasury memorandum (probably the work of one or both of these two) recommended that '... priority of intelligence should more than anything else distinguish the Government papers from those that are opposed to it, BUT THE CONTRARY IS NOTORIOUSLY THE CASE'. It was suggested that, instead of individual departments announcing what they wanted when they felt like it, the Treasury Secretary should coordinate press relations for the Foreign Office, War Office and Admiralty (as well as a the Treasury, it is assumed). An official in each department should monitor all press coverage every morning, note hostile points or arguments and, as rebuttal, send the Treasury a statement of relevant facts or 'a hint of the line which it wished should be taken'.[21] This all has a remarkably modern ring to it. Not only does it start to anticipate departmental press officers, but it also looks ahead to the complaints made by incoming spin doctors or communication directors about the 'departmentalitis' and lack of strategic approaches on the part of their predecessors.

The recommendations made in this document, dated December 1809, early in Perceval's administration, were never implemented, and thus remain one of the great 'might have beens' of the early history of political communication. It also reminds us, of course, of how many radical- and modern-sounding ideas had already been thought of, if not actually tried. Just like Lord Townshend's 'cunning plan' to deploy Defoe as a double agent, a supposed Tory journalist who was actually and covertly Whig, this Treasury circular still has the power to astonish a later generation sometimes prone to imagining that their ancestors were constitutionally incapable of understanding the media of their day.

Instead of the novel press operation recommended in 1809, the old subsidy arrangements remained the rule of the day. Papers such as W. Hughes's *National Adviser* and Lewis Goldsmith's *Anti-Gallican Monitor* (afterwards the *British Monitor*) received direct government help. Hughes, indeed, could claim the personal support of the prime minister, who had written to the Loyal Association – the society on whose support Hughes relied – offering his encouragement for Hughes's newspaper enterprise. Also, during the latter part of Perceval's ministry, George III had finally lost his faculties, and the Prince of Wales had assumed the full powers of the Regency. The Whig opposition, who had relied on him to turn the Tory government out as soon as he became Regent in 1811, now largely switched their support to the Princess; while the ministers, who had previously taken individual positions or backed the old King's views, now broadly converted to the Prince's side. The Prince, who was himself not averse from using money to influence the press in his favour, along with his adviser Knighton coordinated with Arbuthnot in an effort to secure more favourable coverage, particularly in response to pro-Caroline propaganda. There was talk of ministers buying another weekly paper for precisely this purpose. Arbuthnot remembered Street of the pro-government *Courier* attempting to dissuade him from this course of action, on the grounds that '... by attempting to have TWO AVOWEDLY PARTY PAPERS you would destroy the efficiency of each.... [N]o party ever had or ever could have more than one organ'.[22] It is ironic, given all the problems caused by the royal marriage and the York/Clarke affair, to recall that, when Perceval first came into office, the Whigs were worried that the impending celebration of George III's Golden Jubilee would give the ministry an unearned popularity boost. 'This jubilee is a political engine of the ministers', complained Sir Samuel Romilly.[23]

Perceval's assassination at the hands of Henry Bellingham in 1812 could have spelled the end of the ministry as a whole. In the event, after a series of complex manoeuvrings, Whig hopes were once more dashed, and the arrival of Lord Liverpool as Prime Minister ushered in an administration – essentially a continuation of Perceval's – which would endure for almost 15 years and win four general elections.

CHAPTER TWO

LIVERPOOL AND WELLINGTON

Robert Banks Jenkinson, 2nd Earl of Liverpool, had been offered the premiership in 1806, after the death of Pitt. It is also possible that, had he behaved like his Oxford friend Canning and pushed his personal claims, he could have been prime minister instead of Portland in 1807 or Perceval in 1809. He was one of the ablest and most competent of Tory ministers but, unlike his more colourful colleagues Canning and Castlereagh, he managed to avoid the more lurid lights of controversy. No secret duels for him! George III liked him, although Liverpool was to have a much less tranquil relationship with his son, whose chief minister he was throughout most of his regency and reign. Liverpool had been an excellent Secretary for War and the Colonies under Perceval: the minister who, along with Castlereagh but above all others, made it possible for Wellington to win the Peninsular War. Prior to that, he had had two quietly competent terms as Home Secretary under Pitt and Portland, as well as his rather more controversial spell as Addington's Foreign Secretary, negotiating the Peace of Amiens, and probably writing anonymously in *The Times* in support of his own policy. His father, the 1st Earl, had served many prime ministers, bridging the era of Bute and the time of Pitt the Younger, and more than any other seems to have been responsible for training his son to be a professional and able man of business. He also knew a thing or two about the press; he had been one of those junior ministers who were given special responsibility for press management in the early part of George III's reign.[1]

The second Lord Liverpool was not a genius in any one respect, but he was good or very good at almost everything he needed to do. He spoke well in Parliament. His prose style was particularly lucid and perspicuous. He avoided giving the impression of being personally ambitious. He was a

2. Robert Jenkinson, 2nd Earl of Liverpool, by Sir George Hayter, 1823.
© National Portrait Gallery, London.

conciliatory colleague and an emollient leader. His political views, while very traditional, were not far from the mainstream of his time. Like his later Tory successor Lord Derby, while he may not have survived as a household name, his reputation has risen in recent decades. A poll of historians and

3. Arthur Wellesley, 1st Duke of Wellington, by William Salter, 1839.
© National Portrait Gallery, London.

commentators by *The Times* recently placed both Liverpool and Derby in the top 20 prime ministers.

One of the reasons that his ministry survived precisely as long as his ability to lead it (he suffered a very severe stroke while still in power in 1827) was because he allowed one of the most divisive issues of the day to be an open question among his ministers. Rather as Harold Wilson kept Europe as an issue on which his Cabinet could 'agree to differ' in 1974–5, Liverpool permitted the same latitude on Catholic Emancipation for the entire period of his ministry. Parliamentary reform was a closed question, in that it was government policy to consider individual anomalies but not to propose a comprehensive measure.

The Liverpool government's attitude to the press became one of the causes of its poor showing among historians in the century or more after its life. This was largely due to the so-called 'Six Acts', aimed at quelling disturbances after the final restoration of peace in 1815, among which were measures aimed at lessening the impact of the radical press.

But it was hostility from *The Times* on Liverpool's very arrival in office that gave him his first prime ministerial press problem. Its proprietor the second John Walter, while disclaiming personal hostility to Liverpool, told J.W. Croker, the journalist and government supporter: 'I must hesitate at engaging by implication to support a body of men so critically situated, and so doubtful of national support, as those to whom public affairs are now likely to be entrusted'.[2] However, in late 1812, the paper's Edward Sterling wrote a series of letters under the name 'Vetus'. His 'Letters of Vetus', later published in book form, took a swipe at Liverpool personally. Liverpool, like Perceval, was a man of irreproachable morals, and was certainly no Grafton. (Grafton had been the prime ministerial target for the 'Letters of Junius' in the previous century). The intemperate nature of Sterling's attack on this unlikely target's policies and principles was said to be one of the reasons Sterling never secured the editor's chair. Letters between Walter and Sterling display not only the proprietor's criticism, subtly expressed but nonetheless clear, but also Sterling's admission of the letters' 'impropriety'. Sterling had the naivety to write later to Liverpool's colleague Castlereagh, making it clear that he had been writing with the express purpose of securing '… the downfall of LORD LIVERPOOL'S MINISTRY', and its replacement by one headed by Wellington's elder brother Lord Wellesley.[3]

It seems that *The Times* was also keen to criticize Liverpool for failing to display sufficient vigour in prosecuting the war against Napoleon in the Iberian Peninsula: a charge that was never seriously levelled at him by the person in the best position to judge – the Duke of Wellington. There is something of a tradition of politicians and journalists refusing to support new administrations on the grounds that they are unlikely to last. Much the same happened to Pitt the Younger in 1783 (the 'mince-pie administration');

and, before the Falklands War in 1982, many pundits expected the 18-year Thatcher-Major government to be a one-term ministry.

LIVERPOOL AS PRIME MINISTER: THE EARLY YEARS

The first years of the Liverpool government were primarily concerned with winning the Napoleonic war. The first overthrow of Napoleon in 1814 provided a temporary respite, only to be followed by Napoleon's 'Hundred Days' of 1815, after which St Helena beckoned, and peace was assured. The professional bond between Liverpool and Wellington, punctuated by periodic spasms of irritation on Wellington's part (but rarely if ever on Liverpool's), was established when Liverpool was Perceval's Secretary for War and the Colonies; and continued pretty seamlessly into Liverpool's own administration. One shared annoyance about which they both complained was the propensity of the press to prematurely disclose news of troop dispositions and other confidential military matters. There are slightly conflicting accounts of how this was possible. Liverpool himself wrote: 'The editors of newspapers... avow (and there can be no doubt of the fact) that they obtain their information from correspondents in the army: indeed, a mail never arrives without our seeing in the next newspapers copies of letters from officers in the army which bear internal evidence of their authenticity'.[4] Wellington complained to his elder brother Wellesley that his 1812 campaign should be successful unless the enemy were tipped off in advance as to his plans by 'those admirably useful institutions, the English newspapers'. Curiously, however, the *History of The Times* reports that that paper, for one, '... made no specially intimate arrangements with statesmen, but John Walter came into touch with the agents of Lord Wellesley and received through Sydenham and Arbuthnot early news of Lord Wellington's campaigns'.[5]

It should perhaps be noted in this context that Wellesley was one of several political figures considered for the premiership among the complex machinations following Perceval's assassination, and he did not go out of his way to make things easy for Liverpool. Indeed, there was something of a Wellesley-Canning grouping in the Liverpool ministry's early years, which attracted the support of *The Times* as its earlier enthusiasm for the Addington connection waned. Because of the Canning-Castlereagh duel, it was still difficult to construct a government in which they sat in Cabinet together; and although Liverpool was personally closer to Canning, the fact remained that Castlereagh was a more widely trusted figure, and an indispensable right-hand man as Leader of the Commons and Foreign Secretary. Canning and Wellesley, meanwhile, were both personally and professionally (as 'Outs' rather than 'Ins') disposed to have dealings with the press. Indeed, Benjamin Sydenham did not merely work for Lord Wellesley, he was effectively Wellesley's press agent, and the man who put Sterling up to his excessive (and possibly libellous) attack on Liverpool. Legal action was considered, but not pursued.

One aspect of press management which Liverpool shared with many of his predecessors was the matter of Irish press subsidies. The young Robert Peel took over as Chief Secretary for Ireland early in Liverpool's time, and told Liverpool, with prescient qualification, that he was not quite without hope of putting the government's press arrangements in Ireland on a better footing. Even those faint hopes proved optimistic. The picture remained one of large amounts of money being spent with very little to show for it. *The Patriot* and the *Hibernian Journal* continued to benefit from extensive subsidies with very little reward in added support for the government. Indeed, the same might have been said of the press in both islands. Liverpool's overall view of the subsidy system was made clear in a letter to Castlereagh in 1815. Castlereagh, now negotiating the peace, asked Liverpool to intervene to soften the anti-French tone of some papers. Liverpool replied: '... no paper that has any character, and consequently an established sale, will accept money from the Government; and, indeed, their profits are so enormous in all critical times, when their support is most necessary, that no pecuniary assistance the Government could offer would really be worth their acceptance'.[6] Indeed, Liverpool's overall view of the government's position in the press was bleak. He was well aware, he told Castlereagh, of the damage '... which must result from the general line on present politics taken by our daily papers, and particularly those which are supposed to be Government papers'. Moreover, he said, it was notorious that some papers unconnected with the government routinely received foreign news from ministers before the rest of the press.[7]

LIVERPOOL: THE POSTWAR STRUGGLES

Now that peace had returned, economic problems crowded in much more urgently than before. Like Lloyd George in 1918, and unlike Churchill in

1945, Liverpool and his colleagues had to turn their hands to winning the very different domestic battles. The rather negative reputation Liverpool's government enjoyed among later nineteenth- and early-twentieth-century historians was largely a result of the middle years, from 1815 to about 1820. The early years could be seen as a successful conclusion of the long war against Napoleon – though Liverpool rarely got much personal credit. The years from 1820 to 1827 were viewed more favourably – the years of 'liberal Toryism', in Brock's famous phrase;[8] though, again, the credit was often given more to others than to the prime minister himself. But the years of 'repression', of the Six Acts and of Peterloo, ensured for many decades the eclipse of Liverpool's reputation; although it must be said, in fairness, that he was spared the violent personal execration heaped on the members of his own government such as Sidmouth (formerly Addington), his Home Secretary, Castlereagh, the Foreign Secretary and the Lord Chancellor, the Earl of Eldon. However, it is also true that he missed out on some of the praise later meted out to the new Foreign Secretary George Canning, Robert Peel at the Home Office and Frederick Robinson, Liverpool's later Chancellor of the Exchequer.

Liverpool was realistic in appraising the press and its general approach to his government. He was not, however, notably proactive in tackling the problem. Liverpool has not gone down to posterity disparaging the press, as previous and later prime ministers did. As with other problems, he seems to have accepted that it was there, and that the most that could realistically be done about it was to attempt to control and lessen its effects. *The History of The Times* remarks that Liverpool's government, after the end of the war in 1815, made arrangements to transfer responsibility for press management and influence to the Admiralty as well as the Treasury, bypassing the traditional role of the Post Office and the Home Office.[9]

In 1819, Liverpool's administration turned down the chance to buy *The Sun* newspaper despite direct approaches to Liverpool's Private Secretary Robert Willimott. Liverpool's rather bleak view of the efficacy of direct press subsidies made it unlikely he would have wished to take it on, just as Pitt's government seems to have turned down a similar request from *The Observer*, then just three years old, in 1794. As social unrest built up after Waterloo, Liverpool was not at the forefront of those wishing to clamp down as hard as possible on the radical press and 'subversive' literature. But he was not creative in building up alternative strategies. Clearly not a wholehearted believer in the virtues of press subsidies, he accepted as a given that the press was broadly hostile or neutral. On one occasion, in 1825, on the crucial issue of Catholic Emancipation, Liverpool did specifically contradict a report in *The Courier* that he was about to change his mind on the question. Peel, by then Home Secretary, did remark on how unusual a move this was for the Prime Minister.[10] It seems highly unlikely that Liverpool would ever have considered reprising his practice as a young Foreign Secretary of writing articles for the papers, albeit anonymously, to promote his government's policies. In the early years of peace the government struggled to bring in the property tax, a major new tax on land, property and money which was effectively the forerunner of today's income tax. Brougham and the Whigs organized formidable propaganda against the measure. County and parish meetings gave rise to numerous petitions. The government seemed unable to counter all this with similar sophistication. The timing of the postwar return to the Gold Standard has also been seen as a public opinion defeat for the government. Even Liverpool's most favourable modern biographer says: 'Inexperienced in the arts of publicity and old-fashioned in handling their relations with the general public, the government never seemed to make the best of their case. Virtually the whole of the national press was in the hands either of critical neutrals or party opponents'.[11]

When Parliament was asked in 1817 to consider measures for quelling discontent, Liverpool deemed the situation much more serious than in 1794, when Pitt had been considering similar measures. Moves to license reading rooms as well as political clubs stalled in Parliament.[12] Liverpool himself, while still Foreign Secretary, had been as ready as most to stand up for press freedom when it was under threat from Napoleon. When faced with complaints about British press attacks, Liverpool's reply, in his instructions to our envoy Mr Merry, was suitably unequivocal:

> ...the King neither WOULD nor COULD, in consequence of any menace or representation from a foreign Power, make any concession which could be in the smallest degree dangerous to the liberty of the press, justly dear to every British subject. The British constitution admits of no previous restraints upon publications of this description.[13]

However, in very different circumstances, we find Liverpool asking Parliament to consider 'what measures could be adopted for averting the evils threatened... by the outrageous licentiousness of the Press'.[14]

Liverpool's problem has been neatly summarized: 'The fact that Cobbett could outsell every other journal with his "Political Register", while his opponents relied on subsidies, Post Office facilities and free propaganda, was ample testimony that the government could never force the public to read what it alone considered good and wholesome'.[15] In the previous century, Harley's great contribution at the time of Queen Anne had been his decision to engage with the press on its own ground and largely on its own terms, rather than adopting the route of censorship and prosecution. Walpole, too, had by and large followed the same principle, though with a much cruder and more extensive reliance on subsidies. Both had encountered difficulties in aligning legislation (the Stamp Act) with a precise definition of a newspaper.[16] Liverpool and Sidmouth in turn found that the boundary between a newspaper and a pamphlet could easily become blurred. By the time of the more concerted measures of 1819 and the protests at Peterloo, the question remained vexed. Should government follow the path of out-and-out censorship, rather than using economic means, like their predecessors, to rein it in?

The Six Acts were only partly concerned with the press. They were a package of measures aimed at quelling the outburst of postwar popular unrest, passed on 30 December 1819 partly as a reaction to the Peterloo massacre. The other provisions were concerned with seditious meetings, preventing military-style training and the seizure of arms, as well as curbs on intimidation and violence and their instigators. On the press itself, the Newspaper Stamp Duties Bill and the Blasphemous and Seditious Libels Bill attempted to define a newspaper as containing 'Public News, Intelligence or Occurrences, or any Remarks or Observation thereon'; and if they appeared at least once in 26 days and cost less than six pence (two and a half pence in today's money), they were liable to a tax of four pence, ensuring that the price remained high. The temporary suspension of habeas corpus and other provisions would, it was hoped, do the rest. Parliamentary opposition to the measures from the Whigs was stymied by their wish not to appear weak in the face of terror. Even the magistrates' decision to use force, resulting in 11 deaths at Peterloo, was not opposed in principle: it was as a matter of political judgement, not as legal or moral rightness, that the verdict of the political establishment was passed upon the use of force, and on those grounds the government was unlikely to lose its majority, whatever the longer-term damage to its historical reputation.

Among the press, however, the repressive measures of the government were not regarded quite so phlegmatically. It was the Liverpool government's reaction to Peterloo and the subsequent passing of the Six Acts which finally turned *The Times* from guarded neutrality to outright opposition. It had been critical of the measures to suspend habeas corpus in 1817 – but the new legislation backed by the use of force was, in its view, much worse. Liverpool's old print adversary Sterling (alias Vetus) once again returned to the fray – and, it seems, once more perturbed his proprietor by the vehemence of his articles.

LIVERPOOL: THE LATER YEARS

The other great press battle of Liverpool's premiership was one in which he was emphatically not a central character, despite playing a leading role – the King's divorce. George III, long incapacitated, died in January 1820. The Prince Regent, now George IV, did not want to be crowned with his estranged Queen, Caroline: and it was up to George's government to find a way to get him off the hook. As long as he was Regent, the situation could be left in limbo; but the implications for a reigning monarch were more profound. Any hope that George might have mellowed towards his wife, or become reconciled to her presence in the background, was easily dispelled by the comical but revealing later incident where, in an attempt to inform George of the death of the exiled Napoleon, the King was told that his 'greatest enemy' had died. 'Has she, by God?' was his involuntary reply.

The Times, having opposed Liverpool and his colleagues over the Six Acts and Peterloo in 1819, did the same when it came to the matter of the Queen. Liverpool himself had no strong personal views on the question. His job, as he saw it, was simply to extricate the new king from a problem at least partly of his own making. Henry Brougham, the Whig lawyer-politician who had masterminded the election 'press bureau' of 1807, was one of Caroline's foremost supporters and advisers – and his predilection for press management was already well-known in elite political circles. Thomas Barnes was now editor of *The Times*. Although not a familiar figure to the general public or his readers, he was the first in that sequence of editors of the paper who became powers in the land. Henry Crabb Robinson had held the editor's chair before Barnes, and was also an influential figure – but the position of editor itself, with its unique status, was still being developed in his day. Something of that vagueness was captured by Robinson himself. The publisher John Walter, he said, 'calls me the Editor and I pass for such in the office'; but many decisions were taken by Walter and others.[17] Brougham had been cultivating Barnes for some time, and he claimed that Barnes's switch to supporting the Queen was for that most traditional of journalistic reasons: because support for the Queen was what the majority of his readers wanted to hear, and to avert the danger of their going elsewhere if they did not receive it from their regular newspaper.

In the summer of 1820, Lord Liverpool introduced the bill to deprive the Queen of her title and dissolve the marriage. The new King had long since burned his bridges with the Whigs. Their long alliance in his father's lifetime fractured when he kept Perceval in office in 1811, on gaining the Regency for a year, and broke beyond repair when he retained him again and then replaced him (eventually) with Liverpool in 1812, as the Regency became indefinite. The whole affair had thus become a more or less straightforward matter of party politics: Tories for the King, Whigs for the Queen. With their only child, Princess Charlotte, now dead, Caroline came close to becoming an unlikely substitute for that standard Hanoverian figure, the opposition-minded heir to the throne. With the increasingly influential *Times* in opposition as well, the government relied on such trusty hands as *The Courier* and the *New Times* (originally set up by a disgruntled *Times* man who felt his old paper was insufficiently robust in supporting the restored Bourbons in France, and in particular the French 'Ultra royalists' who deemed Louis XVIII too moderate in his rule). The recently founded *John Bull* was also pro-government, if rather shrill and embarrassing in its articulation of the cause: a seemingly permanent and inseparable trait for papers of that title. The government even took the then relatively unusual step of printing pro-King speeches – including one of Liverpool's – to keep up the momentum, such as it was, of popular support for George IV.[18]

The legislation stalled, majorities dwindled, Liverpool abandoned the unwelcome task, and the popular tumult eventually wore itself out. The papers had played their part. The government, characteristically, had made use of the press resources that were available, but had not embarked on a concerted or in any way innovative attempt to mould or change public opinion. Liverpool's heart was almost certainly never in so distasteful a task; and his personal relationship with the King had never been strong. George, who as Prince of Wales had in 1788 sought to buy off the hostile *Morning Post* to silence its criticisms, may well have thought the government's propaganda insufficiently energetic. Thereafter, the Prince had been widely regarded as having a 'close connection' with the paper, whatever the precise nature of their financial relationship.[19] The one-time editor of the *Morning Post*, Henry Bate Dudley, had gone on to be involved with the *Morning Herald*, which he had put at the service of the then Whiggish Prince and his friend Fox. In later life, Bate Dudley would drop dark hints about 'confidential services' he claimed to have performed for Prince George.[20] At this time, the King was considering changing his government, and even approached Grenville (always a seemingly unlikely partner of the Fox-Grey-Brougham Whigs) about taking over as prime minister. In the end, however, the King and Liverpool resumed their uneasy partnership, unbroken until Liverpool's health completely collapsed in 1827. Relations with *The Times* remained strained, however, even after the Queen had disappeared from the political (and indeed from the mortal) scene in 1821.

The increasing importance of *The Times* was perhaps reflected in the parliamentary time given to the question of whether the government had deprived it of official advertisements. Although Chancellor of the Exchequer Nicholas Vansittart initially denied that such a measure had been taken, the question was raised again later, and no further denial was issued. The rising strength of the title meant that it did not suffer greatly from the withdrawal of advertisements. Its increasing political influence was matched by strong circulation – only 500 or so less than the *Morning Chronicle* and *The Courier* combined. What is also notable about the airing of the question in Parliament in 1821 and 1822 is the almost complete silence of the government on the question. One can understand a refusal to comment on direct press subsidies through secret service funds – particularly in relation to the Irish press, where there was always a gap between political practice and public rhetoric. However, the unwillingness to bring questions such as government advertising under public discussion is rather more striking, given the fact that the evidence was available and demonstrable merely by perusing the papers in question.

LIVERPOOL: THE LIBERAL TORY YEARS

Liverpool's view of the appropriate conduct of politics remained traditional to the end. It was not expected at this stage that prime ministers and other senior figures would regularly address political meetings outside parliament: particularly if, like Liverpool, they were peers without elections to fight. The platform speech was not yet part of mainstream politics, although public addresses might be made at special dinners, awards of the freedom of a city and similar occasions. At the same time, relations with the press remained a rare and undesirable topic for political or public discourse. One of Liverpool's own junior colleagues, Robert Plumer Ward, who did some press work and article writing for the ministry, commented on Liverpool's mastery of parliament and his colleagues: '... [N]o man can lead the House or the Cabinet so well; on all subjects every one looks up to him in debate'. But, said Ward, he relied too much on parliament and neglected wider public opinion.[21]

As his administration recovered from the traumas of Peterloo and the Queen Caroline affair, however, it was also renewing itself politically. Vansittart was replaced by Frederick Robinson (Lord Goderich, the future prime minister) as Chancellor. Canning replaced Castlereagh as Foreign Secretary after his suicide in 1822. Peel replaced Sidmouth as Home Secretary. Some of the effort put into retaining the support of newspapers during the period after the worst embarrassments of the royal family's scandals was retained. In 1822, the government even sponsored the publication of an ostensibly anonymous but clearly semi-official pamphlet called 'The State of the Nation' to list its achievements thus far (reducing taxation, cutting government costs), its continuing aspirations and its overall view of policy. In itself, as a pamphlet, it was not a new form of political communication; but it represented an early foray into the management of public opinion in a more systematized fashion, which would lead in time to the election manifesto and the party political broadcast.[22]

The policy agenda shifted from civil disorder and infighting within the royal family to more mainstream issues such as the Corn Laws, parliamentary reform and Catholic Emancipation: and where each of these contemporary debates was concerned, albeit for different reasons, Liverpool's continuing presence at Number 10 was essential. His gradual approach to modifying aspects of the Corn Laws and parliamentary reform (far too gradual for many in relation to reform) was balanced by his continued defence of the status quo *vis-à-vis* the Catholic question: but always expressed in a tone suggesting pragmatism and thoughtfulness, not reflexive hostility. Parliamentary opponents noted that they would trust their case to Liverpool; and he would often be as effective in debate when putting forward their case, before returning to his own, as they were themselves.

ENTER CANNING

Liverpool collapsed from a major stroke in his breakfast room in February 1827. He did not resign immediately: in fact, due to the extraordinary difficulty in replacing him, Canning did not succeed as prime minister until April; but his career was over, and he died in December 1828. Never a colourful figure in the popular imagination, Liverpool had nevertheless escaped much of the vitriol unleashed on his colleagues. Caricaturists did not have much to work on: his tall, thin figure and somewhat gloomy countenance usually had to be pressed into service to distinguish him from more 'evil'-looking characters like Sidmouth, Castlereagh and Eldon, or the more bombastic Canning. Even the poet Shelley spared him the extensive personal abuse meted out to the others in 'The Masque of Anarchy' ('I met Murder on the way / He had a face like Castlereagh...'). The hostility meted out by Sterling's 'Vetus' articles in 1812 was not genuinely personal in tone nor rooted in an animosity specifically directed at Liverpool; whoever had been prime minister after Perceval would have been similarly attacked in order to attempt to clear the way for the ambitious Lord Wellesley.

Liverpool was certainly about as uninterested in personal self-promotion as it was possible to be while active at the top level of politics in his time. In the twentieth century, one of the few biographies of Liverpool was published without anyone apparently realizing that the frontispiece picture was of his father, the 1st Earl.[23] His reputation also suffered at the hands of Disraeli, who famously referred to him as 'The Arch-Mediocrity'. This all helped to set the tone for a consistent undervaluing of Liverpool which is only now being redressed.

The Tory ensemble which Liverpool kept together for 15 years unravelled immediately on his departure. Those, led by Canning, who were generally in favour of Catholic Emancipation, and less openly hostile to parliamentary reform, were prepared to coalesce with elements of the Whig grouping. The so-called 'Ultras', now effectively led by Wellington, who had served in Liverpool's government in its later years, would not compromise on this, and distrusted Canning on a profoundly personal level, both for his ill-disguised political ambition and for his social origins. To complicate matters, some Whigs, including, crucially, Lord Grey, shared these negative views, and would not serve with him. The immediate future lay with Canning, and his supporters were joined by a group of moderate Whigs, including the Marquess of Lansdowne (formerly Lord Henry Petty) and Lord Holland.

Canning, who had aspired to the premiership all his adult life, lasted just four months in the role before he died as a result of complications from an illness contracted at the funeral of the Duke of York at the beginning of 1827. The ministry tottered on for a further five months under Robinson, now Lord Goderich, before it collapsed at the beginning of 1828, to be replaced by a more recognizably Tory administration under Wellington. A few Canningites served for a few months longer – including Palmerston and the future Lord Melbourne – though the then Whig Edward Stanley, the future Lord Derby, left straight away. But, by the middle of 1828, it was essentially Liverpool's ministry without the Canning supporters.

Canning himself had been interested in the press throughout his career. Indeed, this may even have been one of the reasons for the distrust he inspired among so many of the aristocratic elite around him. We have already seen his leading role in founding and editing the *Anti Jacobin*, and the help he was able to enlist from Pitt and young Jenkinson (Liverpool). There may even have been occasional contributions from other senior figures. Earlier still, at Eton, he had been a leading spirit in the production of a school journal, *The Microcosm*. Much later, during the early Liverpool years, he formed the brief alliance with Wellesley already mentioned, their shared disgruntlement at being excluded from the new Liverpool ministry allying them in mischief. Canning is believed to have leaked to the press details of the failed talks aimed at bringing him back into government. He also wrote to Wellesley, Wellington's elder brother, about the 'Vetus' attacks, complaining not so much about their hostility to his old friend Liverpool but at the open favour shown to Wellesley as a more credible alternative Prime Minister.[24]

Canning may himself have realized that his reputation suffered from the perception that he 'meddled' too much with the press. Like Disraeli, he went to considerable lengths at one stage in his career to play down press involvement. In 1806, he wrote to Lord Morpeth:

> I have long entirely ceased to heed anything relating to myself in newspapers, and have so firmly adhered to my resolution, made two years and a half ago, not to have anything to do or say, directly or indirectly, with the gentlemen of the diurnal Press… (the weekly, I need hardly say, is equally out of my reach) – that I cannot attempt to control our good friend and supporter the 'Courier', in any one particular.[25]

Canning's secretary, Stapleton, claimed that he was true to his word to the end; though later, as Foreign Secretary and Prime Minister, he was happy for others (including Stapleton) to act for him in the cause of favourable coverage. The significance of the disclaimer really lies in the fact that it was necessary at all. It is hard to imagine either of the Pitts or Liverpool feeling obliged to deny something which few would have imagined to be true in the first place.

We know that Canning employed the services of Lewis Goldsmith (the man who ran the *Anti-Gallican*) as a sort of confidential agent in Paris after the Napoleonic Wars.[26] We also know that the brief Canning ministry was especially keen to rebut charges, laid by Wellington and his supporters, that it was spending Secret Service money on procuring press support. No less a figure than Lord Dudley (Canning's successor as Foreign Secretary) specifically rebutted such claims in Parliament. Again, this would have been a more damaging charge for a Canning ministry than for some of its predecessors, because of the personality and reputation of the prime minister. He also turned down an offer from William Jerdan, editor of *The Sun*, to act as, in effect, his press agent in the latter part of his career. This may have been because Canning felt he could not afford to be seen to have what we would call a spin doctor because of his already dubious reputation for press meddling.

Canning did innovate to some extent in relation to broader communication with the public. As MP for Liverpool, he fought regular and lively election campaigns, in which public speaking played a part. Unlike today, not all constituencies were actively contested in general elections. Indeed, in some eighteenth-century polls, the number of contested seats was down to double figures. Even prime ministers in the House of Commons did not necessarily have to campaign actively. Canning, however, most certainly did. He never faced an election as prime minister: Liverpool's fourth and final general election had been won in 1826 (the previous ones were in 1812, 1818 and after the death of George III in 1820).

Canning did, however, leave a record of his views on the role of the press and of public opinion, given in a public speech in Liverpool in 1822. Public opinion, embodied in a free press, he said, 'pervades the constitution, checks and perhaps, in the last resort, governs the whole'.[27] In a comparison which could easily have become a historical and cultural cliché, but did not, he compared the new force of public opinion and the press to that equally novel phenomenon of the age; steam.

There is another tantalizing hint of what might have happened had Canning survived longer as prime minister, and felt more secure in the post. Princess Lieven, ostensibly a diplomatic wife but also a remarkable source of intelligence and gossip in international elite circles, gave an account of a conversation with Canning in late February 1827. Liverpool had already suffered his stroke, but retained his office as positioning for the succession got underway. Canning himself was in Brighton, trying to recover from the illness he sustained at the Duke of York's funeral, but also beginning his 'campaign' for the premiership. 'He explained himself at first', the Princess observed, 'so as to make me understand he was the most powerful man in England. He had first inaugurated the power of the press by making it take an interest in affairs. He governed it'. It is both a bombastic and a frustratingly imprecise claim: the tone is more that of Vivian Grey, the arrogant and ruthlessly ambitious young character of Disraeli's early novels, than that of a mature statesman approaching the pinnacle of his career. *The History of The Times* speculates: 'The phrase "he governed it" may perhaps mean that "he HAD governed it" in the period of the "Anti Jacobin" and that its influence was still felt; or that his governance automatically resulted from his general popularity'.[28] Thirty years after the *Anti Jacobin*, the former theory looks unlikely. The more plausible interpretation may be that Canning felt he was in the process of inaugurating a new era of political communication; that what became known as the 'platform' was about to become an important adjunct to parliament, and that the press would be instrumental in the process of publicizing it. If so, he was anticipating developments which would be introduced by future prime ministers: notably Palmerston and Gladstone, both of whom regarded themselves as disciples of Canning.

In another striking phrase, Canning once said of public opinion that, since the revolution of 1688, it had grown from a pygmy to a giant and become a power 'which watches over and governs, and controls, not only the actions, but the words of every public man'.[29] The distinction between actions and words is a crucial insight in the history of press relations. Once it is understood that a politician cannot state and execute policy and then simply wait for public understanding and support to follow, but must ensure that perceptions must be managed as well as actions, articulation and dissemination become as important as action, and a new dimension is added to the conscious conduct of public life. Harley and Walpole understood this instinctively. It may be that later politicians, including Canning, looking back through the prism of long decades of uninterrupted Whig rule, failed to realize that in a previous age, the lessons had already been learned – and forgotten.

THE GODERICH INTERLUDE

Canning's death in August 1827 ushered in the brief premiership of Lord Goderich (formerly Frederick Robinson): the 'transient and embarrassed phantom', in Disraeli's characteristically charitable phrase from his last completed novel *Endymion*. The relative success of Goderich's chancellorship during the last five years of Liverpool's government was marked by his nickname, 'Prosperity' Robinson: lucky the government whose chancellor is so dubbed, and largely without irony too. However, he was not the last chancellor to find the premiership a different matter altogether.

Some papers welcomed Goderich's appointment: the *Globe and Traveller* was particularly warm. However, from its inception, his government proved 'leaky'. This is, of course, a phrase that would not be used or recognized until the twentieth century; but a tendency to feed the press information off the record was already a feature of politically insecure governments such as Goderich's. Like Canning's, it was a coalition; but a coalition without the strong, charismatic focus that Canning had represented. Ministers faced strong Tory opposition from Wellington and others, and almost as strong Whig opposition from some of those who, like Grey, had not entered the coalition. The political hostilities were matched by those between the respective newspaper supporters of the different factions, whose own battles were often remarkably toxic. Brougham was outside the government, and he certainly fed *The Times* a lot of confidential material, which destabilized the government. So too did Charles Greville (the diarist), whose inside track at the Privy Council and strong interest in the press gave him ample scope for influencing opinion.

As Goderich was constructing his cabinet, the *Morning Chronicle* claimed that J.C. Herries's close connection with the Rothschild banking dynasty called into question his appointment as chancellor of the exchequer. Goderich had to go so far as to deny the rumour directly to the press, by the admittedly indirect means of writing a letter to Herries for publication in the *New Times*, while other papers lined up for and against Herries. Meanwhile, the new Cabinet was undermined by press 'leaks' almost from the first. Another minister, William Huskisson, described how, during his first interview with George IV, the King commanded him to read that day's *Times* out loud to him, paragraph by paragraph: '... commenting on it as I proceeded. How is it possible to go on with such a Press, supplied from Brooks's [the famous Whig club] with a comment upon everything that is pending in matters of this delicate nature?'[30]

Despite the King's fury, when it was doubtful whether the Whig group in the Cabinet would be able to remain in the government due to the strength of their objections to Herries's appointment, it was the monarch himself who authorized Lord Landsdowne, leader of the rebellious group, to inform the press that they were remaining in the government. The Whig group had objected to the Tory Herries not so much on the grounds of his link to the Rothschilds, but because he was opposed to Catholic Emancipation. These mixed messages almost led to a falling-out with Barnes, the increasingly influential *Times* editor, whom Tory ministers had briefed earlier to the effect that the Whigs were leaving. He had to be 're-briefed' or 'counter-briefed' to the opposite effect, and Lansdowne had the King's direct permission for George Tierney, one of his colleagues, to do so, while briefing the other papers as well.[31] Meanwhile, the battles between several different newspapers, each purporting to speak for one of the Cabinet factions, helped to make the government look weak and faintly ridiculous. When Goderich himself was accused of using friendly papers to attack Wellington and his colleagues, he replied in the Lords that the press was far too powerful and independent to be influenced in this way, even if the government were so disposed. (The implication, as always in public, was that the government was not so disposed).[32]

One of the inherent problems of coalitions is the need to use the press to convince the public that one side is not getting its way too much at the expense of the other. Efforts were made by senior coalition Whigs to brief papers friendly to their cause, priming them with the information that the Whigs in the coalition were winning their Cabinet battles and all was essentially amicable. Goderich himself, like some later coalition prime ministers, stood ready to do his bit to bolster press support for his partners – for instance, authorizing the Whig Thomas Spring-Rice to contradict stories that Herries had demanded Brougham's exclusion as the price of his own participation. In this instance, *The Times* and the *Morning Chronicle* duly fell in behind the agreed 'line'.

Towards the end of the brief Goderich ministry, however, it appears possible that George IV, through his physician, private secretary and general factotum William Knighton, may himself have been using the press to hasten the break-up of the ministry. By this time, the King's views were almost indistinguishable from his father's stout Toryism, and it seems that even the limited participation of the Whigs in the Canning and Goderich coalitions made him uneasy. Whatever delusions he may have entertained about his own personal presence at the Battle of Waterloo, he still had real respect for Wellington at this stage, whereas Canning had been far from a personal favourite; and George seems to have developed a feeling of contempt for Goderich the more he saw of him as prime minister.

He also seems to have taken against Huskisson (perhaps for his part in trying to block Herries). Over Christmas 1827, feeling his own position weakened, Huskisson warned privately that his resignation was imminent. He found himself receiving mysterious warnings of hostility from a very high quarter. A visitor told him that the information in *The Times* 'had been furnished from Windsor'.[33] This all contributed to a growing feeling from within that the ministry was doomed to a break-up, and the impending session of parliament in January proved an insurmountable hurdle. Huskisson, Lansdowne and Herries regarded themselves as having all but formally resigned, and the King eventually dismissed the government and sent for Wellington. Despite accounts of Goderich crying in front of the King, wringing his hands and being offered a handkerchief, by the end he was determined to carry on and meet parliament, but he never had the chance. Discounting the two-day 'footnote' eighteenth-century administrations of Bath and Waldegrave, which do not figure on official lists of prime ministers, Goderich is the only recognized prime minister never to meet Parliament while in office. Despite his poor showing, Goderich went on to serve under the Whig Grey and then the Tory Peel.

WELLINGTON

Wellington served almost three years as Prime Minister. Like Marlborough, he will obviously never be remembered primarily as a politician, but his ministry, long deemed an unfortunate episode in his career, is now in the process of partial rehabilitation. He is also one of those figures, like Churchill and to an extent Disraeli, to whom quotations are often spuriously attributed. Among the genuine ones, his views on the press are often prominent: and the negative ones are much more frequently given an airing. However, Wellington's views on the press changed during his career and they were, in any event, never the blimpish, unqualified contempt of the military man pure and simple. This is partly because he did not, as some seem to imagine, retire from active service and then 'go into politics'. He had been in politics, on and off, since he was an Irish MP in his early 20s, and had developed his own views accordingly. He was also prepared to acknowledge the limitations of his own earlier opinions of the press – especially after his experience in the top job, and also as leader of his party in opposition in the 1830s.

Because he was also a prime minister who introduced a reform he had spent his adult life opposing – the emancipation of the Catholics – Wellington, like Peel, suffered more venom and vitriol in press attacks from his own disgruntled former adherents than he did from the 'official' opposition. One reaction would have been to revert to reflexive contempt for the press: but, by 1829, Wellington's view was undoubtedly more sophisticated.

In 1810, he had accused the press of 'stultifying England'; by 1827, in the early days of Canning's ministry, he can be found criticizing 'the manner I have been treated by the corrupt press in the pay of the government'.[34] He told Wellesley, his elder brother, that England was governed by 'the Gentlemen of the Press', while Liverpool was still prime minister; and he later told Greville that his fall from power in late 1830 was due to his neglect of the press. At the very least, here is a man who thought often and sometimes subtly about the role the press had played in his life and career. Why else would he have received regular copies of Cobbett's paper from his wife, even if it made him angry on occasion? He was even prepared to rebut stories of his gambling in the *Morning Chronicle*.[35] By the time he was prime minister, Wellington was certainly no more fastidious than his predecessors about enlisting press support. After the traditional Tory papers deserted him in droves after Catholic Emancipation in 1829, he asked J.W. Croker to sound out John Gibson Lockhart, the son-in-law of that stalwart Tory Sir Walter Scott, about buying a paper such as *The Star* to support his rather beleaguered ministry (Lockhart refused). Earlier, the Wellington ministry had reviewed its options with *The Courier*.

Even at its inception in 1828, before its 'apostasy' on Catholic Emancipation, the Duke's ministry was short of press support. The Whig papers, and those who had supported Canning and Goderich, were obviously not well-disposed. But already the 'Ultra-Tory' press was also restive, after the jettisoning of some of the trusted members of Liverpool's administration (notably Eldon, the former Lord Chancellor, but others too) to make (temporary) room for a few of the Canningite and moderate Whig coalitionists. Eldon (despite being in his late 70s, and having served as Lord Chancellor under five prime ministers from 1801–6 and 1807–27) claimed that the Duke's government had briefed the papers to the effect that he had been offered, and declined, not merely a return to office, but even the right to be consulted as to who should be in office. 'Nothing can be so utterly false', the old man grumbled.[36]

Fortunately, *The Courier* played its part on Wellington's behalf. Indeed, it was claimed that the paper had done Downing Street's bidding in 'boosting' Eldon's replacement, Lord Lyndhurst. The *Morning Journal* insisted that Wellington peremptorily ordered *The Courier* to support Lyndhurst by providing an article for virtually verbatim inclusion in the paper. It later alleged that *The Courier* and, indeed, the *Morning Post* existed primarily to promote official statements from Downing Street. 'If any unwelcome news finds its way to the public, the "Post" is instructed to contradict it in the morning, and the "Courier" is ordered to swear to the milliner's [sic] falsehood in the evening... at the nod of some subordinate secretary of the Treasury'.[37]

'I HATE MEDDLING WITH THE PRESS'

One of Wellington's more remarkable political achievements was to keep *The Times* broadly on his side for most of his administration. It seems that this was done in the most time-honoured media management fashion by giving it news and intelligence in advance of its competitors. With *The Times*, this was not despite his decision to introduce Catholic Emancipation, but precisely in order to bring it about. Despite all the manoeuvrings both parties undertook in relation to *The Times* – the Whigs' unofficial spin doctor, Brougham, briefed Barnes the editor about how he saw things and wished his views to be reported – the Whigs and Wellington were ultimately at one on the question of Catholic Emancipation, despite their other political and personal differences and the desire of the Whigs to ensure that they received credit for bringing it about. The wording of *The Times* article on Wellington's conversion, and the reference to the paper's source, are interestingly phrased.

> We rejoice to say again, what we made known some months ago – viz. that we have the very strongest reasons for attributing to the Duke of WELLINGTON (sic) a fixed determination to introduce a bill for the relief of the Catholics in the ensuing Session. We announce this, and we stand to it as our firm conviction, founded on intelligence from a quarter alike incapable of being deceived itself, and of deceiving others.[38]

Wellington had distanced himself from any direct press campaign against Canning (and Goderich) in 1827. He explicitly declined his friend Rev. G.R. Gleig's offer of a series of 'Letters of Junius'-style polemics against the coalition.[39] He certainly was not naive about the press. He was one of a number of future prime ministers who had served (in Portland's time) as Irish Chief Secretary, and his experience of the subsidized Irish press had been as unhappy and disillusioning as it had for the others. Some £20,000 had been spent on press subsidies on his watch, while the unsubsidized press was even more troublesome, going 'either bankrupt or berserk'.[40] While in Ireland as Chief Secretary, from 1807 to 1809, Wellington (or Wellesley as he was then) disclaimed any attempt to manage the press in a detailed manner. He claimed that government proclamations would be given to papers irrespective of whether they received the subsidy. He also expressed the view, towards the end of his time in the office, that the subsidy regime was discredited and not the way forward, while carefully avoiding any direct reference to it in his own official correspondence.[41] But, once prime minister, he was prepared to deploy the available repertoire of news management tools to buttress his own position, and support his policies.

Wellington was firmly in the tradition of eighteenth- and nineteenth-century rhetorical dismissal of the press in public. His ironic references to 'the gentlemen of the press' were so frequent as to be eventually abbreviated; whenever he refers to 'the gentlemen', one knows it is journalists to whom he refers. Later in his career, he acknowledged to friends and colleagues his regret that he had not reacted to the press more skilfully. At a time when Peel (his eventual successor as Tory leader) was proclaiming his own reluctance to meddle with such matters, Wellington, within months of the end of his own ministry, wrote in support of Herries's belief that Peel would need to change his approach.[42]

WELLINGTON AND CROKER

It was during Wellington's ministry that the idea of a government press bureau was revisited. As we saw, in Perceval's time, a blueprint for a much more sophisticated system of press relations had been sketched out, though never implemented. The influential author, journalist and politician J.W. Croker resuscitated the idea 20 years later, in 1829. Wellington had inherited the traditional system whereby the press was one of the many responsibilities of a Treasury minister. Joseph Planta had held the job under Liverpool and the coalition premiers. But he had become too close to Canning for the Duke's entire comfort; and Wellington also professed himself unhappy with his press relations. Eight months after succeeding Goderich in 1828, Wellington told Croker:

> I hate meddling with the Press. The perpetual interference with the Press was one of the rocks on which my predecessors struck. But I am afraid we do meddle, that is to say, the Secretary of the Treasury does; but he does not attend to it, nor does he meddle with that degree of intelligence which might be expected from him. I must put this to rights.[43]

Croker, credited with being something akin to a Tory answer to Brougham when it came to press management skills, also reflected deeply on the growing influence of public opinion, and the broader role of the press and of communication in politics. His proposals differed from those of 1809 in important respects. Among his suggestions was that a Cabinet minister should be responsible for influencing or 'instructing' the friendly papers instead of a mere parliamentary secretary to the Treasury: in effect, though not in name, an early version of a minister for information of the sort later tried in the twentieth century. Croker wrote that it must all be done 'in the most profound secrecy',[44] with the Cabinet minister making the occasional deliberate error to cover his tracks. He continued:

> But I fear it is impossible to hope that a Cabinet minister could be permitted, or found willing, to undertake this delicate task, though… the times are gone by when statesmen might safely despise the journals, or only treat them as inferior engines which might be left to themselves, or be committed to the guidance of persons wholly unacquainted with the views of the ministry.[45]

He also prophesied:

> The day is not far distant when you will (not SEE, or HEAR) but KNOW that there is someone in the Cabinet entrusted with what will be thought one of the most important duties of the State, the regulation of public opinion.[46]

As with the plan of 1809, this advice was never implemented: it would take almost a century and a Great War before anything on this scale was formally attempted. It seems likely that Croker's own scheme would have been destined to fail in any event. The level of secrecy he deemed essential would surely not have been sustainable in the long term: indeed, it was inherently incompatible with the nature and sphere of the activities involved. Also, as we have seen, the notion, implicit in what he says about the past, of a simpler age in which the press and communication could safely be ignored never really existed.

Nevertheless, Croker's thinking was clearly in advance of his contemporaries' views. He was closely associated with the *Quarterly Review* for many years, bolstering its position as the Tory bulwark against the Whiggish *Edinburgh Review*. Positioned some way between journalism and the academic journals of our own age, they wielded huge influence on political thinking: and it was respectable for senior practising politicians to write for a review in a way that it certainly was not (yet) for them to do for newspapers.

Croker was at various times close to three Tory prime ministers: Wellington, Peel and Derby. He was an MP, a minister (First Secretary to the Admiralty) throughout the Liverpool-Wellington years and a useful counterweight to Brougham. Speaking late in life, he would take an altogether darker view of the role of the press in politics:

> My regret and alarm is that I see all ministerial functions either yielded to or usurped by committees of the House of Commons, and even more undisguisedly by editors of newspapers.[47]

WELLINGTON AND *THE TIMES*

Long before that pessimistic verdict was given, however, Wellington prepared, in 1829, to introduce his Catholic Emancipation measure. As has already been hinted at above, his engagement with and management of the press, particularly *The Times*, where this crucial and sensitive issue was concerned, adds much-needed nuance to the one-dimensional popular perception of Wellington as a prime minister who disdained the media entirely.

The intense hostility provoked by James II's attempt to convert Britain back to Catholicism had resulted in the next regime, under William III and Mary II, introducing a raft of legislation aimed at reducing the role of Catholics in the state. In particular, Catholics were banned from participating in a number of key institutions of the state: the old universities, parliament and the monarchy itself. In the intervening century or so, animosity had cooled off, and the feeling was now widespread that the time had come for a less exclusionary approach. Even some Tories, as well as most Whigs, judged a loosening of some of the tightest restictions timely and judicious. The Duke himself recognized that the support of *The Times* was crucial in navigating proposed reforms successfully through parliament, and it was becoming more of an axiom than ever that, for all the other outlets available, *The Times* wielded a more extensive influence than the rest. The ministry ensured that the Foreign Office official Digby Wrangham met regularly with Barnes, the editor, to ensure the paper had privileged access to information as early as possible. The attitude of the ageing George IV was important. He was against the reform, of course; but would he heed his brother the Duke of Cumberland and actively rally the bill's opponents to his standard as their father had done? Wrangham briefed Barnes that it looked unlikely:

> I don't know that I can give you any FACTS to assure the publick of H.M.'s unchanged disposition to support his Ministers, but the fact itself is certain: and you may safely contradict any rumours to the contrary.[48]

This all ensured that *The Times* would not take a Whig oppositionist position and adopt the perennial criticism that the proposed reforms constituted 'too little too late'. The papers whose support the Duke would probably have expected earlier in his career – the *Morning Post*, *Morning Journal*, *Standard* and the *St James's Chronicle* – backed the Ultra-Tory opposition, outflanked in raucousness, as ever, only by *John Bull*. Indeed, when George IV died the following year and *The Times* published a witheringly critical obituary, the outraged *St James's* headlined its own leading article: 'Libel upon the Late King from "*The Times*", the Duke of Wellington's journal'.[49] The paper had said that the only feature of the King's reign that would distinguish it in history was the passage of Catholic Emancipation, precisely the event which he most deplored and regretted, while, in the end, being unwilling or powerless to stop it.

It was Wellington's outspoken claim of the complete absence of any need for parliamentary reform that ended his own premiership, and forfeited the goodwill of his recent press supporters and adherents. Although Wellington won the general election that followed the King's death (general elections were still required after the death of a monarch), it was with a more-than-usually reduced majority. In France, the overthrow of Charles X, more of a restorationist 'Ultra' than his elder brother Louis XVIII, whom he had succeeded in 1824, and his subsequent replacement by Louis Philippe, demonstrated that this was no time for reactionaries. Wellington may have felt that he had 'done enough' for progressive opinion by passing Catholic Emancipation. One of the tipping points against Charles and his minister Polignac in France had been the decision to suspend freedom of the press. Such a blanket ban was never remotely likely in Britain in 1830, despite the fact that governments continued to use the law against radical journals on an ad hoc basis. However, when Wellington lauded the perfection of the prevailing political system in the House of Lords in late 1830, his fate was sealed, and his new press allies bade him farewell. As the bitterness of Catholic

Emancipation faded in the wake of a new political battle, Wellington would find himself moving inevitably back into an alliance with the traditional Tory press, and his always somewhat unlikely partnership with *The Times* came to an end.

In his later career, Wellington would often find himself applying the lessons of his own earlier press relations. For all his sarcasms and dismissals of 'the gentlemen', those lessons often clearly indicated the need for greater engagement; and he was not too proud to admit on several occasions that he had underestimated the power of the press and the consequent need to manage press relations more effectively. While he led the opposition to the new Whig government, and when he briefly held the premiership (and several other offices) again in 1834, pending Peel's return from the Continent, the press in general, and the possibility of regaining the support of *The Times* in particular, were among the issues with which he was most preoccupied. He told Lord Lyndhurst, the Lord Chancellor, of his fears that *The Times* would not support them this time, and he once more lamented to Greville that he had neglected the press too much in earlier days.[50] Indeed, Wellington, along with Lyndhurst, was at the forefront of what were effectively negotiations between the Tories and Thomas Barnes, editor of *The Times*, as to the position the paper would take. The general shock within the political class which was expressed at Lyndhurst and Barnes meeting for dinner reminds us of the still relatively lowly social position of the press in 1834. But the fact that it happened, and that Wellington was prepared to play a role in it too, tells us much more about the changing realities of the power and influence of the press. Without in any way being revolutionaries of press management, Liverpool, Wellington and their colleagues had been instrumental in another major phase of change: not merely in the culture and practice of politics, but also in the constant redefinition of the relationship between prime ministers, their colleagues and the press.

CHAPTER THREE

GREY AND MELBOURNE

L ORD GREY, WHO became Prime Minister in November 1830, had spent almost his entire career in opposition. He had served in the Grenville ministry of 1806–7, succeeding Fox as Foreign Secretary. But he had held ostentatiously and rather disdainfully aloof from the Canning-Goderich coalitions, and was 66 when he finally became prime minister. In his government were several future prime ministers: Melbourne, Russell, Derby (then still Stanley) and Palmerston; not to mention a former premier – Goderich, now Lord Ripon; and the Marquess of Lansdowne, who would be offered and would refuse the premiership more than once. Grey had an agenda: parliamentary reform was not an unexpected outcome of his premiership, as Catholic Emancipation had been for Wellington. He also had a record of disparaging and, where possible, ignoring the press that exceeded Wellington's, even in the Duke's earlier years. At the same time, he had a member of his Cabinet who was perfectly willing to perform the sort of secret duties outlined in Croker's suggestions of the previous year – namely a press bureau and a Cabinet-level chief. Henry Brougham was now Lord Chancellor, and he was happy to combine the traditional duties of the Woolsack with the rather less official role of press manager.

Later in life, in a long and rather bitter retirement from high office, Brougham would stand accused of faking an announcement of his own death just to see how it was reported in the papers. A man who could even plausibly be suspected of this was always going to be an awkward bedfellow for Grey. Nevertheless, Grey was in principle as strong a supporter of the freedom of the press as any of his predecessors. He believed the liberty of the country depended upon it, as well as its strength, happiness and glory.[1] When the MP Joseph Hume moved to repeal the newspaper Stamp Duties in 1827, just after Canning had become prime minister, Grey's son Lord Howick (quite possibly with his father's approval) supported him. However, since neither

4. Charles Grey, 2nd Earl Grey, after Sir Thomas Lawrence, c.1828.
© National Portrait Gallery, London.

father nor son ever showed any subsequent keenness to enact the reform, we must suppose it was based more on loathing of Canning than on love for the press. When it came to press attacks, Grey could assume the garb of the weary philosopher with the best of them: 'The only way with newspaper attacks is, as the Irish say, "to keep never minding". This has been my practice throughout life'.[2]

5. William Lamb, 2nd Viscount Melbourne, by Sir Edwin Henry Landseer, 1836.
© National Portrait Gallery, London.

However, like all prime ministers, Grey was both aware of and to some extent involved in press management. He was content for Brougham to do the detailed work, using his close contacts with Barnes, the editor of *The Times*, to ensure the favour of the paper now that it had abandoned Wellington and the Tories over reform. Although their meetings may not have attracted as much general surprise as Lyndhurst's dinner with a representative of the press, Brougham and Barnes now breakfasted together regularly. For *The Times*, the concern was not the radical nature of Grey's parliamentary reform proposals; it was that they would be too half-hearted.[3] Meanwhile, *The Courier*, which had supported the various Tory ministries since 1807, swung round to the new administration's side. Although the support of *The Times* was undoubtedly based on policy, this did not stop Barnes asking Brougham for a post for his brother John as the new government came in. The proprietor of *The Courier*, Gibbons Merle, also requested a position for himself, to compensate for the difficulties he alleged he had encountered in switching from the Tories to the Whigs. Brougham was willing to oblige, but nothing had been found by the time the ministry ended in 1834.[4]

GREY AND THE PAPERS

There was an interesting passage of arms in the Lords in 1832 over what exactly was meant by the phrase 'a government paper'. While Cobbett had earlier said he believed that Grey's government had three friendly papers – *The Times*, *Courier* and *Morning Chronicle* – Melbourne, then Home Secretary, and Grey himself stated the official line: that the only government paper was the *London Gazette* (which, of course, was the paper of every government, whatever its political colours). Indeed, Grey, somewhat ruefully, claimed that Wellington had received more newspaper support than was being extended to him. He took the view that, because the so-called government papers contained much material critical of ministers, they could not be termed 'Government papers, if, by such a term, the noble duke meant to convey the impression that he or the government possessed any power or influence over them whatever'.[5] Grey's reply is flawed, with its denial of influence seeming overstated at best, disingenuous at worst considering Brougham's regular breakfasts and other activities; furthermore, as for his assertion that the presence of material critical of the government meant that a particular paper could not be a 'government paper', all but the most slavish papers, even in a dictatorship, will contain critical material on occasion. However, it touches indirectly on another phenomenon, without mentioning it. Some of the most intensely fought press battles of the Grey administration were conducted between factions of the government and Cabinet itself, in addition to the more traditional ones against the formal opposition.

Brougham was part of the 'activist' section of the Cabinet on parliamentary reform. All were agreed that reform of some sort there must be. But the pace, the extent and the reaction to obstacles divided them. Brougham, therefore, used his press connections to advance his wing of the party. He and Barnes both believed that public opinion was a vital tool in stiffening the resolve of the Prime Minister. Sometimes, the pressure became personal. *The Times* attacked on a new flank: criticizing Grey for having too many of his own relations in his government. Foreshadowing similar attacks on Lord Salisbury and Harold Macmillan, the articles annoyed the Grey family intensely.[6] Brougham did his best (at great and unconvincing length) to exculpate himself, while Grey allowed himself a short and rather plaintive reply: 'You have somewhere a most injudicious friend and I a most unprovoked and malicious enemy'.[7] The 'somewhere' is a deft touch, given Grey's near-certainty as to the source.

Some observers – especially Tories – professed admiration not just for the extent but also for the skill of the Whig ministry's press relations. The Treasury minister notionally responsible for the press, Edward Ellice, did his part, though he was inevitably overshadowed by Brougham. A future giant of press management, the Foreign Secretary Lord Palmerston, was already honing his skills by inspiring and possibly contributing articles to *The Globe*. Home Secretary Melbourne – another great one for public denials of any 'trafficking' with the press – was happy for his secretary Thomas Young to be active on his behalf. The Commons Leader Lord Althorp also had a secretary with an aptitude for press management, Thomas Drummond, who was referred to by no less an authority than *The Times* itself as the administration's 'chief manager' of the press. In a fascinating article published during the brief first Peel ministry of 1834–5, the paper said:

> The management of the press was one of the arms of the late Government, and if the attempt had been carried on to success, it would have ended in a rotten representation of public opinion, similar to the rotten representation of the people before Parliamentary Reform... The editorship of one paper

was as much a Government appointment as a seat at the India Board or the Admiralty. A committee regularly organised, an inquisition, a secret tribunal, used to hold daily sittings in a Government office, and contrive things for the reward of the servile and the damage of the untractable. The effect of this, where it had effect, was infinitely worse than a censorship.[8]

In a reference to Althorp and Drummond, it continued:

The chief manager of the press (the description is a disgrace to the Ministry) under the late government can be named, and remarkable it is that his post was nearest to the noble person whose plain-dealing and straightforward ways have been the theme of the loudest praise.[9]

The parenthesis, deploring the very existence of press management, is especially notable, showing that the rhetorical pretence that such activity was beyond the pale of publicly acceptable political activity was shared by the press as well as by the politicians.

Of course, the fact that much of Drummond's activity involved favouring other papers did not help the temper of *The Times*. Drummond 'steered' *The Scotsman*, as well as writing for *The Globe* and the *Morning Chronicle*, while constantly criticizing *The Times*. Drummond is found writing to his brother John asking for advice as to which committee rooms *The Globe* and the *Morning Chronicle* should be sent to: 'The "Chronicle" advances rapidly, so does the "Globe". "*The Times*" quails and wavers as such a miserable (*sic*) deserves to do'.[10]

Although this was written in November 1834, by which time the short-lived Melbourne ministry was ending its four-month life, the comments are applied to the Grey-Melbourne ministry as a whole. There is no record of anyone noticing a sudden change of press policy when Grey resigned and Melbourne took over in the summer of 1834. With a certain irony, Drummond later served in the second and much longer Melbourne ministry as Chief Secretary to Ireland, where the issues of press management, as we have already had cause to note, had a savour all their own. Brougham, meanwhile, referred to Drummond much later as something of an amateur compared to his own skills with the press. He was, he said, 'a mere looker to newspapers, and thinks a government secure and right which gains newspaper puffs'.[11] One is more than faintly reminded of the 'spin wars' of the early years of the Blair government, and of the rival operations run by Alastair Campbell in

Number 10 and Charlie Whelan in Number 11, simultaneously disseminating the Gordon Brown line from Number 11. Sometimes, prime ministers must have wondered whether having too many press managers caused more trouble than having none at all.

Even the elite political classes sometimes found it difficult to ascribe papers' loyalties within the Cabinet. The very experienced politician Charles Arbuthnot thought that *The Globe* was firmly in Grey's personal camp in 1832. In fact, Grey did not have a paper attached to him personally, as distinct from his government as a whole; *The Globe*'s closest links at this period were with Palmerston. Increasingly, senior ministers spent their time disclaiming responsibility for press attacks on their colleagues.

While the great measures of the Grey government had been passed, including the Reform Act in 1832 and the Abolition of Slavery Act in 1833, the government's own internal tensions became more bitter and public. Moreover, the wars between papers were more than proxy fights on behalf of the political class: they became intense battles for commercial and editorial supremacy in their own right. As circulations and potential profits rose at the top level, papers like *The Times* and the *Morning Chronicle* fought each other tooth and nail. It was almost as if the politicians were becoming proxies for the papers' wars rather than the other way round. However, there were real issues at stake, even after the passage of the two great reforms; and it was the vexed question of coercion of Ireland which led to the complex series of manoeuvres and disagreements which eventually resulted in Grey's resignation in the summer of 1834, and Melbourne's brief first administration. At the same time, the government was introducing the notorious Poor Law of that year, seen by some at the time as a progressive measure; but one which contributed enormously to our view of early Victorian Britain as a harsh, cruel, unforgiving place to be poor.

GREY: THE VERDICT

The Poor Law, the controversial legislation which introduced the dreaded workhouse to the popular imagination and to contemporary literature, and, in particular, the opposition of *The Times* and of Barnes to its provisions, gave rise to one of the most extraordinary press leaks of all time. Brougham and Althorp were furious at the paper's opposition to the measure, which it saw, along with the eye of history, as unnecessarily cruel to the poor. Brougham and Althorp sent each other short notes on the question of how to combat it. Brougham received one from the temporarily indisposed Althorp while presiding over the Court of Chancery. He read it, tore it into little pieces and put it in the waste-paper basket. We would never have known of it had not someone waited until Brougham had finished, collected the fragments, reassembled them and sent them anonymously 'To the Editor of "The Times", Printing House Square, Blackfriars', and marked it 'Immediate'. The sender added: 'Picked up by a Friend and sent thinking it may be of service as a private principle of action'. The letter itself read:

> Private.
>
> My dear Brougham, The subject I want to talk to you about is the State of the Press, and whether we should declare open war with '*The Times*' or attempt to make peace.
>
> Yours most truly, Althorp.

Barnes let Brougham know of the letter's destination; and eventually the whole affair found its way into the public domain. Intriguingly, when the *Morning Chronicle*, cementing its place as the Whigs' most reliable ally, reprinted the letter, it replaced the words *The Times* with 'the Tories'![12] If the *Chronicle* had been shown the letter, it is unlikely to have been a misreading, as the word 'Times' is clearly legible, with a visible dot over the 'i'. Maybe it was the customary reluctance of a paper to name its rivals; but, since *The Times* was not then a Tory paper, it changed the sense of the story, sharply reducing its news value. A political party deciding whether to be hostile to its official political opponents was hardly news, then or now. The breach with *The Times* over the Poor Law, only weeks before Grey's own resignation, was, however, certainly symptomatic of the ministry's difficulties.

Grey's place in history is secure, although he has rarely enjoyed the prominence enjoyed in popular culture and folklore by other distinctive prime ministers. Melbourne, by contrast, had fewer striking measures associated with his name, and yet, because of his close association with the young Victoria, who succeeded William IV in 1837, he probably has a livelier profile in popular culture.

Grey will always be 'Lord Grey of the Reform Act', however, and it was this measure that Croker believed had such adverse effects on the press and public opinion. Writing to Brougham in January 1854, Croker was of the opinion that there was a direct link between the passage of the Reform Act and the increasing power of the press. Croker tied the growth of newspaper power to other mechanical, educational and commercial changes. But he saw another consequence:

> The Reform Bill established the broad principle of governing by representation, and on that basis has been erected into omnipotence what was formerly a valuable subordinate agent, now called public opinion: she was of old the queen of the world; she has now become its tyrant, and the newspapers her ministers: that is, they assume that they represent public opinion, and of course the people, in a more direct and authoritative manner, than even the House of Commons.[13]

In addition, Croker feared the worst in relation to the politicians' behaviour *vis-à-vis* the press:

> The Reform Bill has made seats, and therefore the profession of public life, so precarious that no man can venture to brave the press, and with what audacity of censure, or the exaggeration of flattery with which it visits individuals, there has grown up, and is still growing, an influence over the conduct of members so imperious that the Speaker, instead of demanding from the Sovereign freedom of speech, had much better ask it from the 'Times'.[14]

Croker himself abandoned active politics on principle after the Reform Act passed: thenceforth his energies were given to what was then termed the 'higher journalism', the world of the review. Of course, it is easy to satirize his view, and refer scathingly to his perception of the inconvenience of democracy and public opinion. However, it is perhaps more constructive to set patronizing rhetoric to one side and consider the applicability of his analysis to political and journalistic behaviour over the following century and a half. Whatever view we take of his doom-laden prognostications, how the effects of Grey's Reform Act – followed by those of Derby, Gladstone, Lloyd George and Baldwin – worked themselves out proved to be of huge importance for the relations between prime ministers and their colleagues on the one side and the fourth estate on the other.

MELBOURNE

Melbourne had promised continuity with Grey, who had tired of further, faster reform by the end of his ministry. However, because of the rather acrid political and journalistic climate of 1834, he found himself accused of using one of his officials who cultivated his own press links, Thomas Young, to undermine Grey's popularity and political position in the press, along with that of other key colleagues. Only a month after Grey's resignation, Melbourne, already established within the firm tradition of publicly disclaiming any direct involvement with the press, had to write to Brougham:

> ... I cannot believe that Young is in any respect the cause of these malignant attacks upon you and upon Althorp... How can he have the power to direct the newspaper as he listeth? What can give it him? Not his situation as connected with me, for the Press has never shown any great deference to Prime Ministers, at least, they never did to Grey, whom they were always abusing with the utmost bitterness, and I have no doubt that you will have a very little time to wait before you will perceive that their sparing of me is but temporary, and that Young's influence is not sufficient to control or moderate them.[15]

A few weeks later, Melbourne told Brougham that he did not know '... what newspapers you designate by the name of the Government Press. I know none which states my opinions or anything like them'.[16]

Melbourne, as we have seen, made an early newspaper debut in the *Morning Chronicle*, attempting a riposte to the *Anti Jacobin*. The verse was not especially inspiring:

> Proceed – be more opprobrious if you can;
> Proceed – be more abusive every hour;
> To be more stupid is beyond your power.[17]

Not an especially triumphant debut: Melbourne was no Canning or Palmerston in this regard. He contented himself with expressing the more traditional public distance from matters of the press, with the expected degree of rather lofty disdain even in correspondence with senior colleagues. However, he did enlist the help of Thomas Young, and when the varnish of rhetoric is stripped away, his actions like those of most prime ministers show an awareness of at least the minimum that needed to be done in the journalistic arena, and a readiness to undertake it.

Indeed, late in his second premiership, Melbourne broke new ground with the press. His first premiership, as we have mentioned, lasted only four months in 1834, and his first administration was the last to be directly dismissed by the monarch – in this case William IV. After a similarly brief initial Peel administration, from late 1834 to early 1835, Melbourne was back: this time for over six years, including the first four years of Victoria's reign. In 1839–40, *The Observer* became an official government paper in a way not seen before. In Liverpool's day, the paper had supported the Tory administration, even during the difficult years from 1815 to 1820, after the end of the Napoleonic Wars. Now, under Melbourne in the 1830s, it was financed by the Whigs, and in what the *Quarterly Review* described as a much more open manner than had been the custom before. It was the first occasion, the *Review* claimed, that a government had been publicly identified with a newspaper (other than the *Gazette*), and *The Observer* had become 'a kind of accredited organ' and had 'publicly assumed a new and absolutely unprecedented character', even claiming the patronage of the Queen and the royal family by a display of the royal arms.[18]

The claim is from a Tory source, of course; and comes at the time when the young and inexperienced Victoria, not yet married to Albert, had allowed herself to become far too readily perceived as a supporter not just of Melbourne personally but of the Whig government as a whole. Her Ultra-Tory uncle Cumberland, however, was now King of Hanover, and the remaining uncles may have been less concerned. Sussex was reasonably Whiggish in outlook, and Cambridge, while probably more of a natural Tory, was far less inclined to splenetic outbursts and plotting than Cumberland.

MELBOURNE AND THE PAPERS

Just before Grey left office in 1834, the ministry had had a chance of buying and controlling the *Morning Chronicle*. Although they turned down direct control of the paper, it was broadly in their camp. By 1839, Cabinet members were discussing the possibility of starting a new morning paper. According to Melbourne, Lord Lansdowne was the keenest on the idea, though others were lukewarm.[19] The fact that such discussions were taking place late in the ministry may well account for the arrangement with *The Observer*. In any event, as the ministry proceeded, the *Morning Chronicle* became more and more closely associated with Palmerston, who was almost certainly already writing or dictating articles for it during his second spell as Foreign Secretary under Melbourne.[20]

Melbourne, like Wellington and Peel before him, and Stanley (Lord Derby) after him, had also served a turn (1827–8) as chief secretary for Ireland, and was therefore *au fait* with the subsidized press. His first few biographers, like Wellington's early ones, tend to shy away from any mention of his dealings with the subsidy system. Intriguingly, Lamb (as Melbourne was then) was himself unaware that secret subsidy arrangements of the sort still undertaken in Ireland were also used with newspapers in England. It seems that this area of politics and journalism really was on a strictly 'need to know' basis, even among ministers. He knew (and we now know), however, that some £1,700 was spent on the Irish press during 1827. He was in correspondence on the subject with his coalition colleague Thomas Spring-Rice in September of that year. Echoing some of the arguments of previous ministers, questions were asked as to the point of the whole system. Successive governments seem to have posed similar questions upon entering office. Was the money well spent? What was there to show for it? What about the papers who did not receive a subsidy: did they not simply become even shriller in opposition? On one point, Spring-Rice told Lamb, he was clear:

> The whole has produced the degradation of the Irish press, without in any degree contributing to the power of the government; and the accomplishment of both these mischievous consequences is produced at a very considerable expense to the country. Ought all this to be continued...?[21]

As on numerous previous occasions, no amount of hand-wringing and agonizing produced much if any change to the status quo.

Melbourne, after these Irish experiences, was not naive on the subject of press management. However, during his two premierships, he encountered different problems with the English press which, however, proved similarly intractable: in particular, relations with *The Times* and, to a lesser extent, with the *Morning Chronicle*. When Melbourne returned as prime minister after the failure of the first, brief Peel ministry to secure a mandate in 1835, Melbourne was in a different and arguably stronger position than in the previous year. He had proved himself to William IV as the only viable prime minister of the two party leaders. He was Prime Minister in his own right, rather than simply a *'faute de mieux'* continuation of the Grey ministry without Grey. He felt strong enough to drop Brougham, not merely as a press manager, but as a member of the Cabinet and Lord Chancellor. He was also without Edward Ellice, his more 'official' press manager from his first ministry, though he continued to benefit from his press help and advice from outside the government. In the Grey-Melbourne ministry of 1830–4, both Ellice and Brougham's secretary Denis Le Marchant almost certainly contributed directly to the *Morning Chronicle*; and Ellice may well have continued to do so from 1835, even though no longer (from his own choice) as a minister.

The problems with the *Morning Chronicle* resulted from the fact that it was favourable towards, and favoured by, the government. It was so closely allied with the Whigs that it became susceptible to factions within the government, particularly as it became more fissiparous in its final years. Among prominent Whigs who wrote directly for it are believed to have been Sir John Hobhouse, Constantine Phipps Marquess of Normanby and Charles Poulett Thomson, as well as Le Marchant. It had also been used by Lord Duncannon to refute claims made in other papers about the circumstances behind the King's dismissal of the first Melbourne ministry. Palmerston, too, was contributing indirectly and possibly directly (as well as to *The Globe*). By 1840, the fruits of this Whig equivalent of China's 'Hundred Flowers' policy, encouraging citizens to openly express their opinions of the regime, meant that Lord John Russell felt obliged to advise Melbourne:

> You ought to control the Press, so far as it is conducted by your own colleagues and subordinates. I wrote from Scotland to complain of the 'Chronicle'. It has been rather better of late, but still far from rational.[22]

OUT, AND IN AGAIN

Melbourne's decision to favour Russell as the successor to Althorp as Commons Leader on the death of his father Lord Spencer was one of the main reasons behind William IV's decision to dismiss the first Melbourne ministry in 1834. For the King, Russell was simply too radical to be a really senior figure in the government. It may well have been the widespread belief that Brougham had been responsible for leaks to the press on the subject of the dismissal, before its official announcement, which helped make up Melbourne's mind not to include Brougham in the Cabinet if and when he returned. Although hardly out of character for Brougham, named by the diarist Greville as the guilty party, Croker claimed that Ellice was the culprit: that, on learning of the dismissal, and Melbourne's intention not to tell his colleagues until the following day, Ellice immediately leaked it both to the *Chronicle* and to *The Times*. To compound the offence, he also attributed it to Queen Adelaide, who was admittedly almost certainly more in tune with the Tories than with the Whigs, but may nevertheless have had relatively little if anything to do with her husband's decision.[23]

It was relations with *The Times* which proved the greater problem, however. The story of Peel's improved relations with the paper will be told in the next chapter; but the rapprochement between *The Times* and the more modern-looking Tory (or Conservative) ministry under Peel ensured that there would be no immediate restoration of relations with the Whigs when they returned. While *The Times* had burned its political bridges with Wellington over reform in 1830, and declared the impossibility of an old-style Tory administration, it was not a blanket party-political proscription. The paper tolerated the duke as a virtual one-man Cabinet pending Peel's return from the Continent, but it did not accept him as a longer-term answer to the country's problems. Lord Lyndhurst, the former Lord Chancellor, and as keen a 'meddler' with the press as his counterpart Brougham, if not quite as ostentatious a media manager, was in regular touch with Barnes, and enabled the ministerial transition to be made.

The fact that it was now effectively open to voters to change not merely the political complexion of their own Member of Parliament, but also the nature of the government, meant elections were taking the first tentative steps towards national campaigning and the formulation of messages with national rather than merely parochial applications. Self-evidently, as Croker had foreseen, this would make the harnessing of the support of the press more important – certainly important in a different fashion – than had been the case in the pre-1832 landscape. Not an auspicious time therefore, to be losing the most influential press voice of the age.

As we have seen, relations between *The Times* and the Whig government had been problematic for much of the 1830–4 government, culminating in the disagreement over the Poor Law. Grey himself, shortly before leaving office, had told Brougham that he was baffled by the paper's malignancy and mischief: 'To what cause this is to be ascribed I know not – but it is a matter in which I cannot interfere, and I much doubt whether any interference would do good'.[24]

MELBOURNE, HIS MINISTERS, AND THE PRESS

Palmerston's increasing interest in 'meddling' with the press – leaking, steering and contributing – also caused problems. Barnes of *The Times* felt that the foreign secretary was giving the *Morning Chronicle* and *The Globe* advance notice of stories and developments: always the ultimate crime in journalistic eyes, if one is not the lucky recipient. The resulting editorial comment did not make happy reading for Palmerston or his government:

> What an offensive union is that of a dull understanding and an unfeeling heart! Add to this the self-satisfied airs of a flippant dandy, and you have the most nauseous specimen of humanity – a sort of compound which justifies Swift in the disgusting exhibition of the Yahoos.[25]

No nuanced or coded criticism there! Meanwhile, Brougham, despite the episode of the torn letter in the waste-paper basket, was not held in quite the same contempt – yet. For another month, the final breach was avoided. When it came, however, it was final: and it lasted for the rest of Brougham's long life. The Poor Law had been a factor; but was there some additional, personal reason? Was *The Times* right in believing that he was deliberately trying to weaken the paper by boosting others and by supporting stamp duty repeal (thus opening up the market and weakening *The Times*)? Perhaps this judgement of Brougham's conduct – true or otherwise – explains the comments in *The Times* at the end of the year about the late government's habitual management of the press.

When Melbourne returned to office in 1835, he was not a particular personal target of the wrath of *The Times*. After its altered relationship with Peel's Tories, the paper favoured a rapprochement between moderate Whigs like Melbourne and Stanley (the future Derby) as leader of the new-look Tories. However, in the meantime, Barnes made it perfectly clear to Lord Lyndhurst's secretary Edward Winslow (whose brother later worked for the paper) that he had 'refused in the most decided terms to have any political connection with the new ministers. Show this to Lord Lyndhurst'.[26] And political persuasion was not enough by itself; Palmerston's politics were fairly similar to Melbourne's, especially on domestic issues, but his 'journalistic' misdeeds would ensure no favour to him.

Overall, *The Times* was able to justify its switch of allegiance away from the government by deploring the fact that the second Melbourne ministry relied for its political and parliamentary survival on the radicals and the Irish, and it directed much of its fire towards the Irish leader Daniel O'Connell. Late in the ministry, as the government started to lose seats in by-elections, the contest did become personalized, at least in the sense that John Walter, the proprietor of *The Times*, stood in opposition to the government's candidate in the Nottingham by-election, and won.[27] It was something of a portent. Two days later, the ministry itself was defeated in the Commons: the beginning of the final denouement of the Melbourne ministry. Less than a fortnight after Walter's victory, Barnes himself died – the announcement of his death, in May 1841, marking the first occasion on which his name had appeared in his own newspaper.

THE MELBOURNE TOUCH

Melbourne, like Grey, was no press innovator. Much of his involvement with the press was passive (as when he was implied to be having an affair with his friend Mrs Norton), or the deployment of the well-worn rhetoric of detachment. While Brougham, Palmerston and others were honing their press management methods, Melbourne and Grey largely left matters to the usual channels: private secretaries and Treasury ministers.

Melbourne, who in his younger days contributed his squib to the *Morning Chronicle* and may also have written reviews for the *Literary Gazette*, does not seem to have made a lifelong habit of it. There may have been a brief period, as he approached and achieved the political summit, when he began to display real interest in how he was perceived, and may have encouraged his secretary Thomas Young to prolong his initial, brief popularity. But it was not the sustained, lifetime effort of a Palmerston; nor the late flowering of a Wellington or a Derby, repenting of their early indifference to the press and compensating for it in later life. It was rather the pragmatic realization that a certain degree of engagement was inevitable; that what had to be done should be done; but that it was not a game to be enjoyed for its own sake. As if in confirmation of this, Melbourne's private secretary and press manager turned on him in the end. Long after his reluctant retirement, and as the former prime minister neared death, Young published some of his letters, almost certainly for personal gain. Young had often been seen as a somewhat sinister figure, his lowly social origins sparking curiosity at his closeness to Melbourne. He was even suspected of becoming embroiled in the affairs of the Nortons, the couple whose wife was at the centre of speculation about the prime minister's own private life.[28]

Melbourne's final political years were so heavily taken up with his close attendance on the young Victoria that the daily grind of party politics and press management may have lost whatever appeal they had once held for him. On the other hand, however, Whig papers like the *Morning Chronicle* and *The Globe* often must have seemed more like factional players within, rather than overall supporters of, the government. Melbourne's relative longevity in office (nearly seven years in all) may have owed a lot to the Queen's favour and to her dread of a Peel administration, but it owed relatively little to his successful management of the press.

CHAPTER FOUR

PEEL AND RUSSELL

NEITHER ROBERT PEEL nor Lord John Russell were natural press managers; but both came to have an involvement with the press which almost certainly exceeded their initial expectations. Peel's introduction came early. As we have seen, he served as Liverpool's chief secretary to Ireland from 1812 to 1818, from the age of 24. One may be permitted a wry smile at the thought of the earnest and solemn young man, fresh from Oxford with the shine yet to be worn off his Double First, encountering the murky world of the subsidized Irish press at such an early age. One might almost suspect Liverpool of possessing a puckish, if well-concealed, sense of humour in making such an appointment.

Ostensibly, the money paid to Irish newspapers was for government advertisements or proclamations: hence the term 'proclamation fund' from which the money was allocated. However, it was but a short step from an official arrangement of this sort to something resembling outright corruption. Once personal pensions were paid to individual editors, and other special payments or subsidies made to specific papers, the water could easily become very murky indeed. Apart from the proclamation fund, as we have seen, the rest of the money had to be found from somewhere else – that is, the 'secret service' fund, which, almost by definition, was not a matter for detailed public scrutiny; and which, like much concerning the relationship between the press and politics, was not deemed a fit or proper subject for public discourse. This, of course, suited politicians in any case; but it all made for a rather uneasy and embarrassing part of political life. To make things worse, almost everyone involved agreed that it simply did not work, and was a waste of the money spent. And yet it continued, presumably on the basis of the familiar political argument that things might be even worse if it were not done.

In Peel's time as chief secretary to Ireland, from 1812 to 1818, three Dublin papers received direct subsidies: *The Patriot* and *The Correspondent* were

6. Sir Robert Peel, 2nd Bt, by John Linnell, 1838.
© National Portrait Gallery, London.

given £500 each, while the *Dublin Journal* was allotted £300. A fourth paper, the *Hibernian Journal*, was also part of the network. However, the effects of government support were sometimes scarcely noticeable. Peel had to threaten to withdraw all support (subsidy and proclamations) from the *Dublin Journal* when it seemingly invented news of a protest against the government's

7. John Russell, 1st Earl Russell, by Sir Francis Grant, 1853.
© National Portrait Gallery, London.

Catholic Relief Bill in 1813.[1] A smaller annual pension of £100 was also paid to the proprietor of the *Clonmel Herald*. The *Belfast News-Letter* received money both before and after Peel's time, though there is no surviving evidence of payments during 1812–18. Often, the 'loyalist' papers spent far more time and energy attacking each other than advancing the government's cause.

By 1815, Peel was so disillusioned with the £1,500 per annum spent on *The Patriot* (with a circulation of around 750) that he wished to close the paper; recompensing the proprietors with a small sum for removing 'this execrable paper'. The next year, he was looking equally critically at the *Dublin Journal*, clearly indicating a wish to close it, or sever all links: but both connections still seem to have been alive when Peel left in 1818. The *Clonmel Herald* was accused in 1812 of supporting the opposition in the Tipperary election, and both the pension and proclamation fund were withdrawn by Peel, only to be reinstated three years later and paid retroactively from 1812! In 1813, Peel contemplated writing for *The Patriot* himself, and also told Croker how invaluable his services would be in that regard.[2] With Irish press subsidies at this time, it really was a case of *plus ça change, plus c'est la meme chose*.

The papers enjoying greater commercial success and larger circulations – the *Freeman's Journal* and the *Dublin Evening Post*, for instance – were all in the hands of the opposition nationalists. It is perfectly possible that, had the subsidies and proclamation funds not been paid, there would have been no pro-government papers at all, and that the opposition would have had endless free shots at goal. With all the flaws of the subsidies system, those involved, including Peel, Wellington and Melbourne, seem to have concluded that the very imperfect something they possessed was still, on balance, better than nothing at all. (By the time Derby took on the role, things were beginning to change). However, on the occasions that Peel returned to the topic after his departure, a tone more of bitterness than of mere world-weariness creeps in. 'I delight in the warfare between the [Ultra-Tory] "Evening Mail" and the "Patriot"', Peel wrote in 1823, in Wellingtonian tones: 'These worthies have done more good than I thought them capable of doing. They have shown what manner of men the "Gentlemen of the Press" are'.[3]

As late as 1826–7, Peel – several years into his time as home secretary – was still found railing against the iniquities of papers like *The Patriot* for stepping out of line and supporting anti-government candidates in Irish elections. Just before the end of the Liverpool ministry, the Irish press was worrying away at the fragile 'agreement to differ' on Catholic Emancipation which Liverpool had sustained with such skill for almost 15 years. Pro-government papers were taking clear and adversarial positions as 'Catholics' (i.e. pro-emancipation) and 'Protestants' (anti-emancipation), and conducting proxy polemics between the two camps. Peel was a 'Protestant', but not an extreme one, and he went along with Wellington when emancipation was introduced. This is to some extent foreshadowed by his ability to echo the approach that Liverpool (also a reasonably moderate 'Protestant' in his personal views) would probably have taken. Peel writes, in January 1827:

> ...[I]f there be two newspapers in Ireland, each countenanced, probably maintained, by Government favour, one abusing the Catholic part of the administration, the other the Protestant, the withdrawal of that favour from both would be much wiser than the continuance of it to both or either.[4]

Peel, who had been notably unsuccessful in severing any of the existing links between government and its chosen Irish papers, also inherited a system in which government titles could receive summaries of the international papers by 'express' delivery, essentially a faster and more expensive postal service, rather than through the Post Office, which was the system used to send them through to the non-government newspapers. Both Wellington and Peel sustained the system, and Peel was not averse from using access to these 'expresses' as a form of stick and carrot to deploy with individual papers to keep them in line.

PEEL'S ASCENT

When Peel completed his six years as chief secretary , he returned to the back benches for several years, before serving two terms as home secretary: under Liverpool; and then, after refusing to serve under Canning and Goderich, in Wellington's ministry. When he was Wellington's home secretary in late 1830, he was almost as frustrated with the ostensibly pro-government *Courier* in England as he had been with the Irish papers. He told Planta, the Treasury Secretary:

> It is quite impossible to go on as we are going on with the Press. We had
> infinitely better have no connexion with any newspaper, than be exposed to
> such paragraphs as I have marked in the enclosed 'Courier'...[5]

There was then a four-year period of opposition, during which Peel
effectively replaced Wellington as the alternative prime minister. When
Grey's government temporarily and briefly forfeited office in 1832, it was
Wellington who was slated to replace him, as the protracted travails of the
Reform Bill process unfolded. By the time William IV dismissed Melbourne
in 1834, Wellington again assumed the premiership – but this time only as a
locum pending Peel's return from ill-timed continental travel. Peel himself
first became prime minister in late 1834, to the accompaniment of one of
the most interesting exercises in newspaper realignment of the nineteenth
century.

Because Peel's public tone was rather lofty and Olympian even by
contemporary standards, he is another of those political figures whom
it is difficult to picture 'meddling with the press'. His background was
not aristocratic: like Gladstone, he sprang from the higher reaches of the
prosperous manufacturer class without ever personally needing to 'get his
hands dirty' in trade. This very slight sense of social dislocation may have
added yet further solemnity to his discourse and certainly made him more
sensitive to the merest suggestion of acting dishonourably or shabbily. His
aversion to being seen as self-seeking or personally ambitious made him
equally contemptuous of others who seemed so. His icy rejection of the
direct appeals for office by Disraeli (and his wife) ensured that there was a
lethal personal element to their future political estrangement entirely absent
from other estrangements with, for instance, Stanley, later Lord Derby.
However, his adaptability (his opponents would have found a more colourful
description) over Catholic Emancipation and the Corn Laws is mirrored in
his pragmatic approach to press management. As long as the rhetoric could
remain lofty, and the tone *de haut en bas*, deals could be done and arrangements
made accordingly.

The young Peel, in company with Palmerston and Croker, had been
happy to contribute to *The Courier*, rather as their predecessors had to the
Anti Jacobin. Indeed, their contributions were even elevated to the dignity
of publication in book form, under the name of *The New Whig Guide*. Peel's
Irish press experiences gave him a lengthier and worldlier perspective on the

matter than appearances might have suggested, and he showed himself ready to embrace new forms of communication as he neared the summit of British politics. The journalistic trio had even managed to bring about a considerable rise in the paper's circulation. It may just be that, despite the distaste which seeps out of his letters from and about Ireland, he rather enjoyed 'meddling' with the press, and found it a suitable outlet for his backbench energies.

PRIME MINISTER: THE SUPPORT OF *THE TIMES*

The support of *The Times* in 1834 was already a much greater prize than it would have been a decade or two previously. *The Courier*, for so long an administration mainstay, was forced to choose sides when the Tories split over Canning in 1827. It jumped ship to the Whigs when Grey came to office, arguably forfeiting a lot of credibility en route. The *Morning Chronicle* was Whig, however much it got caught up in the factionalism within the Whig cabinets. Other papers were still fighting the Tory wars of the late 1820s. *The Times*, by contrast, was on its way to the uniquely powerful position it occupied throughout much of the rest of the nineteenth century, combining commercial success, a growing circulation, political influence, and an increasing role as both the voice and the sounding-board of domestic and international elite concerns. The paper's editor, while in no sense a public figure (and unnamed in its own pages until his death) was someone who could deal with senior politicians as near-equals. The prime minister or the lord chancellor could consort with Barnes without being deemed eccentric or patronizing. We had not yet reached the point where Lord Northcliffe could tell Lloyd George that he could see no purpose in acceding to his request for a meeting. But the days of forelock-tugging chancers writing obsequious letters begging for a subsidy or a personal pension were almost completely gone now.

The early negotiations with *The Times* were largely conducted by Lord Lyndhurst, with a bit of inside help from Greville, the diarist who also served as Clerk of the Privy Council. Wellington was at the same time still maintaining that he 'did not think *The Times* could be influenced'. Greville, despite the Duke's pessimism, 'urged him to avail himself of any opportunity to try, and he seemed very well disposed to do so'.[6] Both Wellington and

Lyndhurst are reported to have described Barnes, at about this time, as the most powerful man in the country. Greville recalled:

> Lyndhurst has just been here – he had seen the Duke, who had already opened a negotiation with Barnes …. I offered to get any statement inserted of the causes of the late break up and he will again see the Duke and consider of inserting one. 'Why Barnes is the most powerful man in the country'. The *Standard* has sent to offer its support – the Duke said he should be very happy…[7]

Walter, too, played a role. When Peel at last returned from Rome in early December, he advised him to make a public declaration of his acceptance of the Reform Act settlement. To pre-empt any notion that a new Tory government would return to pre-Reform views and policies, Walter urged that:

> much undoubtedly may be done in correcting wrong opinions and inculcating right ones; & nothing would tend more to bring about this desirable result than some frank explanation, some popular declaration, PREVIOUS to a dissolution of Parliament.[8]

It was but a short step from a 'popular declaration' to a 'manifesto': and thus was born not merely the Tamworth Manifesto itself, but an entirely new form of electioneering and of political communication. Although Peel was traditionalist enough to insist it be given the formal cover of being issued in the form of a letter to his own constituents, a manifesto for national consumption it clearly was; and the role played by the press in its conception and gestation was extensive.

The press management involved in the Tamworth Manifesto was also sophisticated. Priority was given to *The Times*, the *Morning Herald* and the *Morning Post*, both in announcing the fact that it was on its way and in its actual publication. Consideration was apparently given to including the *Morning Chronicle*, as a way of keeping a bridge to Stanley open. The future Lord Derby had resigned from Grey's government over Irish policy, shortly before the Prime Minister's own resignation. He and his supporters were still nominally within the Whig fold, but had not returned to serve in Melbourne's first ministry. They seemed to have as much in common with the new-look Peelite

Tory party as they did with the Whigs; and, as long as there was a hope of their joining Peel's new government, a line was left open to the *Morning Chronicle*. When that possibility evaporated, so did special consideration for the paper. (The alliance between Stanley and Peel did eventually occur during the second Melbourne government, and Stanley joined Peel the next time round, before leaving over his Corn Law 'apostasy' which split the party. Stanley then became leader of the Protectionists, effectively the next incarnation of the 'official' Tory party). Meanwhile, the proprietor of the *Standard* also offered his services, including a proposal to buy up *The Albion* and *The Courier*, though they do not seem to have figured in the initial arrangements for the launch of the Tamworth Manifesto.[9]

This was media management of a precise and sophisticated kind. Peel, like Wellington, may have transacted the details at one remove from 'the gentlemen'; but his involvement and participation are self-evident. Barnes and Walter had been privy to very detailed discussions as to whether they should round up a number of Conservative MPs to write to Peel, eliciting a reply from him which could then be elaborated upon during the coming election campaign. In the end, Peel decided on the manifesto and an early start to his election campaign, rather than going through these preparatory stages.[10] The *Morning Chronicle*, left out of the loop, could only bemoan both its content ('A more despicable or contemptable [sic] effusion of party cunning never met the public eye...') and the manner of its handling: 'This singular document, received by *The Times* at half past three o'clock yesterday morning, before break of day...'.[11]

OPPOSITION YEARS

It was practically impossible for a ministry to be voted out directly before the Reform Act. It was the working of public opinion and other factors on MPs while meeting or hearing from influential constituents, the direct action of the monarch, or an event such as a sudden ministerial death which led to a change. When William IV dismissed Melbourne, Peel inherited Melbourne and Grey's House of Commons; so the longer-term survival of the new ministry depended on a successful election campaign, in addition to any advantages of incumbency the government might be able to accrue. It was only after the Derby government's Second Reform Act of 1867 that elections leading directly to changes of government became a standard feature of the political landscape. Although this did occur in 1841, it was still unusual for most of the period from 1832 to 1867.

In the event, although Peel picked up many seats, it was not enough; and Melbourne returned to power in the spring of 1835. Even during his short first ministry, he had to work very hard to ensure the continuing support of *The Times*, which, as Lyndhurst reminded him, was by now 'worth ALL the other papers put together'.[12] When the headlines of the King's Speech were obtained by the *Morning Post*, gleefully scooping its more powerful rival, Peel had to work very hard to exculpate himself from suspicion of a direct or 'inspired' leak. He specifically tasked Sir George Clerk with keeping *The Times* on board: 'Sir George Clerk will most readily communicate with any confidential person who may be sent for the purpose by *The Times*'.[13] These efforts were ultimately successful, and Peel wrote directly to Barnes as he resigned after his election defeat in April 1835. With an eye to the historical record, Peel made it clear that he and Barnes were not personally familiar, and that he viewed the paper's support as altruistic and based on policy:

> I should however be doing an injustice to my own feelings, if I were to retire from office without one word of acknowledgement, without at least assuring you of the Admiration with which I witnessed, during the arduous [election] contest in which I was engaged, the daily exhibitions of that extraordinary ability to which I was indebted for a support the more valuable because it was an impartial and discriminating support.[14]

Peel's reward was an editorial comparing him with Pitt the Younger.

RETURN TO POWER

Melbourne's small majority, loss of by-elections and dependence on Radical and Irish support (foreshadowing the Callaghan government of 1976–9 and the second Major term of 1992–7) contributed to his electoral fallibility in 1841, and brought Peel back to the premiership, this time for nearly five years. As has been mentioned, by the time Peel returned, Barnes was dead and the special relationship that had evolved between Barnes's *Times* and

Peel's Conservatives, which had survived the opposition years of 1835 to 1841, needed to be reconstructed and perhaps reconfigured, especially now that John Delane had succeeded to the editor's chair. That such rebuilding was possible was more the responsibility of a future prime minister than of the returning one. Lord Aberdeen, already a veteran of Wellington's cabinet and of Peel's first administration, returned to the Foreign Office in 1841 (he had held it under Wellington from 1828 to 1830), and started to build a relationship with Delane which had a real influence on the politics of the age: ensuring that Palmerston did not have a free run on foreign policy in the press and affecting the balance of press coverage after the Tories split into Peelites and Protectionists over the Corn Laws in 1845–6.

Despite his secure majority in 1841, Peel himself did not entirely neglect the press. Indeed, there is evidence in his correspondence of a close and detailed interest not merely in the doings of the national press, but also in the affairs of the local newspapers of the West Midlands, near his Tamworth constituency. He examined the Stamp Office records in 1841, and is well able to distinguish between the generally supportive *Staffordshire Advertiser*, the 'good paper', in Peel's words; and the 'bad one', the *Staffordshire Examiner*. A year later, responding to a query about the papers to which government advertisements should be sent, Peel is also to be seen singing the praises of *Aris's Birmingham Gazette*: '... a very respectable paper and fully entitled to its due share of Gov. advertisements'.[15]

When Peel had formed his first ministry in 1834, J.W. Croker had renewed his 1829 plea for an organized government press bureau. However, despite Peel's accomplished press management in that period, the suggestion was not formally implemented by that administration, nor was it adopted in 1841. However, by then, Croker was outside active politics, and devoting his energies and talents to the *Quarterly Review*. In this capacity, until their bitter and irrevocable rift over the Corn Laws, Croker was a useful repository for suggestions and 'guidance' from Peel. Shortly after his return to office, Peel asked Croker to include some suggestions for an article about the nature of the modern premiership in a forthcoming piece: '... I wish you could add a paragraph to point out the difference between a Prime Minister in these days and in former times, when Newcastles and Pelhams were ministers'.[16] Characteristically, Peel wanted to highlight the scope for 'service to his country, and the hope of honourable fame', rather than patronage.

The Corn Laws and the Papers

It was during Peel's second ministry that Aberdeen built up his close relationship and rapport with Delane, Barnes's successor as editor of *The Times*. However, relations between Peel and Delane cooled – one might almost say soured. The Poor Law, which had broken the paper's confidence in Melbourne and even in Grey, also became a divisive issue between John Walter, the proprietor of *The Times* and Peel. Indeed, Walter, having won his Nottingham by-election in Melbourne's final days, promptly lost it again at the 1841 general election. There were post-election inquiries: Walter was reinstated, then unseated again, and much bitterness resulted; some of it personally directed towards Peel and the new home secretary, Sir James Graham. Walter believed they wanted him out to forestall opposition to Graham's administration of the Poor Law.[17] Because of Delane's close and growing relationship with Aberdeen, Peel came to feel that it was the proprietor's personal hostility to him that prevented the paper giving general support to his administration. Delane and Aberdeen had extensive dealings in 1844 in an attempt to heal the more general breach, but without success. Peel thus went into the most dangerous and divisive episode of his political life without the support of the most important paper in the land.

Originally introduced after the Napoleonic Wars to keep the price of corn high and protect the livelihoods of the landed upper classes, the Corn Laws undoubtedly pressed hard on the poor, by keeping the price of food too high. Liverpool's government had adopted a gradualist approach to changes in the Corn Laws, as it had on much else. This was essentially what was expected of Peel from 1841. When he changed his mind, and advocated their abolition, senior political figures had fairly simple views on Peel's change of heart. Wellington was clear that it was potatoes and their failure in the Great Famine that had made up Peel's mind to call for the abolition of the Corn Laws; while Melbourne simply called Peel's move a dishonest act, rather to the embarrassment of Victoria and Albert, who supported Peel. In purely political terms, the Tory party split into Peelites, who backed the removal of the Corn Laws, and Protectionists, who favoured their retention. Some of the Peelites – most notably Gladstone – eventually joined the Liberals (as the Whigs increasingly came to be called in the decades to come), while the overall leader of the Protectionists was Stanley, Lord Derby, who resigned from Peel's government over the issue. The elderly Wellington was as unenthusiastic as some of his own followers had been about Catholic Emancipation in 1829, but reluctantly returned the favour of Peel's support then, now that he was at the eye of the storm this time.

For years, the Wolverhampton MP C.P. Villiers had introduced an annual motion for the repeal of the laws. Traditional Tories opposed it because they saw it as an attack on the landed class which had dominated politics for so long. Moderate Whigs had not regarded it as part of practical politics when they were last in office. So where did the balance of opinion in the press lie? When Peel first introduced the measure to repeal the Corn Laws, in 1845, how did it affect newspaper allegiances? Villiers himself told Cobden that the press was not 'a SELF-ACTING machine and wants as the Yankees would say an ALMIGHTY power of GREASE to set it going'.[18] His meaning, of course, was that the media required regular and sophisticated attention in order to keep it 'on message'. The *Morning Chronicle* supported repeal. Richard Cobden and John Bright, Villiers's co-campaigners, wrote prodigiously for the cause. The recognized government papers were the *Morning Herald* and the *Standard*. But, once again, it was *The Times* which was able to secure the biggest coup. The paper itself was firmly in the repeal camp: indeed, it had been critical of Peel for what today's press would call 'dithering'. And then, on 4 December 1845, *The Times* dropped this bombshell:

> The decision of the Cabinet is no longer a secret. Parliament, it is confidently reported, is to be summoned for the first week in January; and the Royal Speech will, it is added, recommend an immediate consideration of the Corn Laws, preparatory to their total repeal. Sir Robert Peel in one house, and the Duke of Wellington in the other, will, we are told, be prepared to give immediate effect to the recommendation thus conveyed.[19]

The effect on large sections of the Tory Party can perhaps be likened to a sudden announcement by the Major or Cameron governments that Britain was about to join the Euro. Even Joseph Chamberlain's announcement of tariff reform in 1903 was not quite as galvanic, because Chamberlain, despite his immense power and dynamism, was not prime minister, and resigned from the Cabinet as he announced his conversion. Peel, like Liverpool, had always been for gradual reform of the Corn Laws. This *volte-face*, without prior 'softening up' of public opinion, was a truly sensational development for this reason alone.

How did *The Times* get hold of the story? George Meredith's novels are not as widely read as they once were, but in *Diana of the Crossways*, he gives us the traditional version: that the young minister Sidney Herbert told Mrs Norton, who promptly scurried off to Printing House Square and sold the story to Delane for £500. (In the novel, Delane is depicted as Mr Tonans, which means 'thundering' in Latin – the paper's nickname 'The Thunderer' meant that contemporary readers would have needed no help to link one to the other). However, it seems much likelier that the leak was a product of the closeness of Aberdeen and the editor. Peel's denial to the Queen may have been literally true. He described as 'quite without foundation' the assertion that the Cabinet had 'unanimously agreed to an immediate and total repeal'.[20] Unanimity was the point: it appears Aberdeen briefed Delane that Wellington had been opposed; threatened resignation; been countered by Peel's confirmation that the Duke's resignation would bring the government down; and had then agreed not merely to support, but to assist in the Lords.[21]

Whether specifically briefed to do so, or simply applying their own analysis, the loyalist *Standard* and *Morning Herald* attacked the story: the former describing it as an 'Atrocious Fabrication by *The Times*'. For supportive papers to be allowed, perhaps even steered, to be incorrect in this way must count as one of the major crimes in news management in any age. And there is perhaps a suggestion that, by this stage, as Peel increasingly wrapped himself in the mantle of the man of principle who was above partisan considerations, the mechanics of party and press management may have seemed unworthy of his lofty attention. More so than in Gladstone's case, absorption in a cause ensured Peel's fatal ineffectiveness as a party manager. As leader of the Peelites, after he left office, he was a frustrating as well as an admired figure to his younger subordinates. His extreme thinness of skin at the merest imputation of unworthy motives almost certainly made him more susceptible to press attack in his later career than before: the opposite of most politicians. By 1845, Peel was urging Aberdeen to consider 'the discontinuance of all communications [to *The Times*] from the Foreign Office'.[22]

PEEL: THE VERDICT

After Peel had carried Corn Law repeal, with Whig support, in 1846 he resigned again, this time for good. Four years later, he died after a fall from his horse. By then, Lord John Russell had been prime minister for four years, Lord Stanley led the main group of Tories and the senior surviving Peelite was Lord Aberdeen. As the party system was reshaped, newspaper allegiances, too, were once again in flux. Peel himself, to a far greater extent than sometimes comes across in his biographies, was an assiduous, if arm's length and somewhat sporadic, press manager. His skilful management of coverage in 1834 helped to ensure that he gained the opportunity to become prime minister in the first place. In the great crisis of his life, however, that of the Corn Laws, while gaining the admiration of his monarch, her husband and numerous subsequent historians, he attracted the bitterest of hatred from his own former adherents. While the leak of his *volte-face* might have looked like a master stroke (and was seen so by Sir Edward Cook, of later *Pall Mall Gazette*, *Westminster Gazette* and *Daily News* editorial fame), in fact he reaped little reward from it, alienated key press allies and probably was not even personally responsible for thinking of it. Sixty years afterwards, his actions over the Corn Laws were still invoked by Arthur Balfour as causing the worst fate a leader could inflict on his party – a split; and after nearly 150 years, in 1992, Foreign Secretary Douglas Hurd, referring to these events, was urging his party – then as so often embroiled in a row on Europe – to give the 'madness' of a Corn Law-style party split over Europe a miss.

RUSSELL AS PRIME MINISTER

The *de facto* Whig leader, Lord John Russell, succeeded Peel in 1846. The Queen, Prince Albert and the Whigs themselves thought momentarily of Melbourne, himself keen to make a comeback, but deemed him too frail and out of touch to be invited back. Russell seems to have approached press management rather as he did politics as a whole: with considerable (if intermittent, in the case of the press) enthusiasm, but not always with great skill. As we have seen, Russell was one of the prime ministers of the age who never felt tempted or obliged to change his party. As much as Grey, he was a lifelong Whig: and, although as an old man the term 'liberal' was much more politically correct (in every sense), Russell was a quintessential Whig.

He was also something of a man of letters and historian; though, unlike Derby's translation of Homer and Disraeli's novels, his writings are little read or remembered now. Indeed, in this respect, he is more like his equally prolific Liberal successor Gladstone, whose many works of theology, classical scholarship and translation also now rest on the shelves largely unread. Even Russell's Victorian biographers (Stuart Reid and Spencer Walpole) are realistic about his limitations as an author, and the conventionality of his views. Hardly surprisingly, much of his work on political, international and constitutional history is representative of what came to be called the Whig school of history.

He showed himself happy to use the press in a more public and visible way both early and late in his career. In 1820, he had written a public letter to *The Times*, signalling support for Queen Caroline and attacking Liverpool's government for its pro-George IV stance, effectively bouncing the Whigs into a pro-Queen policy from that time on.[23] He was also a regular newspaper letter-writer after his final retirement from office in 1866 and party leadership the following year.

RUSSELL AND THE PAPERS

Russell came to feel that he had something of a monopoly on the issue of parliamentary reform. As the principal Commons performer in the unfolding of the 1832 Act, he felt that the issue had been settled; and when, later in his career, calls for further reform grew, he felt that he was better placed than others to decide whether and to what extent those calls should be met. In the end, his brief second premiership of 1865–6 ended with no such achievement, and he was galled to have to watch the more flexible and adroit Derby and Disraeli secure the second Reform Act of 1867.

We have already seen Russell writing to Melbourne urging him to control the press more firmly and effectively. Like many of his colleagues, Russell used his private secretary, C.A. Gore, as a personal press manager or agent, on one occasion attracting criticism from Brougham, of all people, for allowing Gore to publish 'infamous lies' in *The Globe*.[24]

He was almost certainly the first British prime minister to reflect on the relationship between politicians and the press in his own memoirs. (As we saw, Grafton passed over the subject entirely in lofty or wounded silence). Russell wrote that:

> ... Government can exercise and does exercise a great influence over part
> of the Press by communicating from authority intelligence which has been

received, and the decisions which have been arrived at by persons holding high office.[25]

This was not a particularly radical or penetrating insight; but interesting nonetheless as coming from a former prime minister and as an early acknowledgement of the evolving balance between concealment and revelation in this previously covert element of political activity. Indeed, some time before he wrote this, Russell had entertained Delane, *The Times* editor, in his own home: even then (in the 1860s, during the American Civil War, when Russell was Palmerston's Foreign Secretary), this was clearly a landmark, like Lyndhurst's direct encounters with Barnes in 1834.

Overall, Russell seems to have followed a trajectory similar to Wellington's and Derby's: becoming both more aware of the importance of the press and more thoughtful on the whole subject later in his career. During his first and much longer premiership of 1846–52, he had the tacit and sometimes overt support of the Peelites, many of whom deemed his government a lesser evil than one led by Derby and the Protectionists, as it would not even contemplate a return of the Corn Laws or other forms of trade protectionism. He was also at that time the clear choice for Whig leader after Melbourne. It was only after he lost the premiership and (in effect) the overall party leadership, having to serve in coalition governments under Aberdeen and Palmerston while trying to fight his way back to another premiership, that he really engaged with sustained press management.

In 1855–6, during the Crimean War, and with Palmerston consolidating his position as prime minister, Russell gave serious thought to 'acquiring' a newspaper. He was not rich enough to buy one outright: the *Daily News* looked appealing; but Russell, a younger son, had no direct access to the wealth of his kinsmen the Dukes of Bedford. Realistically, therefore, either a consortium, or a 'friendly' editor, looked the next best bet. The *Morning Chronicle* was another possible target; but, in the event, agreement was out of reach. This must have been clear to Russell early in 1856, when the *Daily News* commented that one of his recent speeches was 'scarcely one degree above twaddle'![26] Not, then, the birth of a beautiful political friendship. The choice of Dean Gilbert Eliot of Bristol, related to Russell by marriage, as negotiator had not proved auspicious. One of the other parties to the negotiations said that he 'will make a good Bishop, but a d-mn-d bad journalist'.[27] It may well be that the whole episode soured Russell's mood towards the press in general at around that time. It was in the same year, 1856, that Russell wrote to Lord Clarendon that '... if England is ever to be England again, this vile tyranny of *The Times* must be cut off'.[28]

RUSSELL: THE LONG WAIT

Much of the press coverage of Russell's first ministry consisted either of critical comments from sources external to the government about Cabinet divisions of opinion and policy, or of 'inspired' pieces from ministers like Palmerston who were already more adept at, and interested in, the use of the press. Rather like Melbourne's longer ministry, Russell's was, by the end, living on borrowed time, its political weakness highlighted by the papers. Russell initially resigned after the failure of his Franchise Bill in 1851; Derby (still Stanley then) tried and failed to form a Tory ministry; Russell returned 'on sufferance' and later sacked Palmerston, who duly had his 'tit for tat' two months later, causing the fall of the Russell ministry and the installation of Derby in February 1852.

By this stage, Russell's press position was weak. The *Morning Post* and *Globe* were still in Palmerston's corner, though the *Morning Chronicle* less so. *The Times* was essentially a Peelite paper, thanks to Aberdeen's closeness to Delane. Other papers – the *Daily News* with its liberal leanings, and the *Standard* and *Morning Herald* for the Tories – did not favour Russell personally. The Peelites were still separate from the Whigs, but it was looking likelier that they would eventually join forces with them, not with the remainder of the Tory Party, who now had sole use of the name. The Tories were themselves becoming much more active in seeking to build press support. One can see why, a few years later, Russell came to wish to acquire a paper of his own. He had, rather fitfully, attempted to win *The Globe* over to his corner in the 1840s; but, in doing so, he had encountered the superior skill of Palmerston, and so had entered a contest which the paper doubtless enjoyed, but which Russell was never likely to win.[29]

With the failure of his attempts to gain a paper of his own, Russell's press position between premierships was at times alarmingly weak for a man who aspired to return to Number 10. *The Times*, at the time of the Crimean War, not only saw him as unsuitable for a future premiership: it even deplored his appointment as foreign secretary in Aberdeen's Whig-Peelite coalition, which replaced the first Derby ministry at the end of 1852. The paper decided that Lord John Russell 'has so little of the accomplishments required for his new office that we can only suppose he is keeping it for a successor, most probably Lord Clarendon, who otherwise will not have a seat in the Cabinet'.[30] The fact that they were right about Russell and Clarendon made Lord John even more splenetic. Clarendon, despite being an old press hand almost in Palmerston's league, was a little embarrassed himself, reporting that he had:

> NEVER seen him [Russell] so mortified and annoyed because the friendship between Lord Aberdeen & Delane is, as he said, well known and nobody will suppose that attacks on him would find their way into *The Times* unless they were agreeable to Ld A.[31]

In fact, on this occasion, it is easy to imagine that Aberdeen was not feigning when he said, according to Greville's diary, that 'I have not seen THAT FELLOW [Delane] for several days, but if it will be any satisfaction to John Russell, I will engage never to let him into my house again'.[32]

Russell's bitterness against *The Times* flared back into life periodically in the succeeding years. In 1854, no lesser figures than the Queen and Prince Albert agreed with him that it was time to break the paper's 'news-monopoly'. She told Russell in 1854 that 'she entirely agrees in (sic) Lord John's observation respecting *The Times* which she thinks he and the Cabinet ought positively not to tolerate any longer'.[33]

Prince Albert himself had recently been the subject of an especially virulent press campaign, accusing him of favouring the Continental absolute monarchies and, in particular, manoeuvring behind the scenes on behalf of Russian interests, culminating in accusations of treason and calls for him to be imprisoned in the Tower of London; and, although this was a more general grievance against wider sections of the press as a whole, journalists and editors were certainly not among the royal couple's favourite subjects at the time. Russell, meanwhile, was effectively demanding from Aberdeen a ban on all Cabinet communication with the newspapers. Anticipating countless similar calls from politicians (including Speakers of the House of Commons) over the coming century and a half, Russell urged:

… that no communications should be made to the press not authorised by you, as the head of the Government. Such articles as have appeared in *The Times* for some time past are damaging to the character of the Government, & I must also say most disrespectful to Parlt. Papers and information are withheld from Members of Parlt who ask for them, and are then scattered about by the Editors of the Newspapers, broadcast….[34]

Aberdeen, in his reply, could only agree with Russell.

The Times again carped when Palmerston appointed Russell as colonial secretary in his first ministry; but, by the time Palmerston returned after the second Derby administration, and Russell was once again Foreign Secretary, relations thawed to the point, as has been noted, where Russell was even prepared to entertain Delane in his house. This may have helped somewhat in easing Russell's way back for his brief second and final premiership in 1865. Palmerston's death that year left two possible successors: Russell (by now 73) and William Ewart Gladstone. In the end, Delane went for Russell (who was by now in the Lords, as an Earl in his own right). Gladstone was abler, but Russell was a safer pair of hands, he concluded.

By this time, incidentally, there were already interesting (though unpublicized) crossovers between men pursuing simultaneous political and journalistic careers. One was the future Liberal leader Sir William Harcourt, already a *Times* leader-writer, and about to enter Parliament. Even more intriguingly, the future Cabinet minister Robert Lowe was both a *Times* leader writer and an MP: indeed, a candidate for office in the coming Russell administration on which he was giving his opinions in the paper's leader columns.

PRIME MINISTER AGAIN

Installed in 1865 for what even Russell must have known would be his final taste of the highest office, Russell proved much less forthcoming to the papers than Palmerston had been. In particular, he was able to have his 'tit for tat' with Delane by failing to let the paper have its customary Queen's Speech scoop in 1866, instead ensuring that it was *The Daily Telegraph* readers who had the first look at the government's legislative programme.[35]

Russell was still keen to end his career with a second Reform Bill. Lowe was opposed to Russell on this policy, and was seen by the Prime Minister and his supporters as using *The Times* to thwart his objectives (in which Russell was fully supported by Gladstone as his number two and Commons Leader). Russell made his own attitude clear when he told Clarendon (who, along with Granville, was more inclined to the Palmerstonian tradition of press friendliness) that he was:

> ... aware that Mr Delane was very angry that I did not ask to kiss his hand instead of the Queen's when I was appointed to succeed Palmerston; but I would rather not be in office than hold it on such humiliating conditions.[36]

This may also have been a shot across Clarendon's own bows: he was the only Cabinet minister still prepared to favour Delane. Even Granville observed an uncharacteristic silence during Russell's administration.

Russell's final attempt to crown his reform career with a second act failed. The ministry had relied on support from *The Globe* and *The Telegraph*; and, eventually, even *The Times* came round to the measure, if not to the man. Russell resigned in 1866, and formally announced that he was no longer the Liberal leader in 1867, making way for the age of Gladstone. It is quite possible that, had the measure passed, Gladstone's heroic Commons performances would have ensured that he, not Russell, was given the main credit for it: just as, when Derby's ministry did manage to pass the Reform Act in 1867, Disraeli for a very long time afterwards robbed Derby of his fair share of the credit.

In any event, Russell's top-level career was over. Like Melbourne in 1846, he may fleetingly have hoped at least to be offered a chance to return in 1868, at the end of the Derby-Disraeli government, but few others felt the same way. He was never a skilful manager of the press. He is one of the prime ministers most often cited in the standard accounts as merely expressing aristocratic disdain for journalism. At times, that did indeed reflect his view. But the overall picture is more complex: of a man frustrated at his failure to acquire the personal popularity and press success of some of his colleagues. He surely must have alternated between envying the success of Palmerston in this aspect of political culture and wishing to emulate it, on the one hand; and, on the other, standing by what he may have seen as a principled rejection of the dark arts of press management. His remark about his failure to kiss Mr Delane's hand instead of the Queen's in 1865 is one of the few genuinely witty comments of his to survive. Sadly, however, it is quite possible to picture him writing it with an angry curl to his lip rather than a sardonic smile.

CHAPTER FIVE

LORD DERBY

L ORD DERBY'S MOST recent biographer entitled his two-volume work *The Forgotten Prime Minister*.[1] Yet Derby holds an important place in this study; and is undergoing something of a broader rehabilitation.

Derby, like Liverpool, is now recognized as a much more successful practising politician than he used to be given credit for. Party leader for 22 unbroken years (1846–68: still a record), three times Prime Minister, the only Tory apart from Baldwin (in far less contentious circumstances) to introduce a reform act, a superb orator, probably a naturally wittier man than his more studied successor, a great figure of the turf, a classical and literary scholar of the first rank: it is a real surprise that he was for so long regarded as a mere prelude to the gaudier Disraeli. He was also, incidentally, despite his impeccable Stanley lineage (he was the 14th Earl of Derby), almost certainly one of the few nineteenth-century prime ministers to speak with at least a trace of a northern accent (like Peel and Gladstone).

Derby has conventionally been seen as fundamentally uninterested in the press, and as rather 'above' the necessities of press management. The diary of his son, the 15th Earl, and of his Foreign Secretary Lord Malmesbury, plus occasional 'mots' in Disraeli's correspondence have tended to reinforce this perception; though, as we shall see, the reality was a little more complex – especially towards the end of his career.[2] He did, on occasions, make the almost obligatory declarations of indifference towards and incapacity for the minutiae of press affairs: and, for much of his career, Derby's rhetoric in this respect carried more conviction than did that of several of his contemporaries.

Derby was born and raised a Whig, and was a classic case of a politician who felt that he had never changed party, but that his party had changed and left him. One of the threads that ran through his political life was a tenacious adherence to the established Anglican Church. Increasingly, during the early

8. Edward Stanley, 14th Earl of Derby, by Frederick Richard Say, 1844.
© National Portrait Gallery, London.

part of his career, Whig governments of which he was a member seemed to
put the Irish branch of the church at risk. Having served in the Canning-
Goderich coalition, Stanley (as he remained until 1851) was chief secretary
for Ireland and then colonial secretary under Grey, before resigning over

what he saw as the government's injurious policy on the appropriation of the Church tithes. He 'sat out' Peel's first ministry, offering tacit and selective support then and back in opposition, before joining him in government in 1841, and resigning over the Corn Laws in 1845. The 'Rupert of Debate', with the oratorical skills to shine in any assembly of any age, would have been a great loss to any ministry, and one of his main achievements was to steer the Protectionists from a disgruntled rump of dissidents back to being the official Conservative Party and once more a party of government.

DERBY: THE ASCENT

During Stanley's period as chief secretary, like his predecessors, he needed to come to arrangements with the Irish press. Nor, although times were beginning to change, was he too fastidious to become involved in the subsidy and secret service arrangements familiar to his predecessors. He established and supported the *Dublin Times*, and his Whig successor as chief secretary, Edward Littleton, according to the Earl of Clarendon, said he was in no doubt that it was supported from secret service funds. Of course, Stanley resigned from the Whig government, so his former colleagues felt less need to defend his record than if he had stayed with them.

The timing of the parliamentary discussion of Stanley's press arrangements in Ireland is highly significant. It was raised in Parliament in February 1852, just as Derby (as he had now become) was forming his first ministry. Press subsidies – especially payments involving secret service money – were seen as sufficiently scandalous as to be a useful stick with which to beat an incoming prime minister as late as 1852. Clarendon was corresponding with Brougham at the same time (two old press hands expostulating at Stanley's effrontery at doing the same thing!), and Clarendon described Stanley's conduct as 'unscrupulous beyond measure'.[3] In an echo of previous hand-wringing by Peel, Littleton eventually got rid of the *Dublin Times*: but not because of the support and subsidy arrangement, but because it was 'doing more harm than good' journalistically. He still thought that: 'no better employment of the fund could be made than in enlightening the public and exposing erroneous information and bad principles'.[4]

Richard Earle was Stanley's private secretary at the time of his spell in Ireland, and as colonial secretary. He had apparently made comments about the quality of individual newspaper reporters, for he received a very polite begging letter (for work, not money) from one of the young parliamentary reporters at the *True Sun* newspaper, who would subsequently perform the same role for the *Morning Chronicle*. The journalist, of whose abilities Earle had 'been kind enough to express an opinion in favour', was seeking freelance work over the summer of 1833 as a short-hand writer, to fill in the period when there was no parliamentary business to report. The young journalist's name was Charles Dickens.[5]

During Lord Grey's government of the early 1830s, Stanley (who, it will be recalled, did not become Lord Derby until 1851) was involved in a literary venture of a different sort. Along with Palmerston, Althorp and the future Peelite Sir James Graham, he was part of a high-level team enlisted by Brougham's secretary Le Marchant to contribute to a pamphlet called 'The Reformed Ministry and the Reformed Parliament', published in September 1833. Stanley wrote part of the section on West India slavery (whose abolition was the other great achievement of Grey's government aside from parliamentary reform; by the time the Abolition of Slavery Act of 1833 was implemented the following year, Stanley was no longer in office to receive the plaudits). Althorp revised the Bank Charter section; while Palmerston's topic, naturally, was foreign policy.[6]

In the following year, after he had resigned from Grey's government, Stanley was in a position of considerable power. As Peel formed his first ministry towards the end of 1834, Stanley and his supporters (including Graham) were still nominally Whigs, but looked highly unlikely to rejoin Melbourne's party. Peel, naturally, wanted them to join with his Conservatives to ensure a much stronger party of the centre-right. Like the Peelites in the late 1840s and early 1850s, and the Liberal Unionists in the late 1880s and early 1890s, the relatively small band of Stanleyites held a sort of balance of power. They were disproportionately talented in relation to their numbers, and it was these talents, not the numbers, which gave them their influence.

At the same time, Stanley was elected Lord Rector of Glasgow University. The scene was thus set for a major set-piece speech at his installation, and Stanley was particularly careful to ensure that press reporting of his speech was both full and accurate. Realizing the special attention that would be devoted to what he said, he ensured that *The Times*, the *Morning Post*, the *Morning Chronicle* and the *Morning Herald* had full advance access to his text. The political range of the papers chosen is significant, as well as their prominence in circulation and influence. They were the perfect vehicles to receive and spread Stanley's message: that Britain should be governed from the centre. Peel without Wellington, and Melbourne and Grey without Russell and O'Connell: these were the ideal allies of a centrist Stanleyite vision – a Glasgow/Knowsley Creed to rival or supplement the Tamworth Manifesto of the same month.[7] (Knowsley was the imposing Lancashire seat of the Earls of Derby).

FROM WHIG TO TORY

At the subsequent 1835 election, Stanley again showed he was willing to use the press to his advantage. At this stage, he was still Mr Edward Stanley: he became Lord Stanley through his own (political) choice in 1844, before succeeding to the earldom in 1851. He was still actively involved in Commons electioneering; and, again, he ensured that his political base in Lancashire (extending far beyond his Knowsley Hall home) was secured by judicious use of the press. This time, it was *The Globe* and the *Morning Chronicle* which he favoured, perhaps wishing to keep a line open to his former Whig colleagues, knowing that he was both in competition with, but also in demand from, Peel's Tories.

However, when Melbourne returned to office a few months later, *The Globe* was quick to turn on the Stanleyites, definitely not part of the ministry, and were initially poised between sitting on the Whig government side of the House or the Tory-dominated opposition benches. At this stage, *The Times* was something of an ally, countering *The Globe*'s criticisms with a more supportive line. Indeed, some months later, the paper published a letter from a correspondent simply signing himself 'Runnymede', strongly endorsing Stanley's line between 1834 and early 1836. Claiming that Stanley had foregone Melbourne's own claim that nothing could stop him becoming the next prime minister, in order to put country before party and personal ambition, 'Runnymede' praised him as a pure, noble and natural leader. The flowery phrasing came from a man who was himself intent on a political career. A year later, he entered the Commons. That man was Benjamin Disraeli.

Stanley negotiated the difficult years of transition from semi-detached Whig to close Tory ally, and was then ready to join Peel, as colonial secretary, when he formed his majority government in 1841. Having done so, he may have expected a reasonably lengthy period in which his ministerial responsibilities superseded the need for building up a position through the press as a future party leader and prime minister.

It was Peel's decision on the Corn Laws which threw the spotlight firmly on to the politics of Peel's own position once again. Peel's decision had a number of consequences for Stanley. It made a Tory split almost inevitable. It ensured that Stanley was easily the likeliest choice as overall leader of the Protectionists. And it handed him the advice and support of J. W. Croker, who abandoned Peel as soon as his decision on the Corn Laws was made public. Croker both advised Stanley and promoted him in the *Quarterly Review*, to which he still devoted much of his energy.[8]

Stanley resigned from the Cabinet in 1845, when Peel's decision was announced; and had to build what was effectively a new party, the Protectionist faction, turning it from a rump of the disaffected into a potential party of government. That also meant ensuring that as much of the press as possible supported the Protectionists, not the Peelites. Stanley's own son Edward, like his father, had come into politics early, and was in many ways closer politically to Disraeli than to his own father in these formative years. He also had a greater natural interest in the press; and his diary of these years gives us some sense of the efforts being made to acquire friendly and supportive papers. In 1850, there was an attempt to buy the *Morning Chronicle*, then to influence and favour the *Morning Post*, to establish a supportive weekly, and to contribute to the *Herald*.[9]

The two most prominent insider diarists of Derby's Tory party were Stanley (his son), and the Earl of Malmesbury (twice his foreign secretary). Both of them describe their own efforts to interest Derby (as we shall now call him) in the minutiae of press management, acquisition and influence, with a rather apathetic Derby reluctantly agreeing to go along with the diarists (often acting with Disraeli) in what seemed to him like a reluctant necessity. Croker also encouraged more press effort from (amongst others) the younger Stanley, telling him too how he, Peel and Palmerston had taken a firm hold of the pro-Liverpool *Courier*, and raised its circulation from 6,000 to 20,000.[10]

Malmesbury's considered view was given in 1857, well after the first Derby government of 1852, but before the second and third ones of 1858–9 and 1866–8. He wrote:

> Lord Derby has never been able to realise the sudden growth and power of the Political Press, for which he has no partiality, which feeling is reciprocated by its members. In these days this is a fatal error in men who wish to obtain public power and distinction. Lord Derby is too proud a man to flatter anybody, even his greatest friends and equals, much less those of whom he knows nothing. His son, with greater wisdom (for the day), has taken the opposite line, and with benefit to his popularity and advancement.[11]

On occasions, perhaps because Derby was a little wary of his own son's closeness to Disraeli, Derby used Malmesbury himself as an intermediary in dealing with the papers. In 1851, he praised Malmesbury's tactful handling of Robert Knox, the editor of the *Morning Herald*: 'It is not very easy to write civilly to a man that his paper is conducted with very little talent; and I admire the way you have managed to compliment the Editor, and smooth down any soreness he might feel'.[12]

Malmesbury's comments are interesting for a number of reasons. He was a huge admirer of Derby, and has some extremely flattering verdicts on his character and abilities elsewhere in the diaries. Also, over the comments hover twin presences: Palmerston and Disraeli. 'Pam' and 'Dizzy' were both able, though in very contrasting styles, to apply the requisite flattery. At this stage, Derby was not. Unquestionably, that regard operated in (especially) Palmerston's favour during his political career, and has continued to exercise its influence on the verdicts of historians.

Derby has never been a reviled prime minister: his place in historians' press and online rankings is now fairly high (often well within the top 20 of over 50 prime ministers). It is rather that he does not survive as a character in the collective historical memory as strongly as Disraeli, Gladstone, Palmerston and Peel. The role of the press, surely, was a major contributory factor in this. It was not that large sections of the press 'turned against' him (as arguably the media did much more recently in respect of John Major and Gordon Brown). It simply failed to turn him into a popular 'character' to the same extent.

THE ROUTE TO POWER

Derby's biggest press stumbling block after 1846 was that the increasing power and influence of *The Times* was withdrawn from him. Free trade 'versus' protectionism was the proximate cause; and, although the paper praised him on individual occasions, it was never an enthusiastic or regular supporter. The *Quarterly Review*, by contrast, was so supportive that Croker could be described by Derby's most recent biographer as his 'publicist'.[13] Derby, after 1846, had a sort of informal veto over political articles. However, from the earliest period of his leadership, other sections of the Tory press (the *Standard*, the *Morning Herald* and the *Morning Post*) tended to fall too readily into the hands of the protectionist extremists: the extreme Tory backbenchers, who never looked like a credible corps of ministers in waiting (unlike Derby himself).

In the aftermath of the party split following the Corn Laws repeal, some Tories attempted to link the twin cries of protectionism and anti-Catholicism. Derby's influence was already such that, in 1846, he could intervene successfully with the *Morning Herald* and encourage it to dampen down its overheated 'no-popery' tone. He told Samuel Phillips, the disillusioned ex-*Times* man who edited the *Herald*:

> These articles ... are written with the view of exciting the Protestant feeling of this country against [paying the Irish Catholic clergy]. I cannot say that I approve of such a course....[14]

Indeed, the young Stanley had himself supported such payments as a backbencher as long ago as 1825. According to the most detailed study of Derby in this period, he 'found the affairs of the press bewildering and tedious and did not again try to influence Phillips'.[15]

He also had a taste of his lengthy future collaboration with Disraeli when, after the death of Lord George Bentinck, he had to resolve the question of the party's leadership in the Commons. Disraeli was desperate for the job, barely even able to clothe his ambition in the formal rhetoric of disinterestedness expected at the time. Moreover, Disraeli was happy to use Samuel Phillips, whom Derby had asked to tone down the 'no-popery' campaign, to boost his own chances. In the end, a triumvirate was formed from which Disraeli in due course emerged as Derby's number two and Commons chief. Disraeli, in the meantime, had served notice that his long-established and ill-concealed taste for 'press meddling' could and would be used in his personal interest when he deemed it appropriate.

In the same year, 1851, that Derby was abortively offered the premiership and failed to form an administration, his son was busy with efforts to shore up his party's position in the press. 'It came to nothing', he wrote: '[T]he party in general seemed to regard the newspaper interest as their natural enemy, and any attempt to turn it into a friend as a mere waste of time: my father sympathised with this view'.[16] The younger Stanley also showed a frank and perceptive awareness of the social position of journalists at the time.

> They have the irritable vanity of authors, and add to it a sensitiveness on the score of social position which so far as I know is peculiar to them. Having in reality a vast secret influence, rating this above its true worth, and seeing that it gives them no recognised status in society, they stand up for the dignity of their occupation with a degree of jealousy that I never saw among any other profession.[17]

The young Stanley is describing what happened in 1851, but this was added to his journal subsequently as a gloss to explain the overall aim of his activities, the details of which he decided to omit at the time. He certainly felt pessimistic as to the nature and extent of press support on the eve of his father's first premiership. The *Morning Post* had been a supporter of protectionist and landed interests from the 1830s, but, after a change of owner and of editor, it fairly quickly entered the Palmerstonian camp. Meanwhile, the Peelites acquired the *Morning Chronicle*, which had not, in any case, previously been a Tory supporter, ensuring that the attacks (especially from the politician Sidney Herbert) became sharper. Even the *Herald* was not as close to the Tory Ultras as before, though still broadly supportive.

When Derby did eventually form his first administration in February 1852, the overall press climate was certainly challenging. The response of the increasingly deaf Wellington as the list of Cabinet names was read out was 'Who? Who?'. Although Derby himself had extensive Cabinet experience, there are comparisons with the first MacDonald administration of 1924 and the Blair government of 1997 in respect of the overall dearth of ministerial experience. From many of the opposition papers it was more a case of

'What? Why?'. Another of Derby's biographers believed: 'Few governments in British history had to face such a consistently hostile press as the Derby Ministry of 1852'.[18]

In part, opposition attacks were a result of the realization by the party's leaders that a return to pre-1846 protectionism was no longer practical politics. Derby and Disraeli had to execute a manoeuvre in relation to free trade involving the frequent and eloquent expression of sympathy with their own supporters, while gradually letting it dawn on them that putting the clock back was not a realistic possibility. It was also greatly to Derby's credit that he did not attempt to outdo Lord John Russell when he used the issue of the restoration of the Catholic bishops in 1850 to start a 'no popery' campaign. However, this left opposition periodicals like *Fraser's* and the *Edinburgh Review* ample scope to accuse him of hypocrisy and lack of principle. *The Times* joined in the condemnation. Indeed, for Delane and his team, the tone became positively aggressive just as Derby was about to replace Russell. At the time, there was extensive press criticism of Louis Bonaparte, who was soon to become Napoleon III. All mainstream politicians, including Russell, deplored the tone of the press, both with regard to Louis Napoleon and to 'no popery'. However, Derby broadened the argument considerably:

If, as in these days, the press aspires to exercise the influence of statesmen, the press should remember that they are not free from the corresponding responsibility of statesmen, and that it is incumbent on them, as a sacred duty, to maintain that tone of moderation and respect even in expressing frankly their opinions on foreign affairs which would be required of every man who pretends [i.e. aspires] to guide public opinion.[19]

Derby's *Herald* and the Russell-influenced *Globe* agreed: *The Times* was more recalcitrant. In editorials, it took lengthy issue with Derby's argument (though not indulging in personal abuse), making it clear that, while it had withdrawn its favour from Russell's government and party (with the personal exceptions of the press-friendly Granville and Clarendon), it did not follow that favour would automatically therefore be transferred to Derby's Conservatives. Disraeli had made some attempt at a rapprochement with Delane, and the tone towards the government in general was not vindictively harsh; but they were far from reliably in Derby's corner either.

First Premiership

Despite its relative brevity (ten months), the first Derby government did address the weakness of its press support while in government. In June 1852, Derby's son tells us, the Cabinet spent time on the subject:

> The chief want to the government is the want of a daily or weekly organ, the *Herald* being imbecile, and no other existing. I drew out for the cabinet a scheme, which was proposed through Malmesbury: each member to subscribe 2% of his official salary towards a fund for supporting the press. This passed with little opposition (but though we found money, we never found writers, and part of the sum thus raised was returned).[20]

Derby himself, in 1852, was prepared to 'admit, more than I ever did, the possible powers of the press in a crisis'. A few years earlier, in 1849, Lord John Manners, the future Duke of Rutland,[21] specifically linked the poor position of the party in the press with the general lack of regard shown by the 'country party' for literature and journalism. The sense that Derby and many of his colleagues looked down on the press and those who worked for it indeed certainly had an effect on the way Derby was covered. He was unquestionably one of the greatest orators of the nineteenth century – as good, in his way, as Gladstone and Disraeli in theirs, more stylish and inspiring than Peel and far superior to the likes of Melbourne, Russell, Aberdeen and Palmerston – but even this could be given an adverse twist by papers like *The Times*, who implied that his rhetorical facility was symptomatic of a lack of integrity or conviction:

> Last night the House of Lords heard … with considerable pleasure one of those ingenious and even impassioned orations which Lord Derby is able to … deliver on almost any subject, and perhaps we might add, on almost any side.[22]

On one occasion when his own personal conduct came into question, Derby did show himself to be meticulous in using the press – even local papers – to set the record straight. During his son's election campaign in Lancaster in 1848, a supporter of his radical opponent claimed that his father had said, commenting on the nature of his audience during the 1830 campaign for

Preston, 'I could do without this SWINISH MULTITUDE'. Derby contacted all the local editors, who confirmed that no such statement had been made, and a disclaimer was published in the *Lancaster Gazette*.[23]

Later, during his first administration, he still had ready access to Croker and the *Quarterly Review* to lay out his policies – notably on foreign affairs; and he was able to stop senior journalists at the *Herald* making an unsubtle and damaging statement of his rather precarious position in relation to the abandonment of the policy of restoring protection. However, it was clear to the leadership – including Derby himself – that a stronger press position would be essential both in the coming opposition period and in any future Derby governments. While Derby's own interest and involvement may have been fitful and sporadic, the central perception was already there, contrary to some accounts emphasizing his complete passivity in the wake of activity by Disraeli and others. The support of the *Quarterly Review* was both welcome and well orchestrated by Croker: but it did not reach enough of the broader electorate. The *Herald* was essentially loyal, but not, in Derby's view, ably conducted. More was needed.

OPPOSITION

The government eventually fell in December 1852, over Disraeli's budget. The Aberdeen coalition which followed it was a combination of Whigs and Peelites. Just over two years later, it collapsed and was replaced by the first of Palmerston's two administrations. At various times up to the end of the decade, it seemed a real possibility that the ablest of the Peelites, Gladstone and even Palmerston (more of a Palmerstonian than a Whig!) might join forces with Derby's Protectionists. Disraeli, who had been Chancellor and Commons Leader in the first Derby government, was prepared to make way as Commons Leader for Palmerston (all under Derby at the summit, of course), but not for Gladstone (though he rarely put it as bluntly as this in public). For a politician, it is always easier to make way for someone 25 years older than five years younger. Until Palmerston saw the possibility of himself achieving the highest office, his entry into a Derby Cabinet in a senior position such as Commons Leader was a possibility. This could well have ensured Derby an almost Liverpool-like period of power in the 1850s and 1860s. Gladstone, too, felt temperamentally more akin to Derby than to Russell or Palmerston (though less than to Aberdeen). They were both keen Homeric scholars and all-round classicists and men of letters, with keen intellects, though Gladstone never shared Derby's penchant for joking and passion for the turf. Instead, however, Derby and his party would face just over five years of opposition, until they returned in early 1858.

The first major newspaper effort of 1853 involved a new weekly journal called *The Press*. This was very much an initiative of Disraeli and Stanley (the younger): Derby was obviously consulted, but was not keen. Because many of his lieutenants would be writing for it (Disraeli, Stanley and the other notable politician-novelist of the era, Edward Bulwer-Lytton), Derby feared the potential embarrassment caused by mistakes in what was far more of a house organ than the *Herald* or the *Quarterly Review*. His son records the substance of their conversation in his diary. Derby, he said:

> ... expressed himself decidedly hostile: thought we should be compromised: offence would be given: it was impossible not to hold D[israeli] and even himself responsible for whatever appeared in a paper confessedly their organ: such a connection could neither be acknowledge[d] nor disavowed: Peel, while in office, had repudiated the claim of any journal to represent his ministry: he thought this a sound principle....[24]

It is a fascinating answer. The firm assumption of the impossibility of acknowledging a 'pledged' paper is especially important, marking both the difficulty of a formal press affiliation for a political party, and the implication that the party gains all the disadvantages from a potentially embarrassing paper while accruing little benefit. His comment on Peel is broadly true of the 1841–6 ministry; though, as we have seen, in substance untrue of the first in 1834–5, given the nature of the role of *The Times* in its formation.

Stanley countered that they already had two recognized supporters: the *Herald* and the *Standard*; that they were not very good; that they reflected the 'wrong' part of the party (the 'lowest and least enlightened part'); and that the 'better' part should be represented. (Presumably both parties felt that it was not even worth mentioning the Ultra-Tory *John Bull*, whose displeasure at the advent of *The Press* was made very clear). Derby, perhaps recalling the factionalism of the Melbourne government and the Tory party of Wellington, replied that this would divide the party into sections. His conclusion was that they could go ahead with the publication; but that he should not be involved and his name never used. By his clear disfavour, however, he signalled to rich supporters like the Duke of Northumberland that they should not sink money into the project.

Derby's fears were borne out later when, during the Crimean War, *The Press*, at Disraeli's urging, started supporting a premature peace line in late 1855, while Derby and the bulk of the party continued to support the war. It was one of the most serious breaches between the two men. Malmesbury, Derby's once and future foreign secretary, backed Derby, and even the younger Stanley was becoming less close to Disraeli than before.

The rest of the story of the rather ill-fated paper is Disraeli's rather than Derby's, and will be told later (see Chapter Eight); but Derby had clearly demonstrated not merely his views on the issue, but his unequalled influence within the party. Stanley, meanwhile, may have felt vindicated some years later. He records a conversation between his father and the Queen and Prince Albert in early 1861. His father spoke of the strength of the Conservative Party (between his second and third administrations), to which Albert replied: 'What is the use of that? The country is governed by newspapers, and you have not a newspaper'. The Prince may have been thinking more of the overall state of affairs than he was of domestic politics, since he went on to accuse the entire press of being influenced by foreign governments. When he exonerated *The Times*, Victoria quickly added that they were 'as corrupt as the rest'.[25]

SECOND PREMIERSHIP

When the Aberdeen coalition fell in 1855, there was a possibility that a second Derby ministry might come about more quickly than had been widely anticipated. The papers' attitudes to the prospective successors are interesting to note. Derby could count on the *Herald* (along with *The Standard* and *The Press*), Russell on the *Daily News*, Palmerston (the eventual victor) on *The Times*, the *Morning Post* and the *Morning Advertiser*; while the *Morning Chronicle* merely lamented the fall of Aberdeen. In the event, three more years would pass before the advent of the second Derby ministry.

The story of the Orsini plot against Napoleon III which led to Palmerston's fall is his rather than Derby's and will be told in Chapter Seven. Where Derby is concerned, it is sufficient to note that his prospects were a little brighter as he embarked on his second premiership than when he started his first. The press position was substantially the same; but the tone of non-supportive papers was much less adverse in 1858 than in 1852. *The Times*, despite continuing overall support for Palmerston, was more lukewarm towards him than in 1855, and was prepared to give Derby a reasonably friendly welcome, albeit rather on sufferance. Derby did not take an active role in trying to 'square' Delane, the editor, in 1858. He would be much more personally involved in 1866, when he formed his final administration. Disraeli, however, was in very close touch: giving 'exclusives' on ministerial appointments, on Derby's audience with the Queen and other elements of the formation of the government. Once the government was formed, Stanley and occasionally Malmesbury also 'communicated' with the paper. Ominously, however, the personal contacts with Palmerston and Clarendon remained closer and more regular. Malmesbury was able during March 1858, a month in to the Derby ministry, to describe *The Times* as 'most complimentary'.[26] Even Greville, never a personal admirer of Derby, and with his own close links to *The Times*, noted in his journal: 'The first class of this government is not worse than that of the last, and the second class is a good deal better'.[27]

As long as Palmerston and Russell remained unreconciled, Derby might look forward to a reasonable span in office. It was also possible that Gladstone, still the star of the Peelite group, might join Derby as part of a broader arrangement. If, however, Palmerston and Russell could patch up their differences, and one agree to serve under the other, things would become more difficult. In the meantime, Derby and his team, with protection effectively off the agenda and with the Crimean War over, had to decide what the party's overall approach to government would be, and whether it should attempt to upstage the Whigs and win over the moderate press by addressing the question of a further Reform Bill. Derby had seen that there was no political future in simply rallying the forces of reaction to the Tory banner; and, across a range of policy areas, he looked to provide a distinctive alternative to the Whigs not based solely on opposition to all reform. So striking was this focus upon more progressive alternatives that Lord Campbell, the Whig lawyer, said, early in the second Derby term: 'Democracy has made more progress in England during the last three months than during twenty years of Whig rule'.[28] At about the same time, while the Conservative *Standard* was praising Derby's pragmatism, *The Times*, too, lauded the wisdom of his 'graceful concession' to the prevailing political landscape.[29]

Some sections of the non-Tory press were prepared to support a reasonably moderate Derby Reform Bill. Palmerston, at heart, was uninterested in the subject, and would have supported Derby if it suited him. But, when the time came, Russell could not face the prospect of a successful measure being passed by a Tory government: and this hastened the reunification of the feuding elements of the party. In the end, of course, Palmerston's second ministry came in 1859 and went in 1865 without a Reform Act, as, for different reasons, did Russell's in 1865–6. It would indeed be a Derby ministry which passed one, but not until his third administration in 1867.

In his second administration, Derby followed broadly the same approach to the press as that taken by Grey, Melbourne, Peel and Russell previously: little in the way of direct one-to-one intervention with owners and editors, combined with a willingness to allow very senior lieutenants (Disraeli, Malmesbury, Stanley) to engage with them. However, the press climate was noticeably more benign. The Whig/Liberal papers no longer saw a Derby government as somehow intolerable. Derby, meanwhile, was broadly content to be judged on his parliamentary utterances and his actions, rather than by direct management of (or covert contributions to) the press. He was still old-fashioned enough to be infuriated when the Reform proposals were leaked to *The Times* by Disraeli: through the future Commons leader Stafford Northcote, Derby strongly suspected. In fact, Delane later told Disraeli that the leak came from Edward Ellice (though he probably got the news from Ralph Earle, Disraeli's private secretary!). Whatever the source, the important outcome was that it resulted in support for the bill: not merely because it was leaked, but on its merits. It was given a welcome by the paper's leader-writer Robert Lowe (the future Liberal Cabinet minister). Support also came from the *Morning Herald*, as might have been expected; but also from the *Morning Chronicle* and from *The Globe*.[30]

In the end, the Bill failed, and the reunited Whigs, whom we can now more appropriately call Liberals, later defeated Derby on foreign policy and ended his government. Despite this defeat he was, however, in a much stronger position than a few years ago. The Queen now preferred him personally to Palmerston and Russell. The opposition press largely saw him as a pragmatist and a statesman, not as the last gasp of Tory reaction. Palmerston himself, during his ministry between 1859 and his death in 1865, would often rely on the tacit support of Derby and Disraeli to see off the Radicals (and, on occasion, Russell and Gladstone). Indeed, Palmerston himself thought

Derby's own bill too liberal. When Gladstone wished to go further than he already had under Aberdeen and abolish the Paper Duties, Derby knew that Palmerston privately supported his public opposition.

OPPOSITION AND FINAL TERM

During Derby's next seven years as Leader of the Opposition (despite the capitals it was not really an official position then, but he was clearly recognizable as such), his attitude to the electorate, in effect, can be summed up as: I am at your service whenever you and the country need me. That is not to suggest an abandonment of the regular duties of opposition; but he felt no need for frenetic press campaigns or propaganda initiatives above and beyond what was customary. Even Stanley had cooled considerably on the idea of extra press campaigning by 1862:

> Heard that a new weekly paper is talked of, Disraeli much interested in its success, Lytton also concerned in it... I doubt the experiment being tried, after the failure of the 'Press', and still more doubt its success if it be tried.[31]

These were the years of Derby's excellent translation of the *Iliad*, widely acclaimed on publication. Derby told Malmesbury that he was '... never more astonished in my life than on reading the puff of it in *The Times*'.[32] Another volume, *Translations*, printed privately and later reissued publicly, contained his versions of Greek, Latin, French, Italian and German works. These were also years of worsening ill health: gout increasingly held him in its grip. However, when the chance for a third premiership came, Derby was ready.

After Russell's final resignation in 1866, despite some manoeuvring to induce Derby to waive his claims to the premiership in his son's favour, Derby took his chance. There had been some press and political suggestions that a coalition of Conservatives with anti-reform Whigs and Liberals could be formed. Derby was willing; but baulked at the suggestion that it should be under a Whig prime minister. So although, for a third time, he formed a minority administration, he was in a stronger political position than previously.

The Times, thoroughly disenchanted with Russell both politically and personally, was more warmly supportive than in 1858, and far more so than in 1852. From early 1866, Russell was favouring the *Sunday Gazette* at the expense of *The Times*. Meanwhile, Disraeli had been 'working' on Delane for years. This time, Derby too was prepared to make personal efforts to ensure continued support, especially for the Reform Bill. Early in 1867, before the bill was introduced, Derby spoke personally to Delane, and secured his support for the bill's provisions.[33] Even before this, the paper had spoken of a 'very tolerable ministry', predicting that 'it would be rash to conclude that the fate of the third [ministry] will be that of the predecessors'.[34] Only a few months before, Delane (taking rather a lot on himself even for a *Times* editor) had told Lady Salisbury '… that a Derby-Disraeli govt would not do, that he should feel compelled to oppose it, but that the same objections would not apply to one of which Lord Stanley should be the head'.[35] Instead, Delane had to be content with 'announcing' and approving Stanley's appointment as foreign secretary a week before it happened, occasioning a rather withering comment from Russell to the outgoing foreign secretary, Clarendon:

> I see Lord Stanley is announced as your successor and that Lord Derby has done that which I would not do, namely, submitted his appointment to Mr Delane before submitting them to the Queen. This is a new constitution of itself, and one much to be deprecated.[36]

Lord Russell was correct to name Derby as the prime mover in this instance, which is in itself a noticeable change: on previous occasions, such moves would have been made by Disraeli almost behind his chief's back. Shortly after Derby's entry into office, Delane was invited to visit Derby's London house to see the reform resolutions. One can almost hear the pleasure as Derby tells Disraeli that he has outdone him on his own territory.

> It will be a crumb of comfort to you to know that I had a most satisfactory interview with Delane. He is cordially with us, and will do all in his power to carry us through. He listened most attentively to the whole of our programme, and pronounced oracularly, "I think it will do".[37]

Derby's venture into press management was not wholly successful. The paper's editorial was critical of the initial resolutions, remaining in principle behind the government's measure while pressing for more concessions to the opposition's wishes. However, his task was made easier by the fact that

Gladstone, now effectively Liberal leader, was as reluctant as Russell to court *The Times*. Even the mild Granville urged Delane to approach Gladstone (since Gladstone was unwilling to court him). Delane had to make do with the confidences of Charles Villiers, Clarendon's brother. Had the Liberal leadership played its press hand more skilfully, Derby and Disraeli might have had an even harder struggle to enact the bill. Another future Prime Minister, Lord Cranborne (later Lord Salisbury), was busy attacking his leaders in the *Quarterly Review*; but opposition from the far right was never enough to derail the bill, and eventually the Second Reform Act was passed.

Derby remained Prime Minister until the end of February 1868; but his major achievement was complete. He was the only Conservative prime minister of the century to widen the electorate. He was the minister who abolished slavery, as colonial secretary under Lord Grey in 1833. His place in history is secure on those grounds alone. He had always had mixed views about the press; but, at the end, he had done just enough to ensure support for his greatest measure. His view of 'public opinion', as Gladstone recognized, was essentially parliamentary. One of the greatest speakers of his own or any age, he limited his platform appearances to what was unavoidable – often local or university occasions – and would no more have conducted his own version of Gladstone's 'Midlothian campaign' than he would have taken to the stage. Just before he died, in 1869, he was approached by Lord Colville with a scheme to buy *The Globe*. He replied: 'I cannot conceal from you that, in my opinion, even in a political sense, there is no more unsatisfactory mode of spending money than the purchase of a second class newspaper'.[38]

The first man in British history to be prime minister three times gave fewer 'deathbed' repentances than Wellington for his earlier 'neglect' of the press. In truth, despite the verdict of Malmesbury that Derby's wilful blindness towards the power of the press was his 'fatal error', throughout his career Derby had shown himself prepared to do what he had to, if it was clear that it really was essential, to square sections of the press. He did not enjoy or relish it; he was not especially interested in talking about it. He did it because it was needed.

CHAPTER SIX

LORD ABERDEEN

LORD ABERDEEN'S CAREER culminated in one brief premiership (lasting just over two years, from December 1852 to January 1855) which has defined his entire reputation. However, Aberdeen's considerable press management skills were mainly deployed during his years as a Cabinet minister, under Wellington and Peel, rather than during his time as prime minister – although there were still brief flashes then. While he held the highest office, he did sometimes resemble the hapless, ageing figure of historical reputation; but there were also signs that colleagues – notably Russell – still saw him as someone who could 'control' the press (in particular *The Times*) and effectively decide whether or not the ministry would be subjected to newspaper attacks. He was also prime minister at the time of the aforementioned vitriolic press campaign against Prince Albert in 1853–4, accusing him of being in league with foreign powers, which he was powerless to stop, but on which he was able to offer useful advice.[1] Victoria, like many others who knew of Aberdeen's closeness to Delane, assumed that this could be translated into more general press influence and management.

This part of Aberdeen's contemporary reputation has not really survived: the astute press manager does not sit too easily with the aged wartime ditherer. The foundations of Aberdeen's experience of press management were laid when he was foreign secretary, and he was a worthy press adversary for Palmerston, who was also in the process of taking press management to another level during his three spells in the same office. Indeed, Aberdeen's more traditional hapless image was almost certainly bolstered by his own claim, quoted by Cobden: 'It was the PRESS as Lord Aberdeen told me that forced him into the [Crimean] war'.[2]

A Scottish aristocrat, Aberdeen had held diplomatic office under Liverpool, and had ventured into print with reviews on classical topics for the *Edinburgh Review* and a book on Ancient Greek art and architecture. His

9. George Hamilton Gordon, 4th Earl of Aberdeen, by John Partridge, c.1847.
© National Portrait Gallery, London.

literary and scholarly productions have not survived in the way that Derby's *Iliad* or Disraeli's novels have. Aberdeen's works, like Russell's and most of Gladstone's, were much more of their time, and considerably less likely than Derby's or Disraeli's to be stumbled across today. However, they aided his reputation as a talented and versatile figure, though he lacked the long Commons career of most other prime ministers of the era.

When Wellington formed his ministry in 1828, Aberdeen became foreign secretary, serving throughout its time in office up to late 1830. During the first Peel ministry, he was colonial secretary, but returned to the Foreign Office from 1841 to 1846, again under Peel. For well over 20 years, from 1828 to 1851, apart from the few months of the first Peel ministry, either Aberdeen or Palmerston was at the Foreign Office.

Aberdeen was strongly suspected of writing directly for *The Courier* during his first period as foreign secretary. During the Tory and Tory-dominated administrations between 1807 and 1830, the paper was seen as the closest the government had to an official mouthpiece, and was given exclusive information on that basis. When there was a change of government in Charles X's France, and the Ultra Royalist Jules de Polignac came to power, the government received the news before it became public knowledge, and gave it (we would say 'leaked it') to *The Courier*, along with an accompanying article believed to have been written by Aberdeen himself. Whether by accident or design, Aberdeen's own contribution was omitted. Amidst rumours of shady stock-market dealings enabled by this early access to information, the editor, pleading human error, was summoned to the Foreign Office like a diplomat from an errant nation, to be told: '... FROM THE FOREIGN OFFICE AT LEAST YOU get no more information, so the sooner you take yourself off the better'.

This, at least, is how the story was told by the gleeful non-government papers, the *Morning Journal* and *The Age*;[3] along with an attack on *The Courier* proprietors' financial dealings. As is often the case, however, with government threats to punish newspapers, it appears that *The Courier* retained its privileged position: exclusively breaking the news of the capture of Erzerum by the Russians from the Turks only a week after its Foreign Office dressing-down. Aberdeen (who, one assumes, must have known of the transaction) was often to prove himself a pragmatist in his dealings with the fourth estate. The Aberdeen who told Croker in 1855 that he would not have the least notion how to organize press coverage or a press bureau (the idea Croker had urged on successive prime ministers, with no official result) may have been reflecting the weariness of a septuagenarian whose premiership and top-level career were drawing to a close, rather than the much more active Cabinet minister of Wellington and Peel's government, or even the new prime minister who, we are told, saw Delane daily at the end of 1852 and the beginning of 1853.

We saw earlier that the fall of Melbourne's second ministry more or less coincided with the death of Thomas Barnes of *The Times* and his replacement by Delane. Politicians looking for support from *The Times* in 1841 needed to make a fairly quick assessment and locate just where the real power at the paper lay. Was it more important to win over the proprietors, the Walter family, especially given the youth of the new editor? (He was just 24). Or was Delane already the man to watch? Perhaps Henry Reeve was also essential? Reeve, the friend and later editor of Greville, never edited *The Times*, but he was an influential journalist and reviewer there for many years. Lord Lansdowne was Reeve's favourite politician, but Aberdeen came to respect

Reeve and they cooperated easily. But it was Delane with whom Aberdeen forged the closest bond: and, on the whole, he benefited greatly from it.

The relationship between Aberdeen and Delane was negotiated against a background of great change in the relations between politicians and the press as the era of subsidies finally waned and newspaper circulations rose. 'The gentlemen', as well as the newspapers which they owned, edited or wrote for, were becoming more socially respectable and perceptions of their power and influence increased. As a consequence, transactions of information – exclusives for favourable reporting and more general support – were increasingly foregrounded in relationships between journalists and editors on the one hand and politicians on the other.

It is this consideration which formed the basis of the Aberdeen-Delane relationship. Under Aberdeen, the Foreign Office would routinely give *The Times* as much information as it properly could. In addition, however, Aberdeen himself would also hand Delane stories or pieces of information which would have been regarded as major 'scoops' in any age. As we have already seen, this was the case with Peel's dramatic change over the Corn Laws in 1845.[4] Aberdeen would also give detailed comments on Reeve's editorials on foreign policy, helping to shape policy by so doing.[5] This was a strategy which other foreign secretaries would find useful: not only Palmerston, but Clarendon and Granville were prone to 'steer' leader-writers of several papers in this way. Such was Aberdeen's reliance on Delane that, even when in opposition in 1849, he wrote nervously asking him if he would be away for long on his Italian holiday: 'I hope not for I shall feel no security in the view taken of our Foreign Affairs during your absence'.[6]

Early in Peel's 1841–6 government, the prime minister was pleased to use and take advantage of Aberdeen's 'special relationship' with *The Times* – for instance, to secure favourable coverage of the government's opposition to the proposed Franco-Belgian treaty. However, we recall that Peel's own relationship with the paper was now much worse than at its zenith in 1834–5; and the paper was neither a Tory organ, nor an enthusiast for the government's general domestic policy. Nor was it easy for Tory papers like the *Morning Herald* to stomach the close entente between its rival and one of the most senior figures in the administration. However, almost inevitably, there would be some divergences. Aberdeen wished to repair relations with France, strained under the Palmerston regime. King Louis Philippe was keen to reciprocate. But some papers, including *The Times*, while supportive in principle, could not resist fulminating against individual French actions (in North Africa and the Pacific), just as French papers were all too ready to criticize perfidious Albion: making their respective political masters' lives considerably more difficult.

In the case of Aberdeen, however, individual frustration was pragmatically set aside in the overall interests of the bond – with France as with *The Times*. The diarist Charles Greville gives a lively account of Aberdeen visiting Delane and Reeve in Reeve's office (he worked with Greville at the Privy Council as well as writing for the paper). He tells us how the two young journalists pronounced almost as 'oracularly' on how they would treat Aberdeen's Tahiti policy as Delane did many years later when hearing Lord Derby's reform proposals. After a long consultation, Greville tells us: '... they resolved ... that they WOULD NOT QUITE ABANDON HIM, and though they could not approve of his conduct, they would insert a moderate and neutral article'. Meanwhile, across the Channel, the French statesman François Guizot was meeting with the paper's correspondent there, to try to make amends for having favoured the *Morning Herald*. According to Greville, when Guizot asked what he could do for him, he was told that the paper could do very little because:

> ... in truth the paper was of much greater importance to him than he [Guizot] could be to the paper, inasmuch as it was not above once or twice in a year that any occasion of serving *The Times* could occur, while they wrote every day in the week. 'Well', said Guizot, 'take those papers' (pointing to some on the table) 'and no other English paper shall have them for 24 hours'.[7]

ABERDEEN AND THE PAPERS

In addition to *The Times*, Aberdeen as Foreign Secretary could usually rely on steady support from the Tory papers, the *Morning Herald*, and *The Standard*; and he had a good hearing from the *Morning Post*. He also relied on others' efforts to secure him the best possible journalistic response. Edward Everett, the former American ambassador in London, 'placed' articles for him in *The Examiner*, the *Edinburgh Review* and the *Quarterly Review*; the latter article authored by Croker with direct input from Aberdeen, in support of his policy on the Oregon dispute with the United States. It also appears Aberdeen was capable of a fair measure of deviousness. As part of his campaign against the unwanted Franco-Belgian treaty, having failed in more direct attempts to get articles printed in the French press, he organized a form of 'memorial', allegedly from British merchants, in support of the Franco-Belgian Customs Union, which was then published in the French papers specifically to generate mistrust on the part of France's own merchant community towards the whole project![8]

Having established his largely beneficial relationship with Delane and Reeve, as well as maintaining a good relationship with the other relevant sections of the press, Aberdeen did not make the mistake of letting his concern for a favourable press drop once in opposition. Some of our prime ministers were assiduous in opposition, but less active in press management once in government. Others were active when in power, but dropped their guard in opposition. Aberdeen, like Palmerston, kept up his activity in both spheres. While Palmerston could count, at various times, on consistent support from the *Morning Chronicle* and *The Globe* – in part because he wrote many of the foreign policy articles himself – Aberdeen kept up the essence of his *Times* alliance in opposition, after leaving the Foreign Office and during his short premiership.

THE PREMIERSHIP

While Peel lived, Aberdeen was, in effect, the second man in the Peelite grouping; and, after his death in 1850, the first. The Peelites were even less formally organized as a party than were the Protectionists under Derby (effectively the official Tories from 1852) and the Whigs, still then under Russell. However, despite their relative lack of formal organization, Aberdeen was clearly still regarded as Palmerston's pre-eminent foreign policy opponent during the latter's final spell at the Foreign Office, and he was able to keep *The Times* broadly to his own line during the late 1840s and, crucially, in 1848, the year of revolutions. The line was one of pragmatic conservatism, rather than blanket reaction (the line favoured by Reeve). Aberdeen, probably still not realistically thinking of becoming prime minister, saw his role as leading the opposition to Palmerston both in Parliament and in the press. Aberdeen was never thought of especially highly as a parliamentary speaker; so, perhaps, for this reason too, the newspapers were particularly important to him.

When the premiership hovered into view, however, Aberdeen proved willing. Indeed, as Derby left to see the Queen in December 1852, even the official *History of The Times* is of the opinion that Aberdeen himself prompted the paper's categorical statement:

> ... we believe that it is upon the Earl of Aberdeen that the formation of the new Cabinet will devolve, with the active co-operation, not only of his former colleagues [the Peelites], but of Lord John Russell and the chiefs of the Whig party.[9]

Derby had had his turn; Russell was too tarnished; Palmerston was not yet seen as a prime minister. The only real alternative was the elderly Lord Lansdowne (now 72), who, as later in 1855, seems not to have wanted it enough. Aberdeen himself, who was approaching 69, discovered enough autumnal ambition to wish to press to assist – or solidify – his own chances: especially in the most influential newspaper in the land. He also kept Delane up to speed on the progress of his Cabinet-making: 'Difficult as it is, everything is going on favourably and will, I trust, be speedily completed... [D]o not allude at present to the positions of Lord John or Lord Palmerston'.[10]

Delane was also influential enough to secure a Cabinet place for his close ally, the Radical Sir William Molesworth. Offered a junior post, Molesworth wrote to Delane, who intervened with Aberdeen, and a Cabinet post resulted. The paper had not altogether abandoned more traditional journalistic enterprise, however. We have already seen Aberdeen's irritation when Russell complained to him about the suggestion that his own appointment as foreign secretary was merely to keep the seat warm for Lord Clarendon (see p.xx). (Like many such indiscretions, it was all the more irritating because it was essentially true!) Aberdeen was not the last prime minister whose especial closeness to a particular paper meant that almost anything it said on certain topics was seen as authorized by him, even when it was not. Russell's anger was compounded by the fact that he simply could not see how the offending remarks could have appeared in print unless at Aberdeen's urging, or by his design. Perhaps because he realized the potential of this particular problem to recur, and perhaps also because he shared Bonar Law's later view that intimate press relations were (at least officially) incompatible with the highest office, Aberdeen was less directly interventionist in press matters as prime minister than he had been at the Foreign Office or while in opposition.

His administration's principal press managers were Palmerston (looking a little incongruous at the Home Office) and Clarendon, after he had duly, as predicted, replaced Russell at the Foreign Office.

As the prospects for war in the Crimea grew, the Cabinet's relations with the press began to echo those of Melbourne's last government. Aberdeen, unquestionably, was on what would later be seen as the less belligerent side of the fence. Clarendon favoured a harder line, as did Palmerston. The difference between the Aberdeen Cabinet's press relations and Melbourne's, however, was that, whereas Melbourne's ministers had ventilated their policy differences through various newspapers, Aberdeen's often took issue with each other within the same paper. While never losing sight of the role of other important papers (particularly those with which Palmerston was involved), it happened that Aberdeen's intimacy with Delane was matched by Clarendon's with Reeve; with the result that the battle for pre-eminence in policy was often mirrored by the struggle to keep *The Times* to the desired line. Delane, echoing Aberdeen, pushed the peace line, and the paper was routinely accused by others (including Russell, who did not have a dog in the fight) of being pro-Russian. Some of the vitriol and venom that was to be unleashed against Prince Albert at the end of 1853 and early in 1854 was already aimed at *The Times* much earlier in the year. Indeed, intriguingly, it was just as the paper finally abandoned the Aberdeen line and started to articulate the case for war that other papers started their clamour against the Prince instead of *The Times*.[11] Greville gives an account of some rather acerbic exchanges between Aberdeen and Delane (presumably relayed to him by Reeve) in which Aberdeen

> went off in a tirade against *The Times* and its recent articles, of which he bitterly complained… and talked all the extravagant anti-Turkish and pro-Russian language of which he has been so constantly accused, and which fully justified the charges and taunts of the Tory and Radical Press, altho' they don't know how right they are.[12]

It was at this point that Aberdeen's direct dealings with Delane effectively ceased. The channel of communication was now from Clarendon to and through Reeve. This regular link gave rise to a notable occasion on which Lord Derby was able to launch a convincing attack on what would later be called 'government by leak'. As the news of the British ultimatum to Russia was announced in *The Times* at the end of February 1854, Derby attacked the way the government was using the press to announce important matters of policy. Aberdeen had nothing to do with it: those days were now over; and even he suspected Clarendon. Derby said the leak was incompatible with honourable journalism; and Aberdeen almost echoed him, telling Clarendon: 'I hope you will exert yourself to correct this evil, which has become a scandal not to be endured'.[13]

Aberdeen was able to do little more than sympathize with Albert and Victoria when the press hue and cry against the Prince went into full gear. *The Times* was never at the heart of that campaign; and, even if it had been, Aberdeen's influence, and very willingness to intervene, was waning. He had specifically asked Delane to keep out of it; but it published an article in which Victoria's dependence on her husband was emphasized. Aberdeen's remaining interventions with Delane were much less effective than before; and he himself would soon be under similar attack from other papers.

THE VERDICT

In opposition, the Peelites had taken control of the *Morning Chronicle*, but that was now gravitating towards Palmerston. The Tory, Derbyite press, including the *Morning Herald* and *The Press*, wanted a more vigorous prosecution of the war, as did the radical-supporting *Daily News*. Disraeli himself penned one of the most withering personal criticisms in his *Press*, speaking of Aberdeen's

> ... manner, arrogant and yet timid – his words, insolent and yet obscure...
> [h]is hesitating speech, his contracted sympathies, his sneer, icy as Siberia,
> his sarcasms, drear and barren as the Steppes...[14]

The politician who had given Palmerston a run for his money in the papers as in policy, as they alternated in control of the Foreign Office, ended as the butt of newspapers of almost every political hue. The man who had possessed a privileged line of communication to the most important newspaper in the country no longer retained even a shadow of the influence some still assumed he had held onto. As Aberdeen's resignation approached in 1855, his son felt it necessary to intercede with Delane to ensure that the paper's coverage of his father's political demise was not excessively harsh. Even Aberdeen's son did not expect a favourable political verdict from his father's old ally; but might he ask at least that he be spared personal criticism for accepting the Queen's offer of the Garter? Delane pondered, and granted the suppliant lord's wish.[15]

CHAPTER SEVEN

LORD PALMERSTON

L ORD PALMERSTON HAD one of the longest political careers in British history, comparable only with Gladstone and Churchill among prime ministers. He was a Tory for the first two decades of his life in politics, serving throughout Liverpool's long ministry as secretary at war, an office separate from that of secretary of state for war and not carrying Cabinet status. Indeed, having held junior office under Portland, he held the office of secretary at war from 1809 to 1828. He was one of the Canningites who initially even joined Wellington's government, but, along with the others, Palmerston left after a few months and went on fairly seamlessly to join Grey's Cabinet in 1830. He was foreign secretary three times, for a total of almost 16 years, under Grey, Melbourne and Russell; fairly briefly Home Secretary in the Aberdeen coalition; and finally Prime Minister from 1855 to 1858 and 1859 to 1865. When he died in office, aged almost 81, the last prime minister to do so, he was the oldest in history, though later overtaken only by Gladstone in his fourth term. Palmerston was also the most assiduous press manipulator of all the office holders of the nineteenth century, and has arguably been excelled by very few since.

Although he was a peer, he remained in the Commons throughout his career (the peerage was Irish), which gave him all the advantages of heredity combined with great sensitivity to the minutiae of the evolution of democratic politics. That is not to imply that he was in any sense a radical in domestic policy: far from it. But he was grounded in the rituals of electioneering and the hustings in a way that few of his aristocratic contemporaries needed to be; while having none of the occasional social self-consciousness which might bedevil the likes of Canning, Peel, Disraeli or Gladstone as they had to master the charmed aristocratic circles of nineteenth-century elite political life.

Palmerston was so adept at mastering the needs of press management, and so effective at winning over individual editors and journalists, that

10. Henry John Temple, 3rd Viscount Palmerston, by Francis Cruikshank, c.1855–59. © National Portrait Gallery, London.

one often wonders whether he did it all because he genuinely enjoyed and relished that contact, or simply because he was a sufficiently dedicated and ambitious politician to recognize it as something that would give him the advantage over his colleagues and rivals. Quite possibly, there was an element of both: though one suspects that the latter was the supreme motivating factor. Richard Cobden, who knew a thing or two about using the press, was in no doubt that Palmerston had 'made greater use of that means of creating an artificial public opinion than any Minister since the time of Bolingbroke'.[1]

Palmerston's early press excursions came as he served in those long-running Tory governments early in the century. As we have already seen, he was one of a journalistic trio busily engaged in reversing the flagging fortunes of the government-supporting *Courier* around 1818 and 1819. As we have seen, their contributions were also published in book form in 1819 under the title *The New Whig Guide*. Indeed, it is possible that Palmerston had started journalistic writing for *The Courier* even earlier – perhaps as early as 1806, when he first entered politics. Other efforts were provided in 1815 and 1816, and were among those collected in book form. These (along with his very earliest pieces) were in the satirical 'squib' form which had also formed part of the output of Canning's *Anti Jacobin*, and which also marked Melbourne's youthful contribution in opposition to it.[2] Whereas Peel had already been exposed to the rather murky, cynical world of the subsidized Irish press as chief secretary, this was likely to have been Palmerston's first sustained journalistic endeavour: and he subsequently embraced it more enthusiastically and with more prolonged success than any of his fellow prime ministers of the age, even Disraeli.

A few years later, in 1823, still secretary at war, he was involved in the attempt to establish a local newspaper in Hampshire. The *Hampshire Advertiser* was the result, and his involvement, if sporadic, continued for some time. It appears that Palmerston may have helped to subsidize the paper for a while; and his Hampshire neighbour Wellington may also have been among the network of supporters. Within a few years, as Palmerston's political affiliation shifted, the *Advertiser* had become something of a local embarrassment to him. As foreign secretary in the Grey-Melbourne government, the paper accused him of constant 'desertion of principle for the emolument of office'.[3] For this reason, he seems to have been involved in the funding of another local sheet, the *Hampshire Independent*.[4] Palmerston at this stage was wary of public knowledge of his press 'arrangements': he enjoined secrecy as to his own financial involvement; and the note in his own handwriting regarding the *Hampshire Independent* reads 'agreed provided I have no connection with the paper as proprietor, and my £50 is taken as a gift'.[5] The newspaperman and early press historian James Grant, writing a few years after Palmerston's death, said he was 'privately assured at the time' of a much larger initial contribution from Palmerston of £1,000.[6]

Palmerston's caution at this time was reinforced by a spat with Croker in the Commons, in 1831, which elicited his rather remarkable claim that 'I for one do not write in the newspapers'. Luckily for Palmerston, Croker's own involvement in their earlier Tory projects – *The Courier* and *The New Whig Guide* – were as incriminating for Croker himself as for his opponent: a case of what would later be termed 'mutually assured destruction' in an age where press 'meddling' did not fit within the frame of acceptable public political activity.

THE FOREIGN SECRETARY AND HIS PAPERS

It was as Foreign Secretary in three spells between 1830 and 1851 that Palmerston really expanded his press activities. The sheer range of the papers with which he was closely associated is remarkable. Although not friendly with all at the same time, he was variously closely involved with *The Times*, the *Morning Post*, the *Morning Chronicle* (fellow Whigs referred to him on occasion as 'Viscount *Chronicle*') and *The Globe*. There are *Globe* articles in Palmerston's handwriting in the Palmerston papers. He had links with *The Examiner* and the *Edinburgh Review*, and even wrote and planned articles for the *Allgemeine Zeitung* and the *Augsburg Gazette*.

Lord Grey had already realized (as had Liverpool before him) that the days of government 'control' of newspapers through direct subsidy, placing of advertisements and preferential post office arrangements were passing. As Grey had observed, governments might still acquire papers with tiny circulations; but, as soon as circulation and profits increased, so did the desire for independence of view. Although Britain may have avoided the heaviest examples of what Fred S. Siebert called the 'Authoritarian Press' (in his *Four Theories of the Press*, published in 1956), by the 1830s, circulations and profits were rising so quickly that the *Libertarian Press* was becoming fully established, and its powers and independence were increasing commensurately.[7]

Liverpool and Grey may have diagnosed the problem and the change correctly, but Palmerston was arguably the first to systematically and assiduously counter the effects, by accepting that press management was becoming more a matter of pragmatic negotiation rather than of instruction or subsidy. This also, of course, explains the admiring, affectionate tone of early press histories, memoirs and biographies towards Palmerston. In the press histories and memoirs of Grant, Robinson and Lucas (for details, see the bibliography), for instance, all three authors have included anecdotes about Palmerston's friendliness and condescension not merely towards proprietors and editors, but also towards individual reporters from local and national newspapers. This also explains the sheer number of individual newspapers with which Palmerston was to be involved during his long career.

Palmerston was often upbraided by representatives of countries like France and Austria, asking why he did not do more to prevent articles hostile to their countries being published in British newspapers. He summarized his response in a distinction between positive and negative influence on papers. He depersonalizes it by referring to 'my office', but it is a very personal statement nonetheless:

> [T]he only influence which my office possesses over the *Courier* or any other paper is POSITIVE not NEGATIVE. I could get [the Editor] to insert any article I wished to-day but I have no means or power of preventing him from inserting any other of quite a different kind to-morrow. I can impel but I cannot control. The only communication that takes place is that every now and then when we have any particular piece of news, it is given to the editor and he thereby gets a start of his competitors, and on the condition of receiving these occasional intimations he gives his support to the Government. But no editor would bring his daily articles to a public office to be looked over before they are printed and no public officer who had any sense in his brains would undertake the responsibility of such inspections... Though they look to Government for news, they look to their readers for money...[8]

While Palmerston is almost certainly underplaying the extent and regularity of his involvement, his analysis of the changing priorities of newspapers and the alterations in the balance of power between politicians and the press is nevertheless both shrewd and unusually frank. It was written in a letter to his mistress and future wife, Lady Cowper: but may also have been intended for the ears of Princess Lieven and thus for her numerous international diplomatic and personal connections. Successive French rulers, from Napoleon I through Louis Philippe to Napoleon III, complained bitterly of what they saw as government-sanctioned attacks in influential newspapers; and it is no exaggeration to say that press coverage of France played an increasingly important role in a number of the clashes between the two powers as the nineteenth century progressed.

The Courier remained a player in the Whig-dominated political landscape after 1830, and the easy route for Palmerston might have been to cultivate the paper with which he had already had the longest association. But he saw clearly enough that papers like *The Globe* and the *Morning Chronicle*, as well as, later, the *Morning Post* and, of course, *The Times* were even likelier to enable him to prevail in Cabinet: particularly during administrations like Grey's and Melbourne's, where the leading papers fairly quickly established themselves as proxy arenas for the policy differences fought out within government. It was also claimed that he had severed links with *The Courier* by 1832, because he found it was being influenced by Talleyrand, then serving as French ambassador in London. A few years later, it was Palmerston who was seeking to use the press to intervene in Continental countries, using one of our own diplomats, Sir George Shee, to place articles in the *Allgemeine Zeitung*. He had been offered the chance to 'place' articles in the *Augsburg Gazette*. He was also approached to set up and subsidize a 'constitutional' newspaper in Germany, to oppose the 'absolutist' pro-Russian press. On this occasion, fearing further opposition from the Austrian and Prussian regimes, Palmerston decided it would be better if Louis Philippe took this on, rather than the British government.[9]

METHODS AND TACTICS

Domestically, cultivation rather than subsidy was a much more fruitful route for Palmerston. John Easthope, proprietor of the *Morning Chronicle*, 'waited on Palmerston every day for instructions'; and in 1840, during one of the periodic disagreements between Britain and France over how to handle Russo-Turkish relations, Palmerston handled Cabinet disagreements by 'only condescend[ing] to defend himself in his own anonymous way in the columns of the *Morning Chronicle*'.[10] Lord John Russell, for a time, aspired to adopt Palmerston's own tactics, and sought to use *The Globe* to combat Palmerston's line. Indeed, for a while, the two men fought for a form of press supremacy over *The Globe*, with Palmerston eventually and all too predictably emerging as the victor.

Denis Le Marchant, Brougham's secretary, gave an interesting account in his journal, undated but written some time before 1834, of the major newspapers of the day, and of their political (and personal) allegiances. Le Marchant talks of Wellington's 'sagacious' attitude towards *The Times*, and contrasts it with the less effective overall use of the press by the Whigs. He then runs through the papers with which he himself had dealings. Unsurprisingly it is *The Times* which he regards as by far the most important, not merely in Britain but in Europe. The others are, he says, 'comparatively insignificant': the *Morning Chronicle*, *The Globe*, *The Sun*, *The Courier* and two with which he did not deal, the *Morning Herald* and *The Standard*. Among these insignificant papers, he highlights Palmerston's involvement while Foreign Secretary: 'Lord Palmerston was the patron of the "Globe" and wrote many articles in it on foreign politics. Some of them are spirited. His support of the paper has given it a circulation on the continent beyond that of any other Journal'.[11]

With *The Times*, not yet in Palmerston's corner, influence of another kind could be exerted. Palmerston's engagement with, and interest in, the press was, unusually for the time, mirrored by his wife's. In November 1840, Greville records:

> Yesterday, I got a note from Lady Palmerston asking me if I had written (as somebody had told her) a certain article which appeared in Friday's *Times*, the same somebody also asserting that I was in constant communication with *The Times*. I was able with perfect truth to deny both charges, but I told her that to such questions as these I should never hesitate to give a denial... It shows how sore they are.[12]

With favourable papers, Palmerston used more obvious methods of cultivation. His influence with the *Morning Chronicle* was especially strong; and, as we have seen, he met regularly with its proprietor John Easthope, and with Easthope's editors, to give them privileged information and to 'guide' their articles on foreign policy. Papers were beginning to make fuller use of 'foreign correspondents': however, complications often arose from the fact that such figures were not necessarily full-time journalists in the modern sense. They might also supplement their income by financial speculation – with the resulting temptation to manipulate news to the advantage of their own speculations – and by undertaking diplomatic and consular work as well.

Palmerston's own relations with the *Chronicle* were complicated by the fact that its foreign editor, M.J. Quin, upon leaving his post, asked Palmerston for a vice-consulate, which was refused. There was some personal difficulty, as it appears likely that Quin tried to press his claims embarrassingly hard; but Palmerston's overall relations with the paper were not soured.[13] Quin himself had been of use in the past, and Palmerston had recommended his brother to give 'all the assistance in your power' to Quin, described as a 'respectable barrister', who was travelling to Naples on *Chronicle* business.[14] In other cases, embassies and consulates could be encouraged to favour the *Chronicle* over *The Times* with exclusive, early information.

Palmerston's links with other papers were also kept up – especially *The Globe*, but also *The Examiner* and, for a time, *The Observer*. Later, the relatively new *The Daily Telegraph* declared itself able to 'espouse the principles and measures of Lord Palmerston'. For a while, the *Morning Herald* was also supportive, before slipping back to Tory, Derbyite support; while, as if to show the importance of not relying on only one paper, the *Chronicle* itself was sold to the Peelites during Palmerston's third period as Foreign Secretary. The new *Daily News* was a partial replacement; and the long-lasting link with the *Morning Post* was being cemented in an effort to fill the gap left by the *Chronicle*.

The *Post* came to be regarded, in time, as Palmerston's strongest press supporter after the link with the *Chronicle* was broken: and again there are strong suggestions that proprietorial and editorial aspirations for diplomatic employment may have been part of the mutual bond. Importantly, however, the *Post*-Palmerston alliance was a sign of Palmerston's growing ability to transcend party lines and appeal beyond his Whig constituency. If Derby had ever been able to secure Palmerston's support, the *Post* would undoubtedly have endorsed the resulting combination and remained a Tory paper throughout. Such an eventuality was a distinct possibility until Palmerston began to see his own path to the premiership; and the policy differences between Derby and Palmerston were much smaller than those between Palmerston and, say, Bright and Cobden, who were nominally at least members of the same party. Had Derby secured the support of Palmerston and Gladstone (who felt more personal and cultural affinity with Derby than with Palmerston), he could well have been prime minister for most of the 1850s and 1860s; and some of the press alliances might have been considerably different too. Intriguingly, Peter Borthwick, editor of the *Morning Post*, told his son Algernon (later Lord Glenesk), who later succeeded him in control of the paper, that:

> a member of the [first Derby] Government... proposes to write gratis for the 'Post', and to give us Government information in return for which we are to give the Government our out-and-out support.... But...on no account would we receive any communications unless they were subject to the revision of the Editor.[15]

In the event, the approach was rejected. There are numerous instances in Reginald Lucas's biography of Glenesk of letters from Palmerston to the Borthwicks, 'steering' the way they cover certain stories: notably on important matters such as Palmerston's temporary resignation from Aberdeen's coalition in 1853.

Algernon Borthwick (Lord Glenesk) was himself the centre of an interesting family network of politicians and journalists. He married Alice Lister, whose mother Theresa was the sister of Lord Clarendon and Charles Villiers, neither of whom was a stranger to press manipulation. Theresa was married to Sir George Cornewall Lewis, chancellor of the exchequer and editor of the *Edinburgh Review*. Her other daughter Therese, Alice's sister, married William Harcourt, barrister, *The Times'* leader-writer and later the leader of the Liberal Party in the Commons between Gladstone and Campbell-Bannerman, and de facto overall leader from 1896 to 1898. Such a nexus of family links at the interface between politics and journalism, albeit at the level of proprietors rather than editors or reporters, is a very clear sign of the growing sense of a dialogue amongst equals that was beginning to characterize the relationship between the press and politics. It is both a symbol of the growing intersection of the worlds of high politics and the press, and a reflection of the shifting balance of social and political power between those two worlds.

PRESS VICTORIES AND DEFEATS

It appears to have been Palmerston personally who tempted the *Post* away from the Tories; and the same could be argued for *The Globe*. *The Globe* remained one of Palmerston's closest press links throughout his later career.

The story went that, when people asked Palmerston for 'inside information' about policy deliberations and decisions, he would reply: 'Look at the *Globe*, my dear fellow, this evening'.[16] Just a year after his death, however, *The Globe* started supporting the Tories, after a change of ownership. Part of the reason for the change, and for the fact that it was allowed to fall into Tory hands, was based on policy. But it was also a result of the fact that Russell simply refused to engage with it with the same cordiality and assiduity with which Palmerston had. Personal approaches mattered, and there could be a lot at stake as a result of prime ministerial approaches to press relations. One of the organizers of the syndicate which bought *The Globe* was the Tory MP and future joint party leader Stafford Northcote, whose own interest in the press is often underestimated as part of the relative neglect of his entire career.[17]

During Palmerston's earlier career, *The Globe* was more of a general Whig paper than a Palmerston paper, in which some of the internal disputes of the Grey-Melbourne ministries were fought out. Palmerston eventually prevailed, but the paper was responsive to approaches from Russell and Althorp as well. Later, when Russell was Prime Minister, he rebuked Palmerston for the anti-Russian tone of *Globe* articles in 1850. Palmerston, perhaps predictably, replied:

> I do not write the *Globe*, nor indeed do I always read it. I see the People who write the Foreign articles, when they come to ask to be kept right as to Facts and Events, & that is very seldom, scarcely once in three weeks or a month; but they take their own time & write their own articles.[18]

As Kenneth Bourne drily remarks: 'There are 124 articles surviving in the [Palmerston] Papers for the period 1832–51 – all written in Palmerston's hand and destined for the *Globe*'.[19] Even more remarkably, one of Palmerston's earlier biographers tells us that a series of Palmerston's own articles written for the *Chronicle* were collected and published in book form in 1842 as *Lord Palmerston and the Treaty of Washington*. It was published anonymously, but its contents were 'well understood' to be by the Foreign Secretary himself.[20]

Although Palmerston periodically denigrated it as inferior to the *Chronicle* (in its pre-Peelite days, naturally), *The Times* remained Palmerston's unclimbed peak in his earlier periods of office. During the years in which the link between Aberdeen and Delane had been at its strongest, a number of Palmerston's colleagues had already cultivated the paper and its editor. Palmerston had made his own approaches, naturally; but the relationship was wary and somewhat unpredictable until Delane and Aberdeen finally sundered during the Crimean War. That was Palmerston's chance; and it came at precisely the phase of his career in which the premiership hove into view.

THE PRESS AND THE ROUTE TO THE TOP

Part of the politics of the formation of the Aberdeen coalition, after the fall of Derby's first government, had been the recognition that Palmerston should not simply resume the Foreign Office for a fourth term. However, he had to be included; and the early period of the Aberdeen government marked the time at which Palmerston began to outmanoeuvre Russell while making himself look like a plausible candidate as the next Whig prime minister. He took the Home Office and stayed there, despite a temporary resignation ostensibly over reform in late 1853, just as the Crimean War was coming into view. Russell, meanwhile, took the Foreign Office, only to relinquish it to Clarendon (as the press leaks had indicated he would), then remaining in the Cabinet without portfolio, until an ill-timed resignation on the very eve of the fall of the Aberdeen government itself. Palmerston's forceful advocacy of a bellicose stance against Russia benefited him; whereas Russell's equally hawkish posture went unrewarded by public and press opinion. As Aberdeen's perceived pacifist inclinations became more unpopular, and as sections of the press turned on Prince Albert, the position of *The Times* became especially important. Kingsley Martin has an interesting passage on the paper at this juncture:

> Delane's power is difficult to gauge. Clarendon was not sure whether *The Times* formed or guided or reflected public opinion... [Delane] was not dictated to by advertisers, by party financiers, or by a millionaire proprietor. Moreover, since he had no competitor to fear, Delane was able, for a time at least, to advocate a view offensive to a large number of his readers. When this occurred, he received unstinted abuse, but the circulation of *The Times* did not diminish.[21]

Palmerston's decision to resign over reform rather than the government's attitude to Russia was an astute move. *The Times* was no admirer of Russell. If Palmerston agreed to withdraw his resignation, it would effectively deprive Russell of his chance of reintroducing the measure during the lifetime of that government for fear of losing the increasingly indispensable Palmerston again. A Russell minus a reform agenda was a less potent figure; and so Palmerston could eye the imminent prospect of the premiership as and when the country turned against Aberdeen. Martin's comment about Delane and public opinion is especially pertinent in this regard. Did *The Times* turn against Aberdeen because he was losing public support, or did he lose public support because *The Times* was turning against him? There are echoes of the debate over the respective roles of John Major and *The Sun* in the outcome of the 1992 election.

Whatever the reality of the motivations involved, we have already noted that *The Times*, and Delane personally, were losing faith in Aberdeen throughout 1854, and, by 1855, were content to consign him to political oblivion. For all its past criticisms of Palmerston's foreign policy, and for all Palmerston's closeness to other papers, *The Times* would not favour Russell over Palmerston. Nor yet was there any basis for optimism on the part of Derby and his supporters that it would modify its view of the Tories, for all Disraeli's efforts at ingratiation throughout the 1852 ministry. So, *faute de mieux*, *The Times* would have to look to Palmerston as the likeliest replacement for Aberdeen. What would start as a wary marriage of convenience would develop into a sophisticated and powerful political alliance that would help to sustain Palmerston as Prime Minister for two terms, totalling over nine years and interrupted only by the 16 months of the second Derby administration.

THE PRIME MINISTER AND THE PRESS

When Palmerston became Prime Minister in early 1855, *The Times* was conditional in its support, and not personally warm to the new premier. Indeed, at this stage, it was an arm's-length relationship. Palmerston's War Secretary, Lord Panmure, had no personal dealings with Delane until after he had left office; Alexander William Kinglake, the early historian of the Crimean War, claimed that Panmure behaved like a prisoner of war, with the press as his jailer: 'He received his marching orders submissively from the sheets of *The Times*, proceeded at once to obey them, and so trudged doggedly on…'.[22]

The Times, by this stage, was hawkish and wanted nothing more from Palmerston than victories. It had already turned against the British Commander-in-Chief, Lord Raglan: the dispatches of its famous war correspondent W.H. Russell, exposing the appalling conditions in which the army was having to operate, had seen to that; and this, in turn, prevented the new government from giving Raglan effective public support. (Indeed, this had already started to be the case under Aberdeen and his War Secretary, the Duke of Newcastle).

Clearly, the picture of Palmerston as the master-manipulator of the press is more complex and nuanced than is sometimes suggested. There were times in his third period at the Foreign Office, particularly after the Peelites captured the *Morning Chronicle*, when his press constituency dwindled. The relationship with *The Globe* remained good; the *Morning Post* was broadly in his camp; but *The Times* had remained hostile. Now that Palmerston had secured its reluctant support, he sought to keep it not by his usual methods – steering editors and leader-writers and writing anonymous contributions – but by endeavouring to align his own policy with its recommendations. This is not to say that he pursued policies contrary to his own inclinations: there is little sense, for example, that he or Panmure would have done much to support Raglan anyway. But his freedom of action in his early days as prime minister were more circumscribed than is often realized, given his desire to 'sit well' with the nation's most powerful newspaper.

However, Palmerston could also now count on the backing not only of *The Globe* and the *Morning Post*, but also of the *Morning Advertiser* (the paper which had started the hue and cry against Prince Albert in late 1853)[23] and of the *Daily News*; and he ensured that the new *The Daily Telegraph* was well looked after. He had, incidentally, at the time of the attacks on Albert, indirectly demonstrated to the Royal Family his power over sections of the press. When some Radical and Tory papers had picked up the lead of the *Morning Advertiser*, several of the most influential papers, including *The Times*, came to the Court's defence; not so the *Morning Post*, now widely seen as a Palmerston supporter. It did not join in the campaign on either side. Instead, it preserved an almost eerie silence for several weeks, over Christmas and the New Year and well into January. Eventually, on 25 January 1854, Palmerston told Borthwick:

> I think it would be useful if you were to put into the *Post* the following paragraph: We have observed that some of our contemporaries have endeavoured to connect the resignation of the Home Secretary with some proceedings on the part of the Court. Now we believe we may confidently affirm, without the slightest fear of contradiction, that the resignation of the noble Lord was the result of some misunderstanding between himself and some of his colleagues, and had not the remotest connection with anything on the part of the Court.[24]

Palmerston had shown the royal pair that he was perfectly capable of turning on and off the tap of at least some of the adverse publicity they had faced, and against which they had proved pretty powerless.

Palmerston was not a suppliant to *The Times*; but he was realistic. He later told the Queen, foreshadowing the endorsements of John Major, Tony Blair and David Cameron by Rupert Murdoch in 1992, 1997 and 2010 respectively, that *The Times* was only supporting him now he was Prime Minister because it always liked to be on the winning side.[25] Whatever the truth of this, the time would come when Palmerston was able to apply his usual methods of 'leaking' and suggesting the 'line to take' even with *The Times* and Delane. During his second term, in 1861, Palmerston was leaking the results of his latest Cabinet reshuffle to Delane; and, a year before the end, as another reshuffle was underway in 1864, Delane was writing to one of his staff: 'I don't believe half the Cabinet know it as I write'.[26]

Early in the first Palmerston term, however, the relationship was much less cosy. Delane and *The Times* were keen to promote the interests and careers of two public men in particular: they wanted to see Henry Layard and Robert Lowe, effectively their own part-time employees, in Palmerston's Cabinet. Layard, the excavator of Nineveh, was also a diplomat and an MP. Lowe combined a political career with many years of leader-writing for *The Times*. Palmerston did not oblige, and this made for complications – especially from Lowe, who also went on to be a thorn in the side of Russell and Gladstone. Although Gladstone did eventually include him in his first administration, he was never an easy colleague. Layard, meanwhile, when sent out to the Crimea as Under-Secretary for War, was asked by Delane to deny that he was going 'as the recognised agent of *The Times*', such was the awareness of the link amongst political and journalistic circles.[27]

The Times was more critical of Russell than of Palmerston; and while Russell led an essentially premature peace mission in Vienna in 1855, the paper was thundering for 'less jaw and more war'. Russell was jettisoned and shortly afterwards, in late July 1855, wrote bitterly:

> The present Govt... rests on *The Times* newspaper, and so long as *The Times* supports the Govt they [Whig M.P.s] will support it. – C. Wood owned to me yesterday that the Govt was fall[in]g every day.

On the same day, he told Clarendon that he thought *The Times* 'must be considered in future not the organ but the organiser of the Ministry'. The next day, clearly feeling no better, Russell told Clarendon:

> [Thomas] Phinn a jackal of that paper [*The Times*] is made Sec[retar]y of the Admty, Molesworth an intimate friend of the editor Sec[retar]y of State, a place was intended for Lowe a constant contributor.[28]

If anything, Russell's gloomy comments were a few weeks premature. *The Times* did change its tone from wary, grudging support laced with frequent criticism to enthusiastic approval, but not until 14 August, when it featured a leader which praised Palmerston, in a very decided and significant phrase, as 'an exponent of the popular will'. This was intended as high praise indeed, and was so taken. What makes the endorsement extraordinary, however, is that it exactly coincided with the desired appointment of Lowe to the significant post of Vice-President of the Board of Trade. What makes it even more extraordinary is that it was written by Lowe himself – and with the approval, or at least the tolerance, of Delane. It was not merely an isolated moment of euphoria, soon to be repented of; it set the tone for a much closer, more collaborative relationship with Palmerston that would essentially endure. Although the war had shown some early signs of success, that alone cannot explain the shift. Sebastopol had not yet fallen, and even the same edition of the paper had an article elsewhere, concluding: 'Results there are none'.

So, can such a major about-turn have come about simply because of Lowe being appointed to the position he wanted? It is very unlikely. There were other possible explanations. The strongly anti-Palmerstonian Henry Reeve was in the process of severing his links with the paper. The influential Reeve, second only to Delane at the paper, had always been close to Clarendon (as well as sharing Delane's former partiality for Aberdeen). However, he claimed that his leaders:

> ... were never dictated or even influenced by any authority but my own free will... and though they were often regarded as expressions of the opinion of the Cabinet, or of Lord Aberdeen,... they never in reality expressed anything but my own convictions. If they did, as was often the case, express the opinions of Sir Robert Peel, or Lord Aberdeen, or Lord Clarendon, it is because I commonly found that I took the same view they had formed on public affairs.[29]

Reeve would never have included the name of Palmerston in this list of politicians whose views approximated his own. However, he was on his way out. He was about to succeed Sir George Cornewall Lewis as editor of the *Edinburgh Review*, while Lewis succeeded Gladstone as chancellor of the exchequer, following his resignation from Palmerston's government. But there were other factors too. The breach with Aberdeen, of course, was one. Possibly more significant was the fact that while the circulation of *The Times* had risen from 13,000 to 62,000 between 1840 and 1855, new legislation was coming in – in the form of the removal of the Stamp Act, designed to allow cheaper papers like *The Daily Telegraph* to set up as fresh competitors without having to pay the traditional stamp duty, thus ensuring a price beyond the reach of poorer readers. The paper's accustomed triumphant success, both commercial and political, could be threatened. And, at its simplest, there was a danger of its sources of confidential news, apart from Clarendon, drying up, unless it also had direct links with Palmerston himself. There was the basis of a convenient arrangement, for, as the *History of The Times* succinctly and accurately put it: 'Delane would not give twopence for Palmerstonian views without Palmerstonian news'.[30] At the same time, Palmerston knew that he could not rely solely on the *Morning Post*, at this stage his most reliable and effective supporter. Moreover, he knew that *The Times* would still get shorter shrift from any of the other credible candidates for the premiership: certainly from Russell, and probably from Derby too, at this stage. Disraeli, of course, would have been only too happy to oblige Delane; but, alone, he was no counterbalance to Palmerston, and was unlikely in 1855 to become prime minister any time soon.

Lady Palmerston, perhaps the first prime ministerial spouse to take an active interest and role in press manipulation on her husband's behalf, had already made social approaches to Delane and been rebuffed. Despite the social changes and the rise in some editors' and proprietors' social status, an invitation to a fashionable aristocratic salon was still a useful card to play, and Palmerston was able to benefit from his wife's efforts in this regard in a number of ways. Derby was not especially interested in 'society' as such: his gout, the turf and his literary interests provided him with other priorities for his spare time and Lady Derby did not push the matter. Russell, too, was no social lion. Peel had never been entirely at ease in that milieu, and his wife still less so. Melbourne, of course, had no wife by the time he was prime minister, Lady Caroline Lamb having long since bolted; and Aberdeen was a rather melancholy widower well before his premiership. So it had been a while since a prime minister had been able to use the mechanisms of elite social life as a factor in adding to his coalition of support.

THE COURTSHIP OF *THE TIMES*

Lord Granville, the future foreign secretary, sheds a fascinating light on the changing nature of the relationship between the social and political elite and the world of the press in a letter to the Duke of Newcastle in January 1855. He notes that Delane and Reeve:

> ... have frequently dined with me, and have come to Lady Granville's parties. I have for some time found it entailed personal inconvenience from the impression which it creates, but I am sure that on public grounds nothing can be so mischievous as to exclude from all community of interest with the higher classes, and all intercourse with public men, those who by their pen can exercise such enormous influence for good or bad.[31]

The retired and rather embittered Lord Brougham, once the master press manipulator of the Grey government, sounded a wholly different note. The former favourite of *The Times*, he now saw Palmerston's new alliance with the paper as something altogether more sinister. Writing to another of the paper's fallen favourites, Lord Aberdeen, now also in retirement, he said:

> Observe the DEVIL-WORSHIP of some men. I saw among the persons
> who were enumerated as dining with Pam and others at Molesworth's –
> *The Times* people – that is Mr Twiss and Mr Delane... Is it to be believed
> that nothing oozes out which should be kept secret, in these connexions?[32]

Similar effusions were exchanged in Russell and Disraeli circles, although
Derby was almost certainly much less exercised by it: the days of his efforts
to win over Delane and his paper still lay some years in the future.

Later in the autumn of 1855, *The Times* published a letter, ostensibly from
'A Constant Reader' but, in effect, an editorial couched as a letter to the
editor: perhaps an early example of the editor writing to himself! In a rare
move, it analysed the reasons for the switch to support of Palmerston, and
pondered:

> That *The Times* has been converted by Lord Palmerston, no one will
> maintain who has any recollection of the march of events; and yet, if it had,
> who could find fault with so independent an institution for having given
> way to arguments proved triumphantly true by the sequel?[33]
>
> But the final and most likely alternative – that both arrived more
> or less independently at the same conclusions, *The Times* by means of its
> extraordinary information and consummate ability, and Lord Palmerston
> in virtue of his own genius and experience as the master diplomatist of the
> day, is a likelihood equally flattering to both parties ....[34]

Among those joining the chorus of incredulity at the unexpected alliance were
not merely the other prime ministerial possibilities. Some of Palmerston's
own Cabinet were taken aback. Clarendon, his nearest rival as a press
manipulator, even tried, via his private secretary, to get *The Globe* to include
a critical article about it, but *The Globe* declined: this, at any rate, is what
Greville told the disgruntled Reeve. As it was endorsing Palmerston, the
paper was attacking his new chancellor, Sir George Cornewall Lewis (who,
it will be recalled, was just being replaced by Reeve at the *Edinburgh Review*).

An even more significant figure was also put out by the new partnership
between Palmerston and *The Times*: Queen Victoria. *The Times* had been
attacking the Court (having sided with it when Albert was attacked nearly
two years earlier) over the proposed marriage between Princess Victoria
and Prince Frederick (Fritz) of Prussia, the future Emperor Frederick III.

In their darker moments, the Queen and Prince Albert must have begun to wonder whether Palmerston had the power and the intent to turn on and off press attacks on them whenever it suited him. Victoria went so far as to write to Palmerston demanding to know '… whether it is right that the Editor, the Proprietor and the Writers of such execrable publications ought to be the honoured and constant guests of the Ministers of the Crown?' She advocated a return to the position in which they were largely excluded from elite society, which, she believed, would 'operate as a check on the reckless exercise of that anomalous power the danger of which to the best interests of the country is so universally admitted'.[35]

Palmerston was indirectly being criticized for the fact that he had secured the paper's support, and he fell back, in reply, on the well-worn formula that he supposed they were only supporting him because his was now seen as the winning side.

SHIFTING PRESS ALLIANCES

There is less written evidence of Palmerston's modus operandi in dealing with *The Times* in the remaining years of his premiership for the very simple reason that, unlike Aberdeen, he preferred to deal in person with Delane. As we have seen, Palmerston would write directly to the Borthwicks at the *Morning Post* and to *The Globe*, suggesting in great detail the 'line to take' in a way that was often tantamount to an article in epistolary form. Other papers like the *Daily News* and the new *The Daily Telegraph* (having swung in behind the Prime Minister after a short dalliance with Cobden) could also be relied on to pick up the general line. With *The Times*, Palmerston erred towards this looser approach: suggesting the line to take, but not providing detailed wording or instructions; but he communicated these suggestions to Delane in person. Furthermore, he did not make the mistake of other would-be cultivators of the paper and suspend communications when Delane was away. Instead, he would liaise with his replacement George Webbe Dasent just as assiduously.

Lord Clarendon, too, despite his attempt to stir up *The Globe* against the Palmerston–*Times* alliance, continued in close contact with the paper. With the efforts of these two old hands at media management, the government was able to operate a fairly sophisticated information operation. Both men wrote to Delane in 1857 to tip him off about the forthcoming dissolution of Parliament and the subsequent general election. However, not long after his electoral victory, Palmerston's first ministry came to an unexpected end.

Relations with France had long been a dominant theme of Palmerston's career. When the Italian Felice Orsini attempted to assassinate Napoleon III in 1858, it was discovered that the bomb was made in Birmingham. This occasioned a particularly vicious press war between the two nations' papers. Contrary to his popular image, Palmerston came to be portrayed as truckling to the French emperor and press by agreeing to introduce a Conspiracy to Murder Bill to prevent British involvement in any future attacks such as Orsini's. Palmerston's alliance with Delane was enough to prevent the paper from attacking him; though its support was lukewarm and measured, and was certainly insufficient to stave off a parliamentary defeat. The first Palmerston ministry was over, and Derby prepared to return to power.

It is sometimes forgotten that, towards the end of Palmerston's first ministry, once the Crimean War was over, it appeared to many observers that his career was coming to an end. Criticism of the mediocrity of some of his Cabinet appointments and his age (73 at the time the government fell) gave the impression of a long career petering out in anti-climax. However, as we have noted, the 16 months of the second Derby administration gave the Whigs a chance to resolve their longer-term leadership problem. With the famous party meeting at Willis's Rooms, and the agreement of both Palmerston and Russell to serve under the other if necessary, new prospects beckoned, and Palmerston's career could be extended into a second premiership lasting more than six years. The choice between Russell and Palmerston was made on a number of grounds; but the strength of their respective press positions was not the least of them. Palmerston could count on *The Times*, *The Globe*, the *Morning Post* and *The Daily Telegraph*, and could share the favours of the *Daily News* with Russell, often to his own advantage.

PRIME MINISTER AGAIN

On the fall of Derby in 1859, then it was Palmerston. Then, Victoria might have toyed with the idea of the younger Granville in preference to either Palmerston or Russell (Palmerston was now nearly 75, Russell approaching 67); but that was never a likely outcome. By this time, Palmerston had perfected his manner of dealing with the press in person: leaping up to grab a journalist's hand, praising his articles, exclaiming how proud he was to have made his acquaintance, and so on.[36] It is remarkable how openly near-contemporary journalistic memoirs single out Palmerston for praise: partly, one suspects, simply for being civil to them as well as for making their jobs easier. James Grant, in *The Newspaper Press*, relates how Palmerston would alter the timings and orders of meetings to suit the reporters' convenience. He would go out of his way to help the 'sessionals', the freelancers who only got paid for what they got into the papers. On one occasion, at one of his own elections at Tiverton (this time uncontested), it proved impossible for the sessionals to attend Palmerston's public meeting. Not wishing to miss an opportunity for favourable publicity, Palmerston invited the three dejected sessional reporters, plus two of his own friends, to his hotel room, and delivered his speech to a select audience of five! All were satisfied, good will was obtained, and something of a journalistic legend thus established.[37]

In his second term, Palmerston was able to relax secure in the knowledge that *The Times* was unlikely to jump ship. He could still rely on the *Morning Post* completely, and other papers substantially; but with the proprietor Walter in Parliament, with Lowe still writing for the paper and with Delane onside, he could look to continuing support from the 'Thunderer'. At one stage in 1861, when Delane was suffering from serious eye problems, Palmerston offered him the post of permanent under-secretary for war (on the grounds that it was more of a daylight job than editing the paper). Although Delane declined, no harm was done to their relationship.[38]

Palmerston did not suffer unduly from the potential backlash from *The Times* over Gladstone's reforms of the Stamp Act and the Paper Duties between 1855 and 1861. Although these major changes to the way the newspaper market was able to function occurred on Palmerston's watch, all knew that he himself was at least indifferent if not privately opposed. By the time of his premierships, far from wanting to open up the possibility of a plethora of new, cheaper newspapers, Palmerston must have been pretty satisfied with the state of the journalistic market place as it was and hardly saw the need for drastic change.

In addition to securing Gladstone as chancellor of the exchequer, killing off the last hope of his junction with Lord Derby, Palmerston also managed to appoint Russell as foreign secretary: the two worked together and generally effectively on issues such as the American Civil War and the notoriously impenetrable Schleswig-Holstein question. Palmerston was even able to help

Russell improve his press relations for a while. When Russell went to the Lords (while remaining in office), Palmerston appointed Austen Henry Layard, with his strong ties to *The Times* and Delane, to the under-secretaryship. (He had told Delane within two hours of his appointment). This acted to mollify some of the tensions between Russell and *The Times*. Indeed, in fairness to Layard, he also liaised very closely with *The Daily Telegraph*, developing a close working relationship with Thornton Hunt, its editor at the time.[39]

THE VERDICT

As previously noted, the written survivals of Palmerston's press management are fewer in his later years because so much was done in person. Occasionally, as he aged and was ill, it still took written form. A typical exchange from 1864 shows Palmerston urging Delane not to be too favourable to the Prussians, as war against them over the Schleswig-Holstein complications might need to remain an option. Delane's reply is telling indeed: 'My temporary Germanism like many other inconveniences was the direct consequence of your Lordship's gout which has shut me out from communication with yourself. Your note of today has effected a perfect cure...'.[40]

On occasion, Palmerston's press contacts could even tip him off about possible political developments. In the same year, 1864, Borthwick of the *Morning Post* passed on to Palmerston rumours of the impending resignation of the Duke of Newcastle, which was to lead indirectly to the return to Cabinet of Clarendon, who had been left out to accommodate Russell at the Foreign Office. On this occasion, Palmerston was sufficiently intrigued to write back to Borthwick asking for his source. (Newcastle's was a resignation on genuine health grounds, not over politics: he died shortly afterwards).[41] Meanwhile, Lady Palmerston herself remained in direct touch with Borthwick. Again in the same year, correspondence shows her asking Borthwick not to publish the names of the guests at a recent dinner party; then worrying that he will drop the item altogether, and getting back in touch to tell him exactly what he should and should not include.[42]

Palmerston, having been confirmed in power by an election in 1859, won a final poll victory in 1865, by which time he was nearly 81 and dying. Perhaps appropriately, his last surviving letter to Delane at *The Times* was to tip him off, in July 1865, as to the name of the new Lord Chancellor

(Lord Cranworth succeeding Lord Westbury). By October, Palmerston was dead. He was by far the most thorough and assiduous press manipulator of his century, and this was unquestionably a factor both in his contemporary political success and in his still flourishing historical reputation. While not one of the very greatest prime ministers, he is generally seen as a successful and important figure. Caricaturists endowed him with a certain insouciance by portraying him with a straw in his mouth. The working journalists who came into contact with him liked him and were grateful to him. He formed alliances with some of the key figures in nineteenth-century journalism, and with their papers. From *The Courier*, through *The Globe* and the *Morning Chronicle*, to the *Morning Post* and, at last, *The Times*, he worked at, solidified and benefited from a system of media manipulation more sophisticated than any yet seen at the top of British politics. From the harsh, disliked 'Lord Pumicestone' of earlier years, this all helped him to become a recognizable political 'character' of a sort that became more familiar and widespread as the media changed and expanded. And, even more unusually, while his press work was always serving the broader interest of his policies or his career, he genuinely seemed to enjoy it.

CHAPTER EIGHT

BENJAMIN DISRAELI

B ENJAMIN DISRAELI WAS not a typical nineteenth-century prime minister for all sorts of reasons. He was not an aristocrat. He was Jewish, albeit a Christian convert. He did not inherit major wealth. He was visibly ambitious: never, in that age, seen as an attractive trait in elite political circles, as Canning had found to his cost. His father was a literary man, not a politician or a wealthy merchant; and he found fame as a novelist himself.

He also used to be seen as atypical because of his interest in the press. However, in this regard, we may find him a little closer to the nineteenth-century norm than in those other respects. Yes, he was more than once involved in attempting to set up new newspapers; and he was keen on influencing existing periodicals wherever possible. But, as we have already seen, this was by no means enough to make him exceptional in the annals of prime ministerial press management. Perhaps his unorthodox social position meant that his relationships with proprietors, editors and journalists were different from those of most of his fellow prime ministers. Did this make him more or less effective in ensuring that papers did his bidding? Disraeli is also unexceptional in the fact that he made efforts to conceal his earlier newspaper involvement in the later and more successful phase of his life. Although he was known to have influence (at least) over *The Press* in the 1850s, he went to some lengths to conceal his role in his much earlier newspaper venture, *The Representative*, during the middle and latter stages of his political career. Was this because it was a failed undertaking? Or was there still simply too much social stigma attached to such practices even as late as the 1850s and 1860s: especially for a parvenu?

For a young, ambitious man without connections, automatic entry into Parliament in one's early twenties simply was not possible. While Russell, Derby and Palmerston could expect to slip into the pre-Reform Commons with the minimum of fuss and exertion, and while Peel and Gladstone

11. Benjamin Disraeli, Earl of Beaconsfield, by Sir John Everett Millais, 1st Bt, 1881. © National Portrait Gallery, London.

could use brilliant university careers to aid their chances of an early start, such options were not available to the son of a *littérateur* like Isaac D'Israeli. The alternative methods of attempting to secure favourable public notice, excluding risky enterprises such as military glory, would often involve the written word. For this reason, the young Disraeli, who was quick to remove the parental apostrophe and Anglicize his surname, tried his hand at all sorts of literary forms. The novel, drama, satire, a bizarre 'epic' poem, polemic: all were fair game to a young man in a hurry. And it was but a short step from such juvenile aspirations to aspire to the control and production of a journalistic mouthpiece.

His very first efforts had come in pamphlet form. They were not the sort of works a successful politician would be keen to see republished in later life. The first two were essentially public relations prospectuses on behalf of South and Central American mining companies. In the phrase of the time, they were 'puffs': and puffs not merely for mining in general, but for a particular company in whose interests Disraeli was writing. The third, in the same vein, was a translation of a report put before the Mexican parliament in the interests of – mining! Just as Canning was claiming to call into existence the New World to redress the balance of the Old, by recognizing, as foreign secretary, the new South American republics in the 1820s, the young solicitor's clerk Disraeli and his fellow speculators had their eyes on the possible profits occasioned by the liberation of the South and Central American nations. One of Disraeli's most authoritative biographers wryly asserted that, for a future writer of fiction, these pamphlets marked the ideal debut.[1] They certainly resulted in no commercial success for Disraeli or his partners; and his next enterprise, this time in a more purely journalistic sphere, was also destined for an embarrassing lack of success.

Disraeli presents an interesting contrast with other prime ministers of the age in another respect. Because his newspaper ventures were semi-public, and because he had to shape his career differently from the others, even his earlier, more reverential biographers could not avoid the subject of the press. Indeed, Disraeli's official biographers, William Flavelle Monypenny and George Earle Buckle, whose work was published between 1910 and 1920, were themselves very senior journalists at *The Times*: Buckle served as the editor for many years, with Monypenny his close coadjutor. Writing at a time when the press reticence of Asquith was making way for the more clamant approach of Lloyd George, they did not feel it necessary to veil

Disraeli's newspaper dealings in the obscurity adopted in, for instance, the authorized life of Aberdeen, by his son, where the link with Delane is entirely omitted.[2]

FEET WET AND FINGERS BURNT

The publisher John Murray had already had great success with the *Quarterly Review*, and Disraeli had already collaborated with him in some of his publishing undertakings. Disraeli and John Diston Powles (with whom he had written the mining pamphlets) persuaded Murray to back the proposed new paper, *The Representative*: Tory, but Canningite, not Ultra, in tone. This was in 1825, when Lord Liverpool was still managing to keep the Tories together, and Canning was still foreign secretary. The idea was to overcome the scruples of Walter Scott's son-in-law John Gibson Lockhart about becoming involved with such coadjutors, in order that Lockhart should become editor; while Disraeli remained in the background in a managerial or business role. This was all at a time, it should be recalled, when he had not yet turned 21. Lockhart's hesitancy demonstrates the striking fact that a newspaper editorship of such an untried and unsupported vehicle was decidedly *infra dig*, if not outright scandalous, for a man of his position: whereas when, shortly afterwards, he was offered the editor's chair at the *Quarterly*, no such social stigma was deemed to apply.

Disraeli was never short of ambition, and was equally resourceful in finding the rhetoric in which to cloak such ambition. *The Representative*, he claimed, would overtake *The Times* (already, in 1825, the benchmark for success and political influence) and become the dominant organ in the land. In the event, without a proper editor and apparently without the basic levels of journalistic and design professionalism required, the paper was a lamentable failure. So-called exclusives were impossible to find; articles were tedious and prolix; editing atrocious. It was also launched during what we would term a recession. Its prospects, gloomy, even had the economy been booming, were dire indeed; and it folded after a little over six months in July 1826.

Its influence on the political landscape had been negligible. Its role in assisting Disraeli into a political career was similarly slight. In later life, Disraeli's political enemies were keen to throw the whole *Representative* fiasco at him: however, they seem to have made the elementary mistake of charging him with something he could plausibly deny. They accused him of editing the paper. In practice, he probably had done so on at least some occasions; but he had never held the title of editor, and so blanket-sounding denials of his involvement could be uttered which could be defended as applying to the specific charge of being the paper's editor. In fact, before the paper collapsed, Disraeli had jumped ship and left the others to it. There was no prospect of him investing the capital expected of him into the paper. Once the South American mining venture collapsed, so did Disraeli's hope of access to 'real' money; and so did his involvement. Monypenny and Buckle put the best light they could on their hero's early misadventure:

> ... apart from the failure, there is nothing discreditable to him in the story as far as it can be traced to-day. He had shown amazing energy, amazing self-confidence, and amazing power of winning to his views men older and riper in experience than himself... it was only the feebleness of the first few numbers that destroyed its chances.[3]

Despite the failure of *The Representative*, Disraeli preserved the relationship with Murray for the time being. Their social ties were unimpaired: until, that is, the publication of *Vivian Grey* in 1826, Disraeli's first novel to make it into print, following the unpublished *Aylmer Papillon*. Here, Murray saw (correctly) elements of the story of their venture included in fictional form and (perhaps incorrectly) himself satirized in the character of the Marquis of Carabas. The novel itself, the manner in which it was promoted and the allegations of concealment with regard to the identity and status of its author (it was originally published anonymously), all landed Disraeli in further trouble: this time with the press at large. Many felt that, in order to have credibility, the novel should have been written by someone who knew whom of he spoke: about high society and the other elite circles portrayed in the book. One reviewer also told of 'the shameful and shameless puffery' used to promote sales of the book, also damning the author as 'an obscure person for whom nobody cares a straw'.[4]

At the same time, there was another press mystery: this time about the nature and extent of Disraeli's involvement in a publication called *The Star Chamber*. This was a weekly satirical magazine, publicized three days before the publication of *Vivian Grey* in 1826 by men with sandwich boards parading up and down Regent Street.[5] Disraeli seems later to have denied all involvement with this periodical, not merely the charge of being its editor. However, even Monypenny and Buckle concede that Disraeli wrote for it: fables called 'The Modern Aesop', at least one review and maybe more. But he denied writing its most striking item, 'The Dunciad of Today'; and he also sought to refute the other specific charge of being its editor. (It may not have had one). Lord Blake reserved judgement, but thought it quite possible that Disraeli was indeed the author of 'The Dunciad'.[6]

In what may or may not have been a bit of clever cross-media promotion, as we would call it, a key was published in the *Star Chamber* revealing the 'real' identities of some of the characters in *Vivian Grey*. It cannot have been very hard to deduce that the Duke of Waterloo represented Wellington; and the reactionary septuagenarian Lord Chancellor Lord Eldon was hardly under an impenetrable disguise as Lord Past Century! For all Disraeli's supposed Canningite leanings, Canning himself appears in the text as Charlatan Gas. Indeed, to judge by Disraeli's own *Star Chamber* contribution, he already seemed to be cooling on Canning; apparently regarding him as altogether too Whiggish for safety, and preparing to execute one of the early examples of his lifelong series of political exuviations.

Meanwhile, the *Star Chamber* itself lasted for less than two months; and, whatever the extent of Disraeli's involvement, clearly brought him no nearer to success. The result of this combination of early undertakings was that he had alienated some of the key figures in Tory journalistic and publishing circles: and he had alienated them for good. The influence of Murray and Lockhart, bitter over the whole *Representative* affair, were lost to him; and he would have to attempt to devise a different route to power, influence and (perhaps his greatest priority) fame.

If at first you don't succeed... After a breakdown, and a temporary withdrawal from the rather garish limelight Disraeli had hitherto courted, he resumed his literary endeavours, producing a second instalment of *Vivian Grey*, plus novels such as *The Young Duke* and *Contarini Fleming*. He also wrote satires in the style of the Latin author Lucian: *Ixion in Heaven* and *The Infernal Marriage*. This brought him into contact with his fellow novelist (and future fellow parliamentarian and Cabinet minister) Edward Bulwer-Lytton. Bulwer-Lytton was currently editing the *New Monthly* magazine; and it was in this periodical that Disraeli's two satires first saw the light of day. Disraeli thus walked into another row which involved the worlds of literature and the press, and the nature of the boundaries between them.

Dr William Maginn, who had earlier had links with Canning, and was also part of Croker's network of journalistic contacts, was now the editor of *Fraser's Magazine*. He had no taste for popinjays and dandies who wrote novels about a high society of which they were, in his view, almost entirely ignorant. Maginn set the even younger William Makepeace Thackeray to the task of belittling the two ambitious young novelists, Disraeli and Bulwer-Lytton. A feverish reviewer and magazine war was the result, and some of Disraeli's older and more heavyweight press enemies waded in. Lockhart, now safely installed in the editor's chair at the *Quarterly Review*, also ensured unfavourable coverage. On one occasion, where Disraeli was able to cite misquotation from *The Young Duke*, he did manage to secure an apology: but the underlying enmity of these influential figures remained. Eventually, in later and more successful novels, Disraeli was able to turn the tide and satirize some of these figures too – notably Croker – but at the time of his career when he needed the assistance of such heavyweights, he lost more than he gained by antagonizing them.[7]

In the early 1830s, however, he was to find a very important political backer, on whose behalf he was to undertake his next major sequence of press interventions. Lord Lyndhurst, as we have seen, was one of a group of senior politicians in the early nineteenth century who were prepared to risk the surprise of colleagues by more or less openly consorting with journalists. We saw the surprise in some traditionalist quarters at his semi-public meal with Thomas Barnes, editor of *The Times*, in an effort to secure support for a Tory ministry in the 1830s. Although not as flamboyant, he was in this respect the direct Tory counterpart – in the law, in politics and in press management – of the Whig Henry Brougham, whose press dealings, as we know, were even more open and extensive.

Lyndhurst wished to keep up the pressure on the reinstalled Melbourne ministry in the Tory press in 1835; and so, in return for the promise of a seat in the Commons, Disraeli was commissioned to write articles for the *Morning Post*. There is more than a suggestion, at this stage, that Lyndhurst may have had an eye on the premiership himself. He and Peel were not on the best of terms politically; Wellington had effectively ceded the day-to-day running of the Lords to Lyndhurst. Lyndhurst himself had selected the government's Municipal Corporations Bill (introducing local government in a more recognizably modern form) as grounds for a major fight; and he wanted Disraeli to explain and propagandize for his side of that fight in the *Post*. As such, it became a defence of the peers in what looked like becoming another emblematic 'peers versus people' struggle.[8] Peel won this round; but Disraeli clearly enjoyed his first major excursion into mainstream political journalism, and was ready to resume as opportunity offered. Some of the ideas Disraeli had expounded in the articles also emerged in book form later in 1835, under the title *A Vindication of the English Constitution in a letter to a noble and learned Lord*. (The Lord, naturally, was Lyndhurst).

Disraeli's next newspaper outings were in *The Times*. As well as contributing to the letters column, in one case launching a savage attack on *The Globe* for accusations made against his own electoral tactics in one of his unsuccessful parliamentary campaigns,[9] he assumed the pseudonym of 'Runnymede' for a series of open letters, attacking current and former leading lights of the Whig government throughout the parliamentary sitting of 1836. Disraeli's opportunity was the outcome of the assiduous cultivation of Barnes by Lyndhurst over the previous two years.

The aggressive sarcasm deployed by Disraeli as Runnymede, against the likes of Melbourne, Palmerston and Grey, foreshadows the parliamentary style he would later adopt in his demolition of Peel, and in his many ripostes to Gladstone during their long parliamentary joust of future decades.

Barnes also acted as an editorial censor, not so much on political as on legal grounds. The reference to Melbourne could be seen as relatively benign: not so the barbed reference to his alleged affair with Mrs Norton, which Barnes swiftly removed. At one stage, Barnes told Disraeli, somewhat resignedly: 'You have a most surprising disdain for the law of libel: but I do not object to considerable risk when the stake is worth playing for'.[10] The Runnymede Letters were also eventually published in book form under the title *The Spirit of Whiggism*, containing the memorable, if dubious, aphorism: 'European revolution is a struggle against privilege; an English revolution is a struggle for it'.[11]

Once he had breached the ramparts of *The Times*, Disraeli was clearly determined not to be ejected quickly. Some years before, he had written an allegorical satirical book, *The Voyage of Captain Popanilla*; and he now returned to a similar format in a series of *Times* articles called 'A New Voyage of Sinbad the Sailor, recently discovered'. Perhaps as a delayed or even subconscious response to Barnes's waspish comments, Disraeli was covering some of the same territory he had already addressed as 'Runnymede', but using pseudonyms as transparent as in *Vivian Grey*. There were no prizes for *Times* readers who guessed that 'Shrugshoulders the Grand Vizier' was Melbourne, and that 'the Vizier for Foreign Affairs' was Palmerston.

At around this time, Disraeli had become an admirer of Bolingbroke both as an exemplar of an earlier era of Toryism, and as a writer and propagandist of brilliance; and he seemed to be yearning to recapture the style of eighteenth-century satire in another *Times* contribution, 'An Heroic Epistle to Lord Viscount Mel....e', in the spring of 1837. When he offered a second instalment, even the patient Barnes decided he had had enough.[12] He also attempted another literary homage, this time to the late fifteenth- and early sixteenth-century poet (and playwright) John Skelton, in the form of three long satirical verses, about which Barnes was also lukewarm.[13]

Disraeli was not writing for money: he was consciously writing for fame, for publicity. Barnes, by 1836 and 1837, was happy to reciprocate: not by paying Disraeli, but by reporting his speeches as he attempted to enter Parliament. He did so at the election after William IV's death in 1837; while Gladstone, five years younger, had already been an MP for almost five years. For a twentieth- or twenty-first-century prime minister, 32 approaching 33 is not far from an average age for parliamentary arrival; but it was notably late for nineteenth-century aspirants. However, Disraeli had used the newspapers with some skill, bringing himself to the attention of the Duke of Wellington and Peel, as well as cementing a close political (and personal) bond with Lyndhurst; and opening what he must have hoped would be an enduring alliance with *The Times*. His earlier feud with Lockhart had effectively ensured that the pages of the *Quarterly Review* were closed to him, and would remain so; and it was harder for a Tory (albeit one of a rather unorthodox stamp) to secure influence through the *Edinburgh Review*. One major area of the broader press and of political discourse was thus effectively shut off, in a way that was not the case with most other major political figures willing to write; and thus a high profile in the newspapers became even more important for Disraeli.

At about the same time, Disraeli was toying with the idea of attempting to set up another new paper himself. Undeterred by the adverse effects of his *Representative* experiment, he envisaged himself as co-proprietor of the *Carlton Chronicle*. He wrote to his solicitor Benjamin Pyne in May 1836 telling him to expect the paper to appear '[on] Saturday'. It is as well for Pyne that he did not hold his breath: for it was another of Disraeli's early projects to expire in futility, as a result of his shortage of investment capital.[14] Not until he was a former Cabinet minister would Disraeli again be seriously involved in plans to launch a new paper: this time with at least partial success.

POLEMICIST

Disraeli was still contributing to *The Times* a couple of years later, during the 'Bedchamber Crisis' of 1839. Melbourne's government could have fallen two years before it did, had the new Queen not dug in her heels and refused to give Peel a free hand to make alterations to the composition of her ladies of the bedchamber in taking office. No agreement was reached, and Victoria (not yet married to Albert or benefiting from his advice) was delighted to allow Melbourne to remain in office, and close to her, for another two years.

Disraeli, this time under the guise of 'Laelius', took up the journalistic cudgels on behalf of the Tories, telling the Queen: 'Madam, it cannot be...'.[15] Early the previous year, Disraeli had adopted another suitably self-effacing *nom de plume*: Coeur de Lion. Under this modest pseudonym, he showed signs of having just read the work of Thomas Carlyle (whose *French Revolution* had recently been published). Asking how the Queen's government was to be carried on, he raised the 'great question of a great man, true hero-question'.[16] Fortunately, the Carlyle influence was temporary. The 'Coeur de Lion' letters formed another series for *The Times*, but never emerged as a book.

Later, as the Melbourne government tottered to its close, Disraeli – still, of course, an opposition backbencher – again appeared in the pages of *The Times*, this time as 'Atticus'. In the guise of a letter to Wellington, Disraeli gives him examples of elderly historical figures rising to great challenges. Suspecting Wellington of being content to keep the Whigs in power as late as spring 1841, he urges the Duke to call time on the government.[17] In later years, he was wont to become frustrated with his leader Derby's apparent acquiescence in a Whig government; although Derby arguably showed greater shrewdness than his lieutenant in picking the right moments at which minority Tory governments might be feasible for a reasonable span of time.

Prominence in the newspapers had played a role in bringing Disraeli into Parliament. It played no role, however, in propelling him into ministerial office in 1841. There has been much speculation as to what Peel really thought of Disraeli at this stage, if he thought of him at all. In Gladstone (still at this time the rising hope of those stern and unbending Tories, not the radical Liberal old man in a hurry of later decades), Peel saw a kindred spirit; perhaps a younger version of himself, albeit one with a bit too much 'enthusiasm' in religious matters. For Gladstone, who had already held two junior offices in Peel's first government, there was an easy ascent to the vice-presidency of the Board of Trade, and subsequent elevation to the presidency and the Cabinet. (His own reaction was muted: he wished to govern men not packages, he claimed, in an initial but brief burst of disappointment). For Disraeli, his wife and his devoted sister Sarah, however, there was the nineteenth-century equivalent of the twentieth-century politician's hovering by the telephone awaiting the call from Number 10 recounted in so many political memoirs and biographies. The Disraeli family had little choice but to scan the papers each day for ministerial announcements: and they scanned in vain, for Disraeli was omitted completely.

IDLE HANDS?

The next major episode in Disraeli's complex relations with the press would stem from the vacuum created by his lack of office. Not only were the seeds sown for the great clash with Peel a few years later, but an association between the proprietor of *The Times*, John Walter, Disraeli and the Young England movement was also formed. Walter, it will be recalled, was an MP; and, at the time of Barnes's death and Delane's succession, was in a particularly powerful position at his own paper. Looking back beyond the compromises of recent centuries, the Young England movement glorified an idealized mediaevalism in which classes were seen as cooperating improbably harmoniously, against a backdrop of chivalric glamour and almost heraldic jousts and tournaments. At its most basic and pragmatic, for all its archaism and invocation of that heraldic, mock-mediaeval past and its cultural and historical trappings, it was, for Disraeli, at least in part about maintaining visibility and profile in the Conservative Party in lieu of ministerial office. Of course, that was not the whole of it: but for Disraeli, more than for the likes of John Manners, George Smythe and Alexander Baillie Cochrane, his most prominent colleagues in the 'movement', this was a large element of its attraction.

Perhaps because of this, the careful cultivation of John Walter assumes more importance than, perhaps, has often been realized. Not only was Walter enthusiastic about the romantic and historical overtones of Young England, he also supported the core of underlying policy. Insofar as the one-nation creed of Disraeli's Young England novels represented the 'programme' of the movement, there was an attempt to construct some coherence around the notion of an alliance between the aristocracy and the people in pursuit of social justice. And this was one of the themes that provided common ground with Walter. Recalling his principled stand against what he saw as the cruelty of the new Poor Law (a view which history has largely ratified), we can see a thread of continuity which is in danger of being overshadowed by the more garish and, frankly, absurd elements of Young England. There was also an existing social link between Walter and the movement: Walter's son, the future John Walter III, had been at Eton with Smythe and Manners, and had been on terms of easy familiarity.[18]

Walter was even offered the nominal leadership of the movement, although he declined. In return, he offered the support of The Times, the use of his country home Bearwood and his general seal of approval.[19] As the group expanded its activities, it used all the methods of publicity and self-promotion then available. In addition to the welcome use of Bearwood, Walter offered them space at The Times too, giving them access not only to administrative and secretarial assistance, but also early access to privileged information as it came in. Disraeli and his colleagues further built up a rapport with Peter Borthwick, editor of the Morning Post. Articles could now be written for and placed in two of the most influential papers of the day; and favourable coverage guaranteed at a time when Peel as prime minister was not managing his own press relations particularly successfully, and when the opposition Whig leaders were either neglecting theirs, or using them in their own personal or policy interests more than for the party as a whole (notably in the case of Palmerston).

Disraeli's novels of the period, especially Coningsby and Sybil, can also be seen as part of what we might call a multi-media campaign, though they were obviously much more than that and remain important works of literature transcending their immediate political context. His most recent previous works, Alroy, Henrietta Temple and Venetia, had not been so closely deployed to push a political agenda: they were written for profile, and probably out of more conventional literary impulses. The same is undoubtedly true of his play Count Alarcos. The last of what is often referred to as the Young England trilogy, Tancred is also rather less obviously in the service of a political agenda. Coningsby and Sybil have coloured much of the subsequent writing about Young England, and yet the notion that they constitute a political and social manifesto is inaccurate: indeed, Coningsby in isolation might not even be seen as a primarily political novel at all. Social commentary is present in Sybil; but, as often with Disraeli, pragmatism and opportunism dictated the content of the novels and the way they came later to be seen as a coherent programme is belied not only by a proper reading of the novels, but also by Disraeli's other activities. In 1844, the year of *Coningsby*, Disraeli was little occupied (in public utterance at least) by social issues.[20]

Meanwhile, much of the press and literary reaction, largely now forgotten, focused not on any social policy agenda, but on the movement's easily satirized praise for the old aristocracy. It also quite openly used anti-Semitism as a leading weapon. The minor writer and satirist William North quickly produced an *Anti-Coningsby*, in which he gave this assessment of Young England:

> Give us our old nobility,
> And feudal glories past,
> Unbelieving politicians
> Be from our Senate cast.
> Emancipate the Hebrews
> Conciliate the Pope
> Found mechanic institutions
> And learn to trust in HOPE.[21]

Disraeli's alliance with *The Times* would not prove enduring. He supported Walter when Peel's government attempted to remove him from Parliament in 1844, but the relatively brief period of Walter's maximum influence over his own family's paper had peaked. Delane's authority was growing in the years after he succeeded Barnes in 1841; and when it came to the decisive question of 1845–6, the proposed repeal of the Corn Laws, Disraeli would find that it was Delane's word, not Walter's, which was now law at the paper. The Young England group could still puff each other's works in journals such as the *Oxford and Cambridge Review*; but, in the longer run, as the *Morning Post* leaned further towards Palmerston, and as the Tory party headed for a split, the battle for press influence and support would become tougher than ever for Disraeli and his circle.

PRESS AND PARLIAMENT

The next phase of Disraeli's career would involve a greater concentration on parliamentary politics, rather than on the wider public and press sphere. After his savage attacks on Peel over the Corn Laws, and the split in the Tory party, there was never any question as to the overall leadership of the Protectionists. Lord Stanley, already in the Lords but not yet Earl of Derby, was pre-eminent on the grounds of ability, oratory, experience, social standing and just about all other imaginable criteria. The long-term leadership of the party and that in the Lords was settled for the next political generation.

The position in the Commons was very different. Disraeli was the best speaker by a clear margin; but he was not yet respected, his character and his social standing were suspect, he had never held office and he was seen as a talented maverick and a gadfly, not as a statesman. It was necessary to stop wearing gaudy outfits and jewellery, replacing them with the more conventional statesman's black frock coat, but this was not sufficient to secure acceptance. In any case, there was a ready-made Commons leader available to serve under Stanley in the shape of Lord George Bentinck, a member of the Duke of Portland's clan. Although not previously seen as a committed career politician, Bentinck held the line as a figure all could rally round until his health gave way and he resigned and subsequently died. Disraeli later wrote his life in a manner that combined tribute to his former chief with careful positioning of himself in the party's subsequent internal manoeuvres. Even then, as we have noted, there was a rather tortuous intermediate – one might almost say probationary – period in which Disraeli shared the Commons leadership with Lord Granby, the elder brother of Disraeli's Young England colleague Lord John Manners, and J.C. Herries, that veteran of Tory intrigues past, from the Liverpool-Wellington era. Granby had initially taken on the sole leadership, but resigned after three days.

Disraeli's difficulties were summarized by the Protectionist *Morning Herald*, whose leading spirit Samuel Phillips, himself a Jewish convert, wrote: 'It seems they detest D'Israeli, the only man of talent'.[22] (Note the implied condescension, if not worse, in the retention of the spelling of the surname). The Protectionists, whose first job was to ensure that they were the 'official' Conservative Party before thinking about forming governments, were short of press support. As we have seen, Derby could only really rely on the regular Tory papers the *Herald* and *The Standard*, plus the weekly *John Bull*. By the time Disraeli had finally established his position as sole Commons leader, he was already talking to Derby's son, the younger Stanley, about the party's weak press position, and meditating on how it could be strengthened. One of their earlier notions was to form an alliance with, and possibly buy, the *Morning Post*. By 1849, as Disraeli established himself in the Commons leadership, Stanley was already writing for the paper, and recording discussions about it with Disraeli. They met for a political talk on 19 May 19 1849:

> D. then entered on another subject: the want of a party organ. We agreed to see what could be done provisionally with the *Morning Post*: to try and revive that paper in the first place, and if it succeeded, then to purchase it. I promised two weekly articles, or three if required.

Stanley, in another bracketed section, added to his journal in subsequent years: 'This fell through. I heard no more of it. The *Morning Post* scheme ended in my writing a few articles, but no one else did so, and I gave it up'.[23]

A fortnight later, Stanley records a similar talk: same topic; different paper:

> Another conversation with Disraeli on the press. I found him desirous of buying the *Morning Chronicle* which appears to be on sale. It is not, as commonly supposed, the property of the Peelite party, but was purchased as a speculation, and constituted the organ of that party... The literary reputation of this journal is higher than that of the *Post*, and its purchase besides securing a friend, would silence an enemy.[24]

Again, however, no progress was made; and in the spring of the following year, Stanley reviewed his and Disraeli's press plans of the last 12 months. After the failure of the *Post* and *Chronicle* schemes, they turned, somewhat *faute de mieux*, to the *Morning Herald*: already a supporter, but not, in their view (or Derby's), well run. This time, the plan was to write regularly for the *Herald*, but then to move on to a weekly journal started from scratch as well. However, Stanley and Disraeli could find no suitable parliamentary colleagues willing to join the endeavour:

> We consulted those members of the party who were thought most likely to take an interest in the scheme, but to no purpose. Some were jealous of D.: others disliked the press without knowing why: few liked the notion of paying down money without getting something tangible, like a new vote in

parliament, to show for it. They had no faith in an ultimate result on public opinion.[25]

A few months later, their eyes were on *The Spectator*; the result was the same; and in the following year, 1851, says Stanley, their only support was to be found in the *Post* and the *Herald*. (He omits even to mention *The Standard* and *John Bull*). In March, Stanley visited Croker, who encouraged him to become more involved in writing for the *Quarterly Review*; but astutely observed in the privacy of his diary that 'quarterlies are well nigh superseded by the growing influence of the daily and weekly press, which draws off the ablest writers'.[26] It was during this conversation, when Stanley mentioned his wish that more volunteers could be found to write for the *Herald*, that Croker gave his memorable recollection of the joint work on *The Courier*. Stanley quotes him thus:

I remember that in 1818 or '20, I forget which, but it was before the Queen's trial, our organ, the *Courier* had fallen off greatly both in merit and circulation. Peel, Palmerston and I took it up and worked it daily: and in eight months we had raised the sale from 6,000 copies to 20,000.[27]

When Derby's first ministry came into power in 1852, the refrain was the same:

The chief want to the government is the want of a daily or weekly organ, the 'Herald' being imbecile and no other existing. [*The Standard* was an evening paper.] I drew out for the Cabinet a scheme, which was proposed through Malmesbury: each member to subscribe two per cent of his official salary towards a fund for supporting the press. This passed with little opposition (but though we found money, we never found writers, and part of the sum thus raised was returned).[28]

One further scheme was considered during the life of the 1852 ministry. Stanley was persuaded to meet with Delane's father, who suggested that a series of articles on ministerial policy should be written (to follow up a pamphlet called 'The Ministry and the Session') in an attempt to persuade *The Times* to swing behind the Derby government. Such a speculative venture was too much even for Disraeli who, says Stanley, rejected it at once, for all his other attempts to woo Delane himself by other means.

So, in the event, it was to be a new paper after all: but not in time to be issued during the lifetime of the first Derby government. *The Press* would come into existence in opposition; but, as a Tory and, in effect, a Disraelian newspaper, was to face a fairly short and tumultuous life. Stanley's own estimate of the state of the press at the time (in a letter to Disraeli) gives rough estimates of the party allegiances, and in some cases circulations, of existing papers as follows. In summary, said Stanley, the important papers were: *The Times* with a circulation of 35,000 (in fact it was 40,000), essentially liberal but not aggressively hostile; the *Morning Advertiser*, the publicans' paper which started the hue and cry against Albert in 1853, listed as adverse; likewise the broadly Peelite *Morning Chronicle*, the Palmerstonian *Globe* and the Whig/Liberal *The Daily Telegraph* and *Daily News*. On the side of Derby and Disraeli, Stanley listed the *Morning Post* and its circulation of 2,000, although it was already coming under the Palmerstonian spell; *The Standard*, its circulation between 2,000 and 4,000; and the *Morning Herald*, with a circulation over 4,000 but out on the 'Ultra' wing of the party, and seen as, on occasion, doing more harm than good. (Again, no mention was made of the weekly *John Bull*).[29]

THE PRESS

The name chosen for the paper intended to rectify this deficiency was *The Press*. Disraeli was the moving spirit behind this venture but, after his bad experience with *The Representative*, he was determined not to be publicly and officially associated with it. However, in practical terms, he was its proprietor and also a regular contributor. The efforts to preserve a degree of anonymity and what would be later termed 'plausible deniability' were sometimes a little transparent: on one occasion taking the form of a critique of one of his own speeches as 'much too long and savouring somewhat of the Yankee school of rhetoric'![30]

The paper was a weekly, originally envisaged by Disraeli as a cross between *The Times* and *Punch*. However, it always faced a number of problems: not merely in taking on the Liberals and the Peelites, but also within the Conservative Party itself. Derby, as we have noted, was not in favour. He was as aware as anyone of the deficiencies of the other Tory papers; but he simply did not trust Disraeli enough in 1853 to let him use it as a vehicle for his own ideas, often seen as idiosyncratic in conventional Tory circles. This, in turn, prevented other Tory grandees like the Duke of Northumberland from wishing to invest in it. Predictably too, other senior Tories who promised to write for it proved worse than their word. Stanley, who was Disraeli's only really active coadjutor (Bulwer-Lytton did a bit), tells us that the two of them wrote major chunks of the paper in the early days at least: 'I wrote about a third of the original matter of the first and second volumes: Disraeli likewise worked hard, for a time, with his own pen'.[31]

Stanley also tells us that Disraeli reverted to youthful type, painting wildly optimistic pictures of a circulation of 10,000 to 15,000, and the eventual 'shaking' of the power of *The Times*, having first dislodged the other weekly titles from their lowlier pedestals. It was as a result of Stanley reporting these visions back to his father that Derby put the hint out, via Malmesbury, to Northumberland to keep his money in his pocket. Derby's concern was genuine and understandable. He was a former prime minister, the leader of the party, and a paper known to contain the writings of his number two and of his own son (albeit that knowledge would be confined to elite circles) would inevitably also be taken as reflecting his own views and to have received his own imprimatur. This, combined with a generally aloof attitude to most of the press, ensured Derby's opposition: though he was prepared to ensure it was a silent repudiation, not a public rebuff.

A year into the paper's life, a skeleton staff had been hired; but Disraeli and Stanley were still doing much of the writing. Stanley recounts how Disraeli told him: '...whatever news he got of foreign transactions, he wrote for the "Press" in the style of one translating from a foreign language, so that it might appear to come direct from abroad'.[32] This was attention to detail indeed! The paper itself was part newspaper, part review (the remnants of Disraeli's idea of a cross between *The Times* and *Punch*); and Disraeli consciously looked back to Canning's youthful *jeu d'esprit Anti Jacobin* as an inspiration. A series called 'Letters to the Whigs', signed Manilius, was often attributed to Disraeli; but was in fact by Bulwer-Lytton.[33] To a journalistic ear, the homage to Canning's earlier journal is not auspicious; and, in a letter, Stanley confirms the suspicion, in March 1853, shortly after the launch, that there was too much comment and not enough news: 'They say we are too much of an essay, and too little of a newspaper: that we do not give a sufficient quantity of news, and are rather too exclusively political'.[34]

Weintraub attributes the comment not to 'they', as does Stanley, quoted in the official biography, but to Lord Derby himself, with the further rider: '... as you [Disraeli] are in fact the manager of the machine, I report it to you'.[35] It was a shrewd comment, confirming Derby's ability to understand what makes good and successful journalism, even if it was not a subject that greatly interested him. Stanley enumerated on his own hand a list of the subjects on which Disraeli wrote leaders in the first 11 editions, some of which were in defence of the recently departed first Derby administration, or propagandistic ephemera such as 'Alarming Rumour of the Resignation of Lord Aberdeen'; along with 'Special News about the Eastern Question' and the 'Imaginary Conversations of Eminent Men', in imitation of the Imaginary Conversations of the author Walter Savage Landor.[36]

By the end of 1853, the circulation of *The Press* was around 2,250, hardly an imminent threat to *The Times*; and it was losing money, though not disastrously. The first editor, Samuel Lucas, was replaced in reasonably amicable fashion by D. T. Coulton after just over a year, and he remained in post until his death in 1857. He was a success, taking over leader-writing responsibilities from Disraeli, following regular briefings supplied by him. Other alumni of the paper included R.H. Hutton, editor of *The Economist* and *The Spectator*, J.R. Seely, author of the influential 'Ecce Homo' essay, and T.E. Kebbel, the future biographer both of Derby and Disraeli. Disraeli's own daily involvement ceased, according to Monypenny and Buckle, in 1856, though he clearly retained an overall supervisory role; the paper was sold on Derby's return to the premiership (and Disraeli's to the Exchequer) in 1858; and it finally closed in 1866, the year the third Derby administration came to power. At least, as Monypenny and Buckle observed, it managed to outlast the coalition government it was created to undermine.[37]

One of Disraeli's recent biographers has written: 'Disraeli enjoyed journalism, indeed one cannot help feeling that had he not been a politician he would have been a journalist'.[38] This is clearly true in part, though he would surely have chafed at the anonymity imposed on figures such as Barnes, the former *Times* editor, and even on Delane who, although prominent in elite social circles, was not named in the pages of his own paper. One wonders whether, rather, journalism was more of an enjoyable means to an end: something he was happy to embrace, but which, as with Winston Churchill, George Lansbury and Michael Foot, was never quite enough in and of itself. Possibly Jonathan Swift is a nearer analogy: Swift saw himself as a man of letters who should have been a man of power; Disraeli was a man of letters who saw a way to use writing to become a man of power. Delane's biographer Edward Cook tells us that *The Times* editor said to Palmerston, when Lord Derby published his translation of *The Iliad*: 'Now you could not have done that'. (Palmerston replied that he was too busy translating bishops).[39] Similarly, for all his articles for *The Globe* and other papers, Palmerston could not have written for the press with the same *élan* as Disraeli; however, he probably achieved more sustained political success and influence through it than Disraeli was able to exert. It was as if Disraeli was more interested in the performance aspect of press management and influence, as another showcase for his own talents and abilities, rather than as part of an overall strategy to secure his own lasting political success.

Back in 1841, Disraeli had to deny forcefully to his then leader Peel that he had written a letter to *The Times* under the pseudonym 'Psittacus', concerning a long-forgotten manoeuvre over the Speakership, just as Melbourne was about to fall. Even Lord Blake could not decide if he was telling the truth,[40] and we still cannot be absolutely certain. The long public denial required for concealing his close involvement in *The Press* (albeit flimsily where elite circles were concerned) must again have pulled him in multiple directions as the need for discretion jarred with his own love of performance and notoriety. His own recognition of the social unacceptability of being publicly identified as writing for and directly managing a newspaper was, because of his humbler social origins, doubtless more acute than Palmerston's, though even he had similar qualms, as has been seen. One gains the impression that Palmerston was particularly acute at diagnosing what needed to be done in his own interest, and then doing it in the most expeditious manner. Disraeli, for all his renowned political flexibility, may have found this harder. Derby took a third view: he would do what he thought suitable and appropriate, and no more: it was then up to intelligent people to make their own decisions on whose policy was correct, and vote accordingly.

FROM MANAGING THE PRESS TO PRESS MANAGEMENT

When Derby formed his second government in 1858, Disraeli had divested himself of *The Press*. One wonders whether, had it been more commercially successful, and had he not partially lost interest in the detail of it, he would have been tempted to retain possession. Derby would not have welcomed such a move. However, once it had been sold on, Disraeli realized that he would need to redefine and improve his relations with Delane at *The Times*.

Years earlier, Disraeli had committed the unpardonable sin of suggesting to Delane whom he should choose to review his biography of Lord George Bentinck. The asperity of Delane's rebuff entailed the eating of a good portion of humble pie by Disraeli, involving his own later description of the idea as a 'stupid suggestion'.[41] His subsequent efforts to secure favourable coverage of the 1852 Derby government had not been wholly unsuccessful; but were never likely to dislodge Aberdeen and later Palmerston as Delane's principal political contacts. Nonetheless, Disraeli had been able to write, without excessively sugaring the pill: 'We are very sensible of the admirable tact and great effect of your articles'.[42] By 1858, Disraeli's frustration at the strength of the bond between Delane and Palmerston led him to speak publicly of how 'the once stern guardians of popular rights simper in the enervating atmosphere of gilded saloons'.[43]

This less-than-subtle reference to Delane's attendance at Lady Palmerston's parties did not, of course, prevent Disraeli (and it was Disraeli this time, not Derby himself, as happened later) from briefing Delane closely on policy and personnel in 1858, as the second Derby ministry entered office. Derby also corresponded with Delane, but not as extensively as in 1866 and 1867; and there was no recorded face-to-face meetings at this stage. Disraeli, Malmesbury and Stanley were the chief press briefers of the second Derby administration; balancing Palmerston, Clarendon, Granville, Wood and, when he was in office, Villiers in the Whig ministries. It is an exaggeration to regard Palmerston as running a Rolls-Royce media management strategy while the Tories were driving a clapped-out Trabant. However, external realities and parliamentary numbers ensured that, this time round, the government's creditable attempt to tackle reform simply could not survive the reunited Liberal Party. With the Palmerston-Russell split now behind it and the services of Gladstone finally secured, the new-look Liberal Party, as it began to be called, was able to dictate the timing of the end of the second Derby administration. It is curious to recall that, when Derby's second government was being formed, *The Times* 'revealed' that Gladstone would be chancellor and Disraeli foreign secretary: and, of course, Gladstone did later accept office from Derby, albeit the less-than-mainstream post of commissioner to the Ionian Islands. (A nod, perhaps, to Derby's and Gladstone's shared love of classical scholarship, in which Disraeli would not have been seen as an equal partner).

MARKING TIME

In Disraeli's next period of opposition, from 1859 to 1866, there were no bursts of press energy and no further realistic attempts to found a new paper, although the idea had not quite died. This was the period during which Prince Albert made his famous comment to Derby about England being governed by newspapers, 'and you have not a newspaper'; though Stanley's journal also records an improvement in relations with the Tory *Standard*, describing the editor in 1861 as 'an intelligent and moderate man'.[44] This seems to betoken a recognition that a bit more work probably needed to be put in to nurture the loyal, if sometimes irritating, Tory loyalist journals. The proprietor of *John Bull* had been annoyed at the very idea that *The Press* had even been thought necessary, and solicited further financial support from party grandees. Another small Tory paper was the *Weekly Mail*, described as 'the only cheap London weekly CONSERVATIVE Paper from 1858'. It too solicited Disraeli for money.[45] Meanwhile, in 1862, Stanley recorded:

> ...Heard that a new weekly paper is talked of, Disraeli much interested in its success. Lytton also concerned in it, Sir H. Wolff the chief promoter...
> I doubt the experiment being tried, after the failure of the 'Press', and still more doubt its success if it be tried.[46]

The *Morning Herald* and *The Standard* remained the mainstays of Tory journalism in these years, however. As they themselves recognized, they had hardly been zealous advocates of the changes in the duties on papers, which we will discuss further in the next chapter, but they had benefited from them. By 1859, they were looking to use new machinery, opening the possibility of printing 'from 16,000 to 20,000 copies per hour'.[47] Disraeli started cooperating more closely with the papers, which were jointly owned. He collaborated with the editorial staff to guide the tone and content of their leaders, in return for what was in effect a party subsidy. The plan was for the party to buy 1,000 copies of the *Herald*, while *The Standard* was deemed more self-sufficient. By 1862, Disraeli was examining their balance sheets.

They were not profitable, but economies were expected, and a new, more productive relationship seemed to ensue. Meanwhile, the journalist James Birch was telling Disraeli that he had tried, when involved in setting up of *The Daily Telegraph*, to make the paper a supporter of Derby and Disraeli, but had been outmanoeuvred by 'the Palmerston party', which 'intrigued and succeeded in obliging me to secede...' from its columns.[48]

THE GREASY POLE

By the time the third Derby government came to power in 1866, the press climate was a little more auspicious partly because of circumstances beyond the Tories' own control. As we have seen, the picture changed almost overnight when Palmerston's sure press grasp was replaced by Russell's more uncertain grip. Stanley even recorded a rumour in December 1865 that Delane had fallen out with John Walter III over how Russell's government should be treated, and that Delane had resigned. Of course, he did not do so in the end, and there is scant trace of the row in the biographies of Delane or in the *History of The Times*.[49] The existing Tory papers were growing in influence and circulation, and arrangements with the party leaders were better. Derby, knowing that this would almost certainly be his final premiership, was wise and pragmatic enough to know that he would have to devote more personal attention to the press than he had before. After the failure of Russell and Gladstone's Reform Bill, there was also, perhaps, a feeling that the Tories really should be given a chance; and this time, the ministry was in power for two and a half years: a year and eight months under Derby up to February 1868; and a further ten months or so under Disraeli. John Morley, in his biography of Cobden, wrote: '*The Times* was Palmerstonian because the country was Palmerstonian, just as by-and-by it became Derbyite because the country seemed Derbyite'.[50]

We have already seen how Derby took personal responsibility this time round for attempting to deal with, and to 'square', Delane and *The Times*. The results were mixed, and Disraeli still had his own part to play in leaking and briefing. On the big question of the administration, however, while Derby met Delane one-to-one for a briefing for the first time, Disraeli's role would be the more time-consuming one of winning the Commons battle. Just as Lyndon Johnson had the Southern standing and seemingly conservative

Democrat record that enabled him to pass the Civil Rights and Voting Rights Acts, and just as Richard Nixon could 'safely' go to China as a previously 'red-baiting' Republican, so people seemed to feel that a radical Reform Act could be safely passed by Derby and Disraeli, while Russell and Gladstone were not trusted even to pass a more moderate one.

Meanwhile, as Derby's career neared its end, Disraeli prepared finally to take the reins both as party leader and, for a while at least, as prime minister. As he did so, he set what he must have hoped would be the lasting tone for his relationship with Delane. After an editorial spoke of him as 'evidently the fitting successor to Lord Derby',[51] Disraeli made only two changes to Derby's final Cabinet, one of which was the necessary replacement of himself as Chancellor by George Ward Hunt. In his dealings with Delane, Disraeli adopted an intimate, almost conspiratorial tone, as if they were the only two who had thought of such a stroke, against the advice of lesser men. He spoke of 'the successful manner in which OUR Chancellor of the Exchequer has been received… What you said decided me'.[52] However, all would not remain so harmonious and straightforward.

The *History of The Times* says the paper 'moved steadily over to the Liberal side' during Disraeli's brief first premiership. This was partly due to a clever hand played by Gladstone on Irish church reform, and on the need for economy, and was so pronounced that, when Disraeli was forced to call an election, '*The Times* entered upon the election almost as a Liberal party organ'.[53] This should caution us against a ready assumption that press management had moved from the sporadic under Derby to the masterly under Disraeli. If anything, the reverse was true. In the key relationship, that with *The Times*, Derby was more successful and effective from 1866 to 1868 than Disraeli for the rest of 1868. By December, just months after talking intimately to Delane about his Cabinet appointments, Disraeli was musing bitterly on the power of *The Times* as Gladstone basked in the glow of favourable coverage and of the resulting three-figure parliamentary majority.

THE WAIT FOR REAL POWER

Because we know that Disraeli remained as Leader of the Opposition for over five years, and then formed a second government that lasted for six, even remaining for a further year as opposition leader once more, it is easy to overlook the fact that this election defeat could have marked the end of Disraeli's career, he was about to turn 64, and had been prime minister, albeit briefly. Like Derby, Russell and Palmerston, however, he resolved to continue beyond what looked to some an ideal retirement point. In this, they would all, in their turn, be outdone by Gladstone, who was still prime minister almost 20 years after his first 'retirement'.

In the leading biographies, there is relatively little about Disraeli's press activities between 1868 and 1874, though in fact this was a period of some promise for the Conservatives. Although *The Times* was out of reach for the present, it will be recalled that the Liberals had lost support from some of their titles after the death of Palmerston. Russell lost *The Globe* in 1866; there were signs of a rapprochement with the *Morning Advertiser*, with its access to publicans and the trade; and the *Morning Post* was also there for the taking with Palmerston gone. Borthwick at the *Post* had always liked Palmerston's mixture of conservatism and international robustness and in the search for a replacement, Disraeli was more than likely to outdo Gladstone in appealing to that constituency. Meanwhile, some familiar names were disappearing as the newspaper landscape changed, and cheaper papers sprang up in the wake of Gladstone's removal of paper and stamp duties. The *Morning Chronicle* closed even before the death of its favourite, Palmerston, in 1862. The *Morning Herald* succumbed to commercial difficulties in 1869, the year of the death of Lord Derby, and Disraeli's first full year as Leader of the Opposition.

When the tide eventually turned against him in 1874, Gladstone himself reflected bitterly that, at that year's election, which he lost heavily, he had been 'borne down in a torrent of beer and gin'; and it was at least in part to the *Advertiser* that he was referring. Gladstone was seen as hostile to the liquor trade and over-reliant on temperance support, and, as early as December 1869, there were signs of co-operation between Disraeli and the paper, with opportunities already being afforded for Disraeli to put forward his case in its columns.[54]

Perhaps the biggest success, however, lay in winning over the increasingly important and influential *The Daily Telegraph*. This major feat took longer and was consummated rather later. Throughout Gladstone's first premiership (1868–74), the *Telegraph* was fundamentally, and at times enthusiastically, supportive of him. Indeed, it seems they were particularly keen to assist him during his first ministry, knowing as they did that his two foreign secretaries, first the Earl of Clarendon and then, after 1870, Lord Granville, were still in very close cahoots with *The Times*. However, Gladstone did not reciprocate. While Disraeli was making overtures to the paper, Gladstone had little to say to it, especially after his defeat in 1874 and his 'retirement' from the party leadership at the beginning of 1875. His replacements were Granville and Lord Hartington, and the *Telegraph* was unlikely to embrace Granville, rightly seen as Delane's favourite, while Hartington, despite his Cavendish heritage, was at the time far from being a political figure to aspire to compete with Gladstone or Disraeli for public prestige.

The final break between Gladstone and the *Telegraph* did not occur until Gladstone's return to the political scene with the Bulgarian atrocities campaign of 1876. However, Disraeli had sown useful seeds in opposition, performing with regard to the press the routine that successful oppositions tend to follow: await the end of a political honeymoon, take advantage of mistakes and of the complacency of office and then start formulating the details of a positive alternative. Despite his age, Disraeli had the patience to forego the chance of office without power in 1873, waiting instead for the final collapse of the government the following year. The irony, of course, is that this strategy, pursued by Derby in 1851 and 1855, used to infuriate the younger, more impulsive and impetuous Disraeli. When he came into power as the head of the first majority Conservative government since the second Peel government of 1841–6, his press position was much stronger than might have seemed likely in 1868. Assessments will differ as to whether this was attributable more to Disraeli's skill and persistence with the papers; Gladstone's seeming neglect, policy differences and the increasing conservatism of some proprietors; or simply the feeling that the country was moving from a Gladstonian to a Disraelian mood (rather like Morley's reference to the move from a Palmerstonian to a Derbyite country in the later 1860s).

The Standard and the *Evening Standard* were also now flourishing Tory papers, and while Stanley, who had succeeded his father as Earl of Derby in late 1869, was at this point a somewhat semi-detached member of Disraeli's team, he was also able to rely on press efforts of different kinds by several of his other colleagues. The future Lord Salisbury's review contributions were not always helpful or supportive; often far from it, and they would diminish as he succeeded his father as Marquess. But he would be a real journalistic force if won over fully. Stafford Northcote, with whom Salisbury would share the leadership for the four years after Disraeli's death, was also a knowledgeable and influential figure in the world of the Tory press. W.H. Smith and John Gorst were at home in that world: Gorst working especially closely with the *Standard*.[55] Disraeli's private secretary Montagu Corry too played a useful role as a confidential channel between Disraeli and the press. The papers also served as a means of test-driving social reform, which was seen as a handy dividing line between the parties and as a way of attracting the voters recently enfranchised by Derby's last government (along with those who might yet gain the vote in future reforms).

As part of a wider publicity and propaganda offensive, Northcote encouraged the establishment and dissemination of *The Sun* (not the same paper as its namesake from Lord Liverpool's era), so that the Tory message could be spread in rural areas beyond the regular reach of papers like *The Standard*. *The Sun* was effectively a paper not merely supporting but run by and on behalf of the party, and may have been seen as a development stemming from Northcote's own personal efforts to found a newspaper in the Devonshire area, his constituency base.[56] Thus, as Disraeli's second ministry took the places of the 'exhausted volcanoes' of Gladstone's government, there were signs of a Tory press position heralding long periods of media dominance in the decades to come. But what of *The Times*?

REACHING THE TOP

Disraeli's relationship with *The Times*, as we have seen, had gone through numerous phases: but then, so had Palmerston's, and he had sealed the deal in the end. For Disraeli, too, there was a reasonably happy outcome. The decline and fall of Gladstone's first ministry in 1874, and his subsequent abandonment of the Liberal leadership, marked a staging-post at which those editors and proprietors who felt an increasing conservatism of outlook could gradually or quickly change allegiance. The Bulgarian agitation of 1876, which drew political dividing lines swiftly and sharply, also hastened the process. Gladstone was genuinely shocked by the Ottoman Empire's attempt not only to quash glimmerings of Bulgarian independence from Muslim rule, but to use extreme torture and violence in suppressing it. Disraeli, by contrast, seemed excessively lenient to the Ottoman point of view. During the era of Palmerston and Derby, there was little of fundamental political substance dividing the leaderships, especially domestically. Indeed, as we have seen, Derby and Disraeli were able to outflank not merely Palmerston but even Russell and Gladstone on the left over the issue of reform. The same had been true, to an extent, in the era of Melbourne and Peel, until the retired Melbourne felt Peel had been far too radical on Corn Law repeal. Now, however, there was not only a much keener personal rivalry between Gladstone and Disraeli, but genuine and major differences of policy. When Gladstone took up the case of the Bulgarians, opposing the Turks and, by implication, softening opposition to Russia, it began to look to many conservative-minded figures in journalism as if there was a radical movement on the march, led by one of the two most important statesmen of the day, albeit a statesman not at that moment the official leader of his party.

The Times did not decisively turn against Gladstone during his first premiership; though the tone became warier. By the beginning of 1875, however, when he was already 'semi-retired' from the Liberal leadership, he was discerning outright hostility: '[A]n article in The Times this morning is undisguisedly aimed at getting rid of me'.[57] In fact, the article was probably the result of an 'inspired' leak from what might later have been called 'a source close to the Gladstone family', as Gladstone did indeed announce his retirement on that very day (January 14 1875). By this time, Disraeli had been back as Prime Minister for nearly a year. He had always enjoyed good personal relations with Delane. When asked whether he enjoyed Disraeli's flattery, Delane once replied that he did not, but that he liked 'to think I was thought of sufficient importance to make it worth his while'.[58]

By 1874, Delane was able to conclude that a majority Tory government indeed reflected the settled will of the country at that time, and gave Disraeli broad support. Disraeli was keen to retain the paper's favour, and so offered it exclusive intelligence, to the irritation of the other Tory-supporting papers. (This clearly foreshadows Tony Blair and Alastair Campbell privileging the newly won Sun over the loyalist Mirror in the era of New Labour). Queen Victoria, unconsciously echoing her late husband's comment to Derby in 1861, worried in 1876 that Disraeli had not got sufficient press support. She feared that The Globe was 'badly written' and that John Bull was far too 'ultra and extreme in its religious views'.[59] Now herself enthusiastically pro-Disraeli and anti-Gladstone, she need not have worried. Her prime minister's press position was as strong as any since Palmerston's in his heyday. Indeed, some of the papers who had switched to his side were readily able to justify the move by using the old politician's standby: it was not they who had changed, but the politicians. Disraeli was simply continuing Palmerston's aggressive foreign policy, with the extra rhetorical colouring of empire. That shrewd journalistic observer Derby, the late prime minister's son, assessed the position in late 1876 as: '*Pall Mall*, *Telegraph*, *Post* and *Standard* for; *Times* uncertain and trimming; only *D. News* and *Echo* against us'.[60] Two years later, Victoria drew up a similar list of supporters (of Disraeli's views and her own) who were 'very strong in the right sense'.[61]

Derby was right. Delane was certainly not unequivocally pro-Disraeli, and certainly not reflexively anti-Gladstone, when the great Liberal re-emerged to lead the Bulgarian campaign. That will be examined in the next chapter, but Disraeli could not simply rely on automatic and uncritical support. Disraeli could easily be portrayed as too pro-Turk; Gladstone ran the risk of seeming too Russian. Gladstone was able to harness real moral force and passion; while Disraeli risked appearing like a latter-day *ancien régime* politician: all cynicism, quips and world-weariness. Delane took the middle view: deploring the attacks on the Bulgarians, not wishing to prop up the Ottoman Empire, but at the same time not wishing to harm British interests to the benefit of Russia. Such a nuanced position might be easy for an academic historian: in the most important journalist in the country it sounded too uncertain a note for many, and was seen as vacillation. Some attributed it to his failing health (he resigned in 1877, and died two years later).

AUTUMN DAYS

Delane's successor, Thomas Chenery, held the post until 1884, thus seeing out Disraeli. His instincts were Liberal: more so than Delane's; and so Disraeli's final years of relations with *The Times* would not be untroubled. However, Disraeli was assisted by the increasing conservatism of the proprietor, John Walter III, and by the fact that any new editor of the paper would need time to establish his personal stamp of authority. Walter became more involved with the day-to-day running of the paper for a period. Chenery himself was more interested in international than in domestic politics; but there was a feeling that Disraeli could lose the paper's support before the 1880 election.

Disraeli had grumbled at Chenery's appointment, particularly bemoaning the fact that a figure like Chenery, much less of a social lion than his predecessors Barnes and Delane, was unlikely to be as socially prominent as his predecessor. Disraeli himself had gone to the Lords in 1876. In doing so, he had given Delane one last scoop, by telling him of his intentions: but it was a tip-off the failing Delane had not picked up on, simply not understanding the significance of Disraeli's words. 'My session will be over of Friday, August 11', the Prime Minister had said. 'I shall go to Osborne on the 12th, and I shall not return to the House of Commons'.[62] Disraeli was far too subtle to use the word 'never', but that is what he meant; and it was as Earl of Beaconsfield that he returned to the fray.

However, by the end of the government, for all Disraeli's continuing press support elsewhere, *The Times* was again in danger of slipping from his grasp. The paper had been critical of Gladstone's Midlothian campaign of late 1879, with its attempt to carry the message direct to the electorate in public meetings and its attacks on 'Beaconsfieldism' and its iniquities. (Perhaps Gladstone thought the use of Disraeli's lordly title made his foreign policy sound even more wicked!). However, by the spring of 1880, as the election hove into view, Lord Acton was writing to Gladstone's daughter Mary: '[Abraham] Hayward will tell you what I learn from other sources, that Chenery really wishes to bring "*The Times*" round [to the Liberals]'.[63]

Hayward was a literary man and political publicist, who had been involved with the Peelite circle that took on the *Morning Chronicle* many years earlier. Like some of those with whom he dealt then (possibly including Gladstone), he had eventually completed the full switch to liberalism; and was now an important liaison between the party and *The Times*. The paper's own official history recounts that, by the time of the 1880 election, this project had been achieved to the point where it occupied 'a central position, with a bias towards Liberalism'.

After Gladstone returned to the premiership with another sizeable majority (and despite the Queen's efforts to send for the official leaders, Granville and Hartington first), Hayward was meeting Chenery in the depths of the night, briefing him closely on the views and positions of the prime minister and his two displaced leadership colleagues. Hayward told his sister:

> It was a great point to secure *The Times*; so, after being told the exact state
> of things [by Gladstone, Granville and Hartington], I went off in the middle

of the night to *The Times* office, where I saw Chenery, the editor, an intimate friend of mine; and the first leading article in *The Times* of today was the result.[64]

EXHAUSTED VOLCANO

Disraeli remained as Leader of the Opposition for the final year of his life, but, aside from occasional glimmers of misguided optimism as to a sudden collapse of Gladstone's second government, he cannot seriously have expected to return as prime minister. His health had been poor for years: worse than Palmerston's had been or Gladstone's was to be at the same age. Gladstone could expect five or six years in power – even though he started dropping hints about another retirement within a very short time of his return. Disraeli was in no real position to launch a new campaign to win back the defaulting members of his press coalition. In a sense, he did not need to. With the exception of *The Times*, Disraeli bequeathed to his immediate joint successors, Salisbury and Northcote, a healthy phalanx of Tory-supporting or Tory-leaning newspapers. But would it be enough?

In his Midlothian campaign, Gladstone had taken politics 'out of doors', and had been reported, presented and perceived as doing so, in a way no previous top-level figure had before attempted. Disraeli had neither the energy nor the inclination to follow suit. His own direct participation in the 1880 election had consisted solely of a letter for publication, while Gladstone was experimenting with new methods of political communication and persuasion. As Stephen Koss pithily phrased it: 'Gladstone proved it possible to stir the country without stirring the press; and Disraeli, after stirring the press, was rejected by the country'.[65] Of course, Gladstone's Midlothian campaign speeches and appearances would have had far less national impact without press reporting, for all that the speeches were published almost immediately in book form. However, this reflected a less grandiose view of the role of the press: as 'media', in the modern sense; as mediators of activity independent of their own views, rather than as shapers and promoters of opinion. The relationship between politicians and the press was changing again. It was a change that Gladstone played a significant role in, and it was a change too many for Disraeli, coming overly late for him to be able either to shape or to benefit from the process.

CHAPTER NINE

WILLIAM GLADSTONE

W ILLIAM EWART GLADSTONE's political career broke many records. He is the only man to have held the premiership for four separate terms. He was Britain's oldest prime minister, in his 85th year, when he finally retired in 1894. He had one of the strongest intellects of all premiers (the strongest, according to his Tory successor Lord Salisbury). His official career spanned almost 60 years, from his first junior office in late 1834 to the end of his final premiership in early 1894; and his Cabinet career spanned in excess of 50 years (1843–94); comfortably exceeding Palmerston's (1830–65) and Churchill's (1908–55). He was in the Commons, like Churchill and Charles Villiers, for over 60 years (Villiers was the only one of the trio to have unbroken service). He is widely regarded as one of the three or four greatest prime ministers in British history; and as perhaps the greatest of all peacetime prime ministers. He was arguably the finest chancellor of the exchequer, an office he held four times, twice while he was also prime minister. We have already seen him making breakthroughs in political communication (the Midlothian campaign) and in press regulation (the removal of the Stamp and Paper Duties), and we will examine these fully later in this chapter. But how effective was he at press management?

In a review of the literature on the nineteenth-century press, Gladstone emerges, in this as in so many other respects of his career, as a hugely complex figure. Some accounts, notably the one in the *History of The Times*, see him as an unwilling press manager, delegating a distasteful task to others and viewing it as unbecoming his high office. Others among more recent biographers speak of his ability to acquire a mastery of publicity while seeming to disdain it: 'Gladstone's awareness and use of the press was much more acute than has hitherto been allowed'.[1]

He was a prolific journalist, but not in the manner of Disraeli, or for that matter Palmerston. Apart from his numerous books, he wrote extensively

12. William Ewart Gladstone, by Sir John Everett Millais, 1st Bt, 1879.
© National Portrait Gallery, London.

for the reviews, but less so for the newspapers. There were contributions to the *Contemporary Review*, the *Quarterly Review*, the *British Quarterly Review*, the *Church Quarterly Review*, the *North American Review*, the *Edinburgh Review*, the *Fortnightly Review* and the *Foreign and Colonial Quarterly Review*. Many of these were later published in several volumes of what Gladstone called his 'Gleanings'. He wrote an article on the Franco-Prussian War as a serving prime minister, still a highly unorthodox move at the time. He had even, while at Eton, edited and contributed to the *Eton Miscellany*, the school organ. Ironically, just as Disraeli had an eye on Canning's *Anti Jacobin* when he founded the 'Press', Gladstone seems to have regarded the *Eton Miscellany* as an offshoot of Canning's juvenile *Microcosm*.[2] He did not entirely abstain from newspaper contributions, writing early letters and making contributions to the *Liverpool Courier*, and to the *Liverpool Standard*. He also, notably, wrote for the *Morning Chronicle* in defence of Prince Albert when he was under attack from other sections of the press.

He executed, or authorized, one of the most extraordinary leaks in political history, rivalling or surpassing Aberdeen's bombshell on the Corn Laws. What became known as the 'trial balloon', the leaking of a story on a deniable and retractable basis to test political and public reaction, found an early and dramatic form in what became known as the 'Hawarden Kite'. This was when Gladstone's son leaked the intention to announce Home Rule for Ireland: just as controversial and momentous in the 1880s as Corn Law repeal was in the 1840s, and with similar effects on the unity of the party involved. He was arguably the first (but by no means the last) prime minister to adopt the tactic of favouring the provincial press, and on occasions the Press Association, as a means of bypassing what he came to see as the increasing unfairness of the metropolitan newspapers. He was also sufficiently interested in the potential of new media of communication to be the first prime minister to make a recording of his own voice, which still survives. (We think we know Peel and Derby had detectable northern accents: we can be sure there was at least a hint of it in Gladstone's accent, because we can hear it for ourselves).

RISING HOPE

In common with Disraeli, and like his own Liberal successors Campbell-Bannerman and Asquith, Gladstone's official biography was written by a professional journalist, albeit one who had turned politician: John Morley. J.A. Spender wrote Campbell-Bannerman's, and co-wrote Asquith's with a family member. Disraeli's, of course, was written by Monypenny and Buckle, both senior *Times* figures. Derby did not receive an official biography; but one of the first two unauthorized ones that came out was written by the professional journalist T.E. Kebbel. This alone gives the lie to the idea that there had been no social change in the relations between politicians and the press. A combination of the moral tone Gladstone was able to strike throughout his career and the fact that so many of his writings were on theological and classical topics has perhaps made it difficult for some biographers and historians to engage with the more operational, pragmatic side of Gladstone's press dealings. As Stephen Koss notes, when it came to newspapers: 'the popular impression was that Gladstone was above that sort of thing'.[3]

Famously, Gladstone's first choice of career after Eton and a Double First at Oxford (coupled with the presidency of the Oxford Union) was the Church. Peel, the offspring of manufacturers, had been a rather high-minded figure in his youth: but Gladstone must have seemed still more so. Peel was of the older school, deploring excessive 'enthusiasm' in religion. Derby was the same, despite his rock-solid commitment to the Anglican Church. Disraeli and Palmerston were accused of many things, but never of undue high-mindedness or priggishness. Gladstone, however, had no fear of 'enthusiasm', in religion or in any other cause he found worth supporting. His pragmatic father wished him to go into public life: but into Parliament, not the Church.

Nevertheless, Gladstone was always interested in politics and public affairs, and among the first and last public acts of his life were contributions to newspapers. As early as 1826, not yet 17, it was recorded that he had 'lately been writing several letters in the *Liverpool Courier*' in defence of his father, a prominent local figure who also served as an MP, who was being attacked for what Morley calls 'sundry economic inconsistencies'.[4] Writing as 'Friend to Fair Dealing', he did so without his father's knowledge and enjoyed his father's speculations as to the identity of his defender. He also defended the 'Liberal Tory' position on the economy and the Corn Laws, supporting William Huskisson and arguing that he was 'as much opposed to the Levellers and visionaries of the one side, as to the Bigots and Monopolists of the other'.[5]

Exactly 70 years later, he would still be writing to the papers: to the *Daily Chronicle* in 1896 on the Armenian massacres, 20 years on from his rousing campaign over the Bulgarian atrocities. Indeed, although he was nearly 87, some saw, even then, a possible return to the Liberal leadership, and Gladstone's article and views were major contributory factors in the resignation of his Liberal successor the Earl of Rosebery. Still later, in January 1898, the year of his death, he wrote recollections of his school friend Arthur Hallam for *The Daily Telegraph*.

The schoolboy Gladstone also threw himself into the *Eton Miscellany* with genuine enthusiasm and interest. He was joint editor and saw himself following in the footsteps not only of Canning and Frere's *Microcosm* of 1786–7, but also of Praed and Moultrie's *Etonian* of 1818: the two most famous previous examples of Etonian school journalism, as practised by future political figures. W.M. Praed had been a precocious literary talent who went on to combine literary, journalistic and political activity before premature death in his 30s. Even the pious Morley, however, regards Gladstone's early editorial venture as some way behind its predecessors in verve and style. He was safe in doing so, as Gladstone himself later wrote in his diary: 'I cannot keep my temper in perusing my own (with few exceptions) execrable productions'.[6]

Canning died in 1827, while Gladstone was at Eton, and was the subject of eulogies from his young follower in prose and verse. Canning had his own parliamentary bond with Liverpool, and John Gladstone was one of his most prominent local supporters and colleagues, so there was a personal element to the contributions; and it is worth remembering that, although Gladstone would be later labelled by Thomas Babington Macaulay as 'the rising hope' of those 'stern and unbending Tories', the Tory tradition from which he started was towards the left of Lord Liverpool's Tory spectrum: not, as is sometimes implied, the beginning of a journey from the Tory Ultra-right to the Liberal left.

After his highly successful Oxford career, it was, however, as a protégé of the decidedly Ultra-Tory Duke of Newcastle that he entered Parliament in 1832 as member for Newark; and it was this patronage (later severed over a divergence of views) which has sometimes coloured views of Gladstone's early Toryism. He was indeed decisively against the first Reform Bill of 1832; and, after attending a reform meeting in Warwick in 1831, was inspired once again to write to a newspaper, this time the *Herald*:

If, sir, the nobility, the gentry, the clergy are to be alarmed, overawed, or smothered by the expression of popular opinion such as this, and if no great statesman be raised up in our hour of need to undeceive this unhappy multitude, now eagerly rushing or heedlessly sauntering along the pathway to revolution, as an ox goeth to the slaughter or a fool to the stocks, what is it but a symptom as infallible as it is appalling, that the day of our greatness and stability is no more and that the chill and damp of death are already creeping over England's glory.[7]

In the following year, 1832, as he awaited the outcome of his first election campaign at Newark, and feeling decidedly uneasy at the subsidized drunkenness associated with getting the vote out, or 'pints for votes' as it might be termed today, he also wrote a series of articles for the *Liverpool Standard*. Despite his own electoral success, the overall picture was of a huge endorsement of the Whigs and reform, and a wholesale rejection of the Tories. Gladstone struck a defiant tone in his articles, but was privately still as pessimistic about the state of the country as he had been the previous year.

Gladstone's joint diary editor and modern biographer H.C.G. Matthew spoke of Gladstone's 'acute and purposeful flair' for press relations; but he, echoing Gladstone himself, attaches this description to the main portion of his political career, from first becoming chancellor in 1852 to final retirement as prime minister in 1894, rather than seeing it as characteristic of Gladstone throughout his political life. Gladstone himself wrote in a letter to J.A. Froude in 1861:

The whole subject of working through the press for the support of the measures of the financial departments is very new to me. I have commonly been too much absorbed in the business of the offices I have held to consider as much as I ought of the modes in which my proceedings…would be commended favourably to the public notice. I will with your permission bear the subject in mind.[8]

At the time, Froude had recently taken over the management of *Fraser's Magazine*, and was effectively offering Gladstone its support. It seems true that Gladstone did not think particularly thoroughly on the subject in his earlier career. There is, of course, a trajectory in political and public careers (as, indeed, with so-called celebrities today) in which the earlier stages may be spent seeking publicity and coverage; whereas the stage is later reached at which one's words and actions are automatically newsworthy, and the shaping of coverage becomes more important than its creation. This was certainly true in Gladstone's case; and his own distinctive role in the opening up of the newspaper business was to make him an additionally attractive subject in any case.

STERN AND UNBENDING?

In his earlier career, while starting to involve himself in 'the higher journalism', the world of the reviews, Gladstone was also involved like Disraeli in writing books, but on vastly different topics. His first two were on the relations between Church and State, and church principles: the first occasioning Macaulay's 'rising hope' tag, already quoted, and provoking dismay as well from the distinctly secular and more conventionally pious figure of Peel, his party leader. Peel simply could not comprehend how an up-and-coming, talented young Tory could wish to involve himself in such subjects, becoming an unnecessary focus of criticism and debate.

Gladstone's early review articles were often book reviews (as, of course, at least ostensibly, were Macaulay's own). From 1843, the year in which he was promoted from vice-president to president of the Board of Trade, he was publishing in the *Foreign and Colonial Quarterly Review* and the *Quarterly Review*, later branching out into the *Edinburgh Review* to write, among other topics, on his own translation of the first two volumes of Farini's *Lo Stato Romano*, an attack on the idea of the papacy retaining temporal as well as spiritual power. The Farini translation itself, and his contribution to the *Edinburgh*, along with a public letter to Lord Aberdeen condemning the King of Naples for excessive zeal and violence in putting down revolt, are often seen as among the early signs of his move towards a more liberal view of politics, and his career as 'the People's William', for which he is primarily remembered.

Gladstone's initial forays into review journalism covered ground similar to the topics of his first two books. Two early examples concern 'Present Aspects of the Church' and 'The Theses of Erastus and the Scottish Church Establishment', both for the *Foreign and Colonial Quarterly Review*. The early books and articles are perhaps tempting grounds for ridicule in a less earnest and more secularized society; but they were written against the backdrop of Gladstone's ongoing attempts to reconcile his wish for a church career with the demands of political life. Gladstone looked for ways to reconcile the two, and worked out these ideas in books and articles. This was all against the background of the Oxford Movement, the attempt to reconnect the somewhat arid Church of England tradition with the best elements of its pre-Reformation roots, and the eventual secession of John Henry Newman and then Henry Edward Manning, one of Gladstone's closest friends, to Catholicism. In using the reviews thus, Gladstone was not really attempting to carve out a media profile for the sake of advancement or fame, though such an accusation would often be levelled at him later in his career; it is at least possible that there was something more personal and sincere going on.

At the same time, Gladstone was showing early signs of using print as a means of advancing more temporal concerns. The former prime minister Lord Goderich, now Earl of Ripon, had been Derby's predecessor as colonial secretary in Grey's government: he was now Gladstone's chief in Peel's. While Ripon was president of the Board of Trade, Gladstone, as vice-president, contributed an anonymous article to the *Foreign and Colonial Quarterly Review* on 'The Course of Commercial Policy at Home and Abroad'. This was to be the first of many occasions on which Gladstone would use his pen in support of his own policy while in office. He followed it up, shortly after his resignation over religious education policy in Ireland in 1845, with a pamphlet called 'Remarks upon Recent Legislation'. While pamphlet publication was part of the discourse of politics, writing anonymously for a review while in office was a relative novelty. However, it would have been viewed at the time as a much less startling development than, let us say, a public disclosure of Palmerston's anonymous newspaper articles or Disraeli's daily involvement with *The Press*. Still less shocking would have been his review of Lord John Russell's poetic 'Translation of the Francesca da Rimini', or of the novel "'Ellen Middleton', in the *English Review*. He also started publishing on classical subjects in 1847, with a *Quarterly* article on Lachmann's Trojan study 'Ilias'. Within a few years, he was also writing for the *Gentlemen's Magazine* and *Fraser's Magazine*.

One is struck, like all students of Gladstone, by the range and scope of his interests, and by his self-belief and confidence in being prepared to express his views on them publicly to a relatively small but informed audience of review readers. Disraeli wrote for fame; Derby and Russell out of interest and intellectual engagement. Gladstone, at this stage, was much nearer to Derby and Russell in this regard, but with the extra layer of earnestness of approach that both Derby and Russell, in their different ways, found rather alien. Gladstone's resignation from Peel's Cabinet, too, had that same air of earnest pedantry about it. He resigned not because he disagreed with the funding of Maynooth College to advance Catholic education in Ireland, but because he had previously disagreed with it, and gone on record as doing so. This struck Peel and almost everyone else in practical politics as absurd. However, when Derby resigned at the end of the same year, 1845, over the much more clear-cut issue of Corn Law repeal, Gladstone came back to replace him for a few months until the end of the government the following year. He was still not a figure of the very front rank, nor yet a politician with an unusually high public profile. However, he was now one of a handful of Peelites who would have a disproportionate influence on the futures of the Tory and Whig parties.

MAN OF IDEAS

The question of anonymity is one that recurs in relation to nineteenth-century prime ministerial forays into journalism. There are clearly differing degrees of anonymity. Queen Victoria herself provides a fascinating example of this with an article she submitted to *The Times* in defence of her self-imposed isolation after the death of Albert. A letter signed 'Anonyma' was sent to the paper in 1864, in reply to an editorial urging her to make herself more visible and accessible to her subjects, defending and explaining the necessity for such a low profile in widowhood. It was hand-delivered to Delane, in the Queen's own handwriting:

> The Queen will ... do what she can – in the manner least trying to her health, strength, and spirits – to meet the loyal wishes of her subjects, to afford that support and countenance to society, and to give that encouragement to trade which is desired of her.
>
> More the Queen CANNOT do; and more the kindness and good feeling of her people will surely not exact from her.[9]

Did the Queen expect people to assume she had written it herself? With the media literacy and media self-obsession of the twenty-first century, we would surely assume so. Through the eyes of a *Times* reader of 1864, it is less certain.

For those 'in the know', like Lord Clarendon, that seasoned and veteran press manipulator, it was 'considered very *infra dig*. for the Queen'.[10] Granville, too – another politician who could not be accused of being an innocent in the world of the press – tried to dissuade her secretary Charles Grey (son of the Prime Minister) from delivering it. Delane had the last word, replying to 'Anonyma' in another editorial later; but the Queen would not be moved. It was 1866 before she opened Parliament in person, and, that same year, visited Wolverhampton to unveil the famous equestrian statue of Prince Albert that still provides a focal point for its centre.

Gladstone, too, encountered the same dilemma. Was he merely nominally anonymous as a reviewer? Lord Aberdeen told Gladstone that his *Quarterly* contributions were anonymous in name only, citing an Aberdeenshire squire who said he knew certain articles were by Gladstone because 'everybody said so'.[11] When Gladstone was opining on contemporary and classical literature, archaeology and even certain aspects of religion, there was little at stake politically. When, however, he was holding forth on foreign or commercial policy, the stakes were higher. We have seen the evasions of Disraeli and Palmerston, and Canning's slightly sulphurous reputation as a press 'meddler'; and it is clear that newspaper writing was still unacceptable as a directly attributable activity. Review contributions, however, afforded the opportunity for elite communication, without the accusation that one was exceeding the boundaries and conventions of mid-nineteenth-century political communication. It was only later, as Gladstone became more radically inclined, that he was prepared to make semi-public and even overt criticisms of the 'clubland' and metropolitan press, and to start making explicit condemnations of the 'classes' as opposed to the 'masses'. (One wonders, incidentally, whether the antithesis also serves as proof that Gladstone pronounced both words with the northern short 'a' for euphonious effect).

PAPERS FOR THE PEOPLE?

The campaign against newspaper taxes and duties, consciously designed to remove the economic obstacles preventing the poorer members of society from being able to afford a newspaper of their choice, though not as well remembered as the campaign against the Corn Laws, was conducted by some of the same people: notably John Bright and Richard Cobden. Although often not given the same prominence in accounts of Gladstone's political journey from right to left as, say, his disgust at repression in Naples and (much later) Bulgaria, it does mark an important part in what one of his modern biographers termed his 'progress in politics';[12] and the repeal measures he introduced as Chancellor remain among his most important achievements in politics.

His consideration of advertisement duties in 1853, ahead of his later reforms, almost inevitably produced a coalition of opposition between the established papers and those politicians who were closest to them. Gladstone's greatest opponent in the coming years would not be Derby or Disraeli, but Palmerston, soon to be his own chief, supported by other Printing House Square allies such as Granville. The other established papers – the *Herald*, the *Post*, the *Morning Advertiser*, the *Chronicle* and the *Daily News* – were as vehement as *The Times* in opposing the early stages of Gladstone's reforms: although they feared that a remission of the advertisement duty on supplements would favour, not damage, *The Times*. Predictions that the national revenue would suffer were countered by the simple argument that, if the advertisement tax were abolished, there would be more advertising, which would ultimately also benefit the Treasury.

For the reformers, the advertisement duty was but the first step. The stamp duty itself would be next on the horizon; and, although it happened shortly after Sir George Cornewall Lewis had taken Gladstone's place at the Exchequer, it, too, was consigned to history the following year, 1855. Bright was able to quote *The Times* against itself, on 'the absurdity of a tax which, as it is a tax on news, is a tax on knowledge, ... a tax on the progress of human affairs, and on the working of human institutions'.[13]

The final part of the trilogy of reforms awaited Gladstone's return to the Exchequer. In his 1860 Budget, which, along with that of 1853, is deemed his greatest, he moved for the removal of the duty on paper, further opening the way towards cheaper newspapers. In moves foreshadowing later constitutional wrangles, the Lords blocked the measure after it was passed by the Commons. Gladstone retaliated by including it as a formal Budget measure in 1861, and it duly passed. The legislative framework that had encompassed the British press for the last century and a half had been removed, and even Gladstone himself said he thought he would not live to see the full consequences of the measures work themselves out. If he had never held office again, and never become prime minister, Gladstone had assured himself a unique place in the history of British politics and the relationship between politicians and the press.

When it came to the repeal of the Paper Duties, Palmerston could hardly have made it clearer that he was at best indifferent, bluntly informing his chancellor that he was on his own and that it would not be turned into a confidence (or survival) issue for the government. Indeed, Palmerston was happy for it to be seen as a battle between a revenue-cutting Chancellor and a prime minister anxious to spend more on defence and foreign interests. As recently as 1858–9, Gladstone had been on a diplomatic mission for the Derby government. Now, he was in *de facto* alliance with the Radicals against his own Whig-Liberal Prime Minister. By then, the newspaper market had already opened up, *The Daily Telegraph* was showing its potential for rapid growth and Gladstone, almost inevitably, was the politician of choice for many journalists and editors in the post-Stamp age. He had been more cautious in allowing any impression of a radical alliance when addressing the Advertisement and Stamp Duty changes during his first period as chancellor. Perhaps, in seeing off the Paper Duties too in 1860–1, he felt the irrevocable nature of the party political decision he had made in 1859 in joining a Liberal government, and was therefore proportionately likelier to follow the logic both of his policies and of his political position further through to their logical conclusion.

By giving the possibility of life to the likes of *The Daily Telegraph*, had Gladstone burned his bridges with *The Times*? Under his Stamp reforms, all papers were subject to a small postage tariff, based on the paper's weight. *The Times* was heavier than its competitors, and the differential was a halfpenny: not, on the face of it, a huge amount. But it was the opening up and levelling out of the market, of course, that was the real change. As long as Palmerston survived, *The Times* would almost certainly retain its strong bond with him; but all was to play for thereafter: both between the parties, and among Liberals and Whigs. In any post-Palmerstonian battle for party leadership, the paper was unlikely, as we have seen, to be overly excited at the short-term prospect of Russell. In the longer term, the paper's links with Clarendon and Granville remained strong, but neither was widely seen as the next Liberal prime minister after Russell; and, so far as one can ever read the mind of a long-dead figure, for neither was the leadership the subject of a fixed and long-held ambition.

Prime Minister

By the time the party leadership and premiership began to seem possible, therefore, Gladstone could reasonably expect, without yet having made a sustained effort to court *The Times*, to be acceptable as the next Liberal chief; and, in time, after its fairly brief period of support for the last Derby government, to acquire the paper's support for the premiership. And so it transpired. In 1868, as Gladstone neared the premiership, he was able to count on a strong press position overall. The established Liberal papers, as well as the relatively new *Telegraph* and *The Times*, were all in his corner. So, what was to be Gladstone's personal approach to press management as party leader and prime minister?

Before reaching the summit, shortly after his first period as chancellor, Gladstone had been approached about a paper called *The Empire*. He was asked to invest fairly heavily in it (it needed £10,000 to continue), in return for which Gladstone would have a paper as much in his camp as *The Press* was in Disraeli's. Gladstone's reply is clear:

> ... I have never at any time thought it compatible with the exigencies and duties of my more immediate sphere of action to contract that kind of responsibility for the conduct of any newspaper wh. is implicitly a pecuniary loan or contribution for its support.[14]

He also implied that, even if he had thought it compatible, other papers (the *Morning Chronicle*?) would have a prior claim on his money:

> ... there are newspapers in existence wh. perhaps would have a prior claim upon me were I to depart from my rule but I feel myself prevented by the strongest reasons from abandoning it.[15]

His moral dividing line was not involvement *per se*, but the financial element of such a relationship. Just before Gladstone became prime minister, a new weekly called *The Chronicle*, founded in 1867, was in trouble. An appeal was made, via Glyn the Chief Whip, to Gladstone. Although no direct proof appears to exist, it seems that Gladstone did not supply or authorize the £1.500 in Stephen Koss: *The Rise and Fall of the Political Press*, Vol. 1., pp. 176–7, requested, and the paper folded less than a year after its birth.[16]

PRESS STRATEGY

Although some may have assumed that Gladstone would be too fastidious to deal personally with individual members of the press, this was not the case. On becoming prime minister in early December 1868, Gladstone adopted a policy with regard to Delane, for example, that differed little in substance from that followed by Palmerston, Derby and Disraeli. He wrote personally to Delane on the day he kissed hands (with the Queen, not Delane, despite Lord Russell's earlier worries!). He instructed him to liaise directly with the chief whip, George Glyn; and later wrote to him with the list of Cabinet appointments. 'You may like CERTAINTY at a time such as this', he wrote in a tone which, coming from a different politician, might almost suggest a faint element of teasing. The next day, *The Times* was able to publish the list (with one exception, in line with its earlier predictions). That very night, Gladstone, Granville and Delane all met at dinner; and Delane was able to record that Gladstone had been 'most attentive' to him.[17]

However, this did not herald press relations of Palmerstonian intimacy, although Gladstone and Delane continued to meet on occasion in Gladstone's Commons room. Most of Gladstone's personal press dealings were initially conducted fairly formally through Glyn; and he was content to let the older press hands, Clarendon and Granville, carry out the more informal contacts as they had done under several previous prime ministers.

The Times had an even more interesting link to the first Gladstone Cabinet in the form of Robert Lowe, who now held office as chancellor of the exchequer. Gladstone and Lowe never enjoyed particularly congenial relations; but, with Lowe on the inside, Delane must have felt as close to the government, if not to the Prime Minister personally, as he had in Palmerston's day. Gladstone seems to have added something of a note of impersonality to prime ministerial press dealings: having come to the pragmatic realization that privileged communications and providing 'information as soon as any is ripe' were necessary; but not, despite the recorded dinner with Granville and Delane, seeking the regular, intimate meetings undertaken by Aberdeen, Palmerston and (on occasion) Disraeli. In this, as in other respects, he may have modelled himself on Peel; his practice was not dissimilar to that of the later Derby; and it certainly lacked the tone of slightly peevish frustration that often crept into Russell's press dealings.

Gladstone, although never expressing it clearly, seems to have felt, rather like Bonar Law, that degrees of intimacy which had been acceptable at other stages of his career were not so now he was at the top. Edward Levy, the *Telegraph* editor, was a reasonably close associate, and Thornton Hunt (son of the essayist Leigh) probably a closer one. There is diary evidence of cooperation between Gladstone and Hunt during the reform endeavours of 1865–7, both in government and opposition; and the *Telegraph* remained firmly in his camp for quite a few years to come. The diaries also show a similarly close liaison with Hunt during Gladstone's difficult Oxford election campaign in the summer of 1865, just before Palmerston's death.[18]

WINNING AND LOSING THE PRESS BATTLE

The battle between Gladstone and Disraeli for people's votes, with big majorities for Gladstone in 1868 and 1880, countered by a similar one for Disraeli in 1874, was to an extent, though not entirely, mirrored by movement in the press. Glyn commented to Gladstone in 1868, during Disraeli's first, short administration:

> I think the 'Post' and the 'D. News' will go quite right. The *Telegraph* I really cannot make out at all but I think it will not dare to break with you. With Delane I have no direct intercourse but I think he will not back Disraeli, and that he feels the end is coming rapidly.[19]

By 1873–4, as public opinion turned against Gladstone, it was inevitable that there would be shifts of allegiance among the press, if only as part of a 'winning side' mentality. But it was more than that. As we have seen, the *Morning Post* moved back to Disraeli because he started to look and sound much more Palmerstonian than Gladstone; and that was enough for Borthwick. For the *Telegraph*, the shift was over a longer timescale, and was not a reaction to the unpopularity of Gladstone's first government. The paper remained in Gladstone's camp in 1874; but started to open the door to Disraeli as a result of Gladstone's withdrawal and retirement.

The Bulgarian crisis of 1876 was a further watershed. Because we are accustomed to viewing Gladstone's career through the prism of his eventual emergence as in many ways a rather radical Liberal leader, the Bulgarian agitation seems like a staging post on the way to Home Rule. But for his contemporaries, it would have appeared much less explicable. It was seen by many in the press as a decisive embrace of radicalism: siding with the Bulgarian underdogs, struggling to be free of the yoke of Ottoman Turkish rule. He would show the same instinct three years later, in embracing the cause of the Afghans. For *The Times*, there was indeed the 'winning side' aspect, as well as the waning of Delane's powers in the 1870s, and the power vacuum before his successor Chenery asserted himself on domestic politics, to account for the paper's switch to Disraeli, and then back again to Gladstone in 1880.

There was a rather plaintive note in the correspondence of Gladstone with Edward Levy (now Levy-Lawson) of the *Telegraph*. When the *Telegraph* supported Disraeli's purchase of the Suez Canal shares, Gladstone wrote: 'I fear you and I are diverging rather widely, but you have probably at least the advantage of having 999 out of every thousand on your side'.[20]

When, some years earlier, the *Telegraph* had bought out and taken over the failing *Morning Chronicle*, Gladstone, still Chancellor, may have been disappointed (he had attempted to bolster its position by non-monetary means in the 1850s, and implied, as we saw, that it would have had first call on his pocket had he felt it right to subsidize a paper), but he must have thought that its readers and its support for him would remain safe in the hands of the *Telegraph*. Now, he could not be so sure. And, after the Bulgarian campaign, he could be in no doubt at all that, while the *Daily News* remained loyal, the *Telegraph*, too, was lost.

TERRIBLE ON THE REBOUND

The Bulgarian agitation first touched Britain as a press phenomenon. The *Daily News* was the first to make a big impact with stories of Turkish atrocities against the Bulgarians whom they had ruled for 500 years, but who still yearned for freedom and Christian rule. It was taken up by W.T. Stead's Darlington *Northern Echo* and C.P. Scott's *Manchester Guardian*. As we have seen, *The Times* was also perturbed by the atrocities, but was never quite in full campaigning mode, with Delane's attempts to find a middle way widely seen as one of the symptoms of his decline in the final days of his editorship. This was the 'breakthrough moment' for Stead, an increasingly influential figure in the following years, leading to his move to London a few years later, where he eventually replaced Gladstone's future biographer and Cabinet colleague John Morley as editor of the *Pall Mall Gazette*.

Once Gladstone had taken up the cry, and issued his famous pamphlet 'The Bulgarian Horrors and the Question of the East', he was fortunate in having the *Daily News* editor Frank Hill as his metropolitan press champion, along with Stead in the provinces, to spearhead what became a new kind of campaign in British politics. Just as Gladstone was to innovate three years later with a very different type of election pre-campaign in Midlothian, in dealing with the Bulgarian question he was able to combine his own rhetorical abilities with those of the press to achieve an impact unlike previous single-issue campaigns. Of course, there had been a very considerable anti-Corn Law campaign in the 1830s and 1840s; but that was in response to a long-standing and much-debated domestic issue rather than to an unforeseen and overseas event, and this marked something of a new turn in how politicians and the press publicized issues and engaged with the public on them.

The same sense of innovation and a turning-point could, perhaps, be traced in Gladstone's own understanding of the press. At this stage, the *Pall Mall Gazette* was not supporting Gladstone and the *Morning Post* was decidedly hostile. Gladstone, in correspondence with Stead, wrote: 'Though I do not think the man of the "Pall Mall" lies for an object, [...] I really cannot but guess that the "Morning Post" is paid'; he meant that they were in the pay or at least under the influence of the Turks, who, he thought, 'perfectly understand the importance of working through the Press'.[21] This was not the first time throughout the nineteenth century when senior political figures (along with Victoria and Albert) felt that elements of the press were being manipulated by foreign powers, usually but not always the French. Whether or not Gladstone was right in this instance is almost irrelevant, since the Turks' case was being articulated in the papers forcefully and effectively by Disraeli's own press supporters, without those papers needing to be directly suborned by the Turks themselves. But there is a sense that Gladstone was thinking more deeply about the potential of the press.

In particular, Gladstone may also have been pondering on the way he could use the provincial press. Although Stead is now primarily remembered as a metropolitan journalist (and is especially strongly associated with London in the historical memory because of his 'Maiden Tribute' campaign against child prostitution), it was in his provincial guise that Gladstone first encountered and collaborated with him. We have already seen Gladstone's keenness to write to and for the local Liverpool papers in the 1820s and 1830s. In 1865, as well as enlisting the national press to assist his own re-election for the Oxford University constituency, he also intervened with the friendly editor of the *Chester Chronicle* to secure favourable coverage for his eldest son Willy, whom he wished to see as MP for Chester. A rival Liberal had to be manoeuvred aside first, and Gladstone did not scruple to enlist the paper's services to that end.[22] Gladstone was in a strong political position locally because of Chester's proximity to the stately home he had acquired the use of through his marriage: Hawarden Castle.

As chancellor, Gladstone had often been on the receiving end of leaks orchestrated by Palmerston. The Prime Minister had intervened with *The Observer* over the issue of parliamentary reform in the early 1860s (in effect, telling the editor to stop praising Gladstone) and had leaked details of Gladstone's budget to Delane in 1865 (to Gladstone's intense vexation).[23] Gladstone had also learned the hard way that it was not practical to write for a review as Prime Minister on a matter as momentous as the Franco-Prussian War without the 'secret' of his authorship becoming public knowledge very quickly. In the the case of his Franco-Prussian War article, the matter was revealed to the *Daily News* very rapidly indeed.[24] What is clear, though, is that, in the years from his second chancellorship to his second premiership, he was broadening both his exposure to, and his involvement with, the press while consciously and unconsciously expanding his understanding of it.

Gladstone's response to the Bulgarian atrocities has on occasion led to him being accused of tardiness and, inevitably, of opportunism. As Richard Shannon points out, Gladstone's first biographer John Morley felt he had to censor Gladstone's later reflections on the campaign and on his own involvement.[25] Gladstone did not rush into the fray of action as soon as the first reports from Bulgaria started to appear in the *Daily News*, penned by the American journalist J.A. McGahan, as the criticisms of his opportunism would suggest; a group of working men reacted strongly and positively to Gladstone's press campaign and it was their protest against the Disraeli government's policy which apparently ignited the fire in Gladstone's mind, providing the bridge from abstract and written indignation to practical action. It was as if he needed to see the effects of the press campaign in a tangible form before it had reality for him, providing the element of realism or pragmatism which made the issue worth pursuing. Morley omitted Gladstone's admission that, on seeing the report of the rally, he realized, sounding rather like Sherlock

Holmes, that 'the game was afoot and the question yet alive.[26] Opportunism it may have been, certainly in a more precise, less morally weighted use of the term. But Gladstone focused attention on the issues in a way no-one else could have done, and thus raised the campaign's profile and impact immeasurably, by means of what we would now call a 'multimedia' campaign, involving pamphlets and articles, but soon escalating to oratory and active public campaigning in large meetings. The cause of the radicals and anti-Turks was also helped by the fact that the Russian Tsar was Alexander II, the relatively liberal-minded emancipator of the serfs, rather than his much more reactionary predecessor or successor.

THE REVOLUTIONARY COMMUNICATOR?

The Midlothian campaign, in which Gladstone toured cities giving speeches of up to five hours in length and largely focusing upon the Bulgarian question and his foreign policy opinions prior to the 1880 general election, helped to propel Gladstone into a further and prolonged political career, which must have seemed almost unimaginable as recently as 1874–5. Gladstone was aware, like other parliamentarians, that the advent of the Press Association in 1868, a joint effort on the part of the papers of the day – in effect a pooling of technical and professional resources – which enabled the telegraphic communication of, for example, parliamentary debates to the provincial press, meant that the regional papers were becoming much more influential on the public and useful to politicians than had previously been the case. Already, editors and politicians were coming to the realization that many readers were not prepared to read column after column of parliamentary speeches, often in very small type. Gladstone himself, especially in opposition, thought hard about how to tailor his political communication both to the potential new technologies, and to a wider proliferation of what we would call media outlets. The pamphlet was still a fruitful medium, as Gladstone had proved during the Bulgarian campaign with the huge sales of his work. Moreover, a pamphlet's release could be coordinated through the press, in what was effectively an early version of a public relations campaign. Even if the pamphlets were not 'serialized' in the modern sense of releasing sections of the work in the daily or weekly papers, the same effect could be produced by pre-releasing information on content and publication dates.[27] And there was a clear willingness on the part of newspapers (and the news agencies) to spread reports of speeches outside the conventional parliamentary format. With a curious symmetry, Gladstone estimated that he had spoken to 87,000 people during the Midlothian campaign, while *The Times* had printed some 85,000 of the words he had spoken.[28]

What was new about Midlothian was not that Gladstone spoke from the platform. This was already commonplace for many front-rank politicians. It was the fact that the campaign was effectively designed as a media event, with specific attention to the deadlines and operational requirements of the journalists covering it and crafted for maximum impact in the morning and evening papers. The outcome of the Midlothian poll itself was not really at issue: Rosebery and other associates were in charge of the logistics of the election; and Gladstone would not have been there in the first place had he been in serious danger of losing. While ostensibly directed at the Midlothian voters, it was in substance the first real effort by a top politician to run a national election campaign through the media. By now, Gladstone was at least as aware as Palmerston of the potential of the press, though his *modus operandi* remained different. He now had his own Press Association reporter, Walter Hepburn, assigned to him and on at least one occasion, echoing Palmerston in his Tiverton hotel room, Gladstone dictated a forthcoming speech to Hepburn on a train. In the event, the train did not stop; the speech could not be delivered to its intended audience; but it appeared on the newswires nonetheless, and Gladstone had his publicity.

The innovativeness and impact of Gladstone's Midlothian campaign is demonstrated by the fact that Max Weber himself, by 1918, was already citing it as heralding 'a Caesarist plebiscitarian element in politics';[29] though, in a way, he missed the point. Weber saw Gladstone as deploying charisma and personal chemistry to achieve supremacy over his audience. In fact, that was a secondary consideration: it was the mediated, less personalized mass contact through newspaper reports that was of more importance to Gladstone in the age before electronic media would make it possible for Hitler and Mussolini to achieve both objectives simultaneously.[30] Some years later, of course, Gladstone's voice was recorded on the phonograph; and although there are reports of recordings of him being played in public, for instance at a fairground stall in Oxfordshire, as well as to public gatherings in the USA, this did not yet represent an exponential leap in the numbers that could be reached (before radio), though clearly it did in terms of the technology of delivery.[31]

There were still other, much more traditional (and to the voters often invisible) forms of electioneering, such as visits to prominent country houses for elite networking and rallying of influential backers. Gladstone did not disdain these methods, but it was his ability to move beyond them, while still employing them, that marks his skill and adaptability as a communicator and campaigner. As we have seen, in 1880, he had the additional difficulty that he was campaigning as the *de facto* Liberal leader, while Granville and Hartington were still in position *de jure*; and he had not only to win the election but also to make himself seem the inevitable man, thus effectively depriving the Queen of her right to choose whom to invite to form the next government.

In the event, of course, he achieved all his objectives: winning Midlothian, winning the general election and supplanting Granville and Hartington to return as Prime Minister. Disraeli was dead within a year, the Tory leadership shared between Salisbury and Northcote, and Gladstone was now clearly the pre-eminent political figure in the land. Already past 70, he combined the premiership with a fourth and final spell as chancellor (the third had been at the tail-end of his first administration), as well as his duties as Leader of the Commons. Not only would he serve as Prime Minister until 1885, he would then return for a brief third term in 1886, then remain Leader of the Opposition for six years, before serving a fourth term from 1892 to 1894.

BACK AS PRIME MINISTER

As Gladstone resumed the premiership in 1880, what did the press landscape look like? The *Daily News* and *Daily Chronicle* were safe for the Liberals, *The Times* back on board for now, the *Telegraph* gone and the *Morning Post* with it. However, there was very good news to follow this second election victory. The *Pall Mall Gazette*, one of the sharpest of the thorns in Gladstone's side in the 1870s and especially since the Bulgarian campaign, was changing hands – and changing sides. The result was a new editorial team which could hardly have been more congenial from Gladstone's perspective: future Gladstone biographer John Morley as editor, and W.T. Stead as his deputy. The *Pall Mall Gazette* became one of the most distinctive Gladstonian voices over the next few years. Its disgruntled former owner, Frederick Greenwood, set up the rival, Tory-supporting *St James Gazette*, which may have carried influence, but did not sell and soon perished. In time, the unlikely but successful team of Morley, the fastidious agnostic, and Stead, the devout man of impulse, broke up, with Stead succeeding to the editor's chair. Much later, as the now octogenarian Gladstone was taking office for the fourth and final time, he granted Henry Norman of what was familiarly known as 'the P.M.G.', a future Liberal MP, what was effectively one of the first ever political interviews:

> Mr Gladstone received me with very great kindness, & said much to me that is of the highest interest and importance....
>
> Mr Gladstone understood distinctly that I asked for his views for publication, & specifically indicated certain things he told me as being... made privately and not to be included in anything I might write.[32]

Clearly, Gladstone understood at least as well as any modern political figure how to mark the boundaries between on and off the record comments. However, before he reached that point, much had happened to change the press picture again. The controversy over the failed rescue and death of General Gordon at Khartoum in 1885 contributed to, though did not directly cause, the fall of Gladstone's second administration; but it certainly aided the process by which his political and press opponents became much more personally vitriolic towards him. It also affected his relations with *The Times*, just as his ally Chenery was replaced as editor by George Earle Buckle, the future biographer of Disraeli. Moreover, it was followed within months by perhaps the single most tumultuous episode of Gladstone's long career, his conversion to Home Rule for Ireland; and by the extraordinary way in which that conversion was communicated to the public.

HOME RULE FOR IRELAND?

Gladstone had grappled with Irish affairs during his first two premierships, addressing a number of important areas he saw as urgently needing reform, not least the Church and the fairer distribution of land among the different sections of the population. But before the end of his second government in 1885, Home Rule for Ireland did not seem to be, as Gladstone himself might have put it, within the sphere of practical politics. Why he came to the decision to introduce it to that sphere during the brief first Salisbury administration of 1885–6 has been much debated. The theories range from an almost visionary perception on Gladstone's part that it was the right thing to do and that it would help Britain in the long term, to a belief that it was an opportunistic, almost cynical, attempt to prolong his own political career and give his party a new 'cry'.

Gladstone himself had ensured that there was rather too much speculation as to his personal future throughout his second term, often speaking of retirement as something that was not far away, or even just round the corner. As he went back into opposition in 1885, he spoke of remaining for the rest of the session, but of reserving his position thereafter. However, with an election looming and the Tory government in a minority, a decision about leadership would soon have to be made. There was additional uncertainty as a result of the third of the major parliamentary reform acts, which Gladstone had passed in 1884, further widening the electorate; and the Liberal 'new men' were pushing for influence over the party and its policies. Joseph Chamberlain, Charles Dilke and their backers were a far cry from the old Whigs like the ageing Granville and the remote Hartington; and Gladstone, as well as being the pre-eminent figure, was also in a sense the only leader capable of holding them all in the same party. In the short term, however, there were signs that Chamberlain would like to keep Ireland on the back burner, push Gladstone into retirement, and tolerate Hartington as leader for a while before attempting to take over the party.[33]

It was against this background that Gladstone's son Herbert left his father in Hawarden and went to London to speak to friendly journalists including Thomas Wemyss Reid, the editor of the *Leeds Mercury*, and Henry Labouchere, the journalist and Radical MP. Indeed, there was something of a network of friendly papers and journalists looking on with some concern at Chamberlain and Dilke's apparent efforts to choke off any Gladstone initiative in Ireland. Papers like the *Liverpool Daily Post*, the *Daily News* and the *Pall Mall Gazette* were issuing warnings to this effect, and ensuring that, among others, C.P. Scott of the *Manchester Guardian* was also kept up to date. Reid, himself a Gladstone biographer in later years, seems to have led the pro-Gladstone efforts, partly in conjunction with Herbert Gladstone.[34] While Herbert was urging Reid to influence the rest of the provincial press in his father's favour, the question remained: what was the specific message on Ireland?

Herbert Gladstone left his own account of the episode, in *After Thirty Years*. There is an entire chapter titled 'The Hawarden Kite', the name given to this endeavour in which Herbert leaked news of Gladstone's conversion to the Home Rule cause to serve as a trial balloon in establishing press and public reaction. He relates how Reid, Labouchere and Edmund Dawson Rogers, founder of the National Press Agency (which supplied material in support of the Liberal cause to 170 papers), urged him that a vacuum of information from the Gladstone camp was the most dangerous policy. Conflicting information was also a danger. Gladstone was briefing Balfour, for the Tories, that he would support them if they undertook a reform policy well short of Home Rule. At the same time, Herbert, himself a convinced Home Ruler, briefed Reid, Labouchere and Rogers on successive days that Home Rule would be the new policy. The briefings occurred on 14–16 December 1885. Herbert's diary entry for 17 December, not surprisingly, reads:

> Fat all in the fire. 'Standard' publishes 'Authentic plan' of Mr. G. and the evening papers and telegraph agencies go wild in the afternoon... So far as I can see the leakage has been considerable... The N. P. A. has sent the whole cat out... Father quite 'compos'.[35]

The entry is interesting for an early sighting of the word 'leakage': not yet established as a regular metaphor for press disclosure, but on its way to being so. Shortly afterwards, in his narrative account, Herbert says his father 'took it all in perfect calmness', and quotes Gladstone's own diary (not yet published) for 17 December as including: 'Telegrams to Press Association, "D. News", and other quarters on the Irish rumours about me'.

On the following day, as well as senior politicians, he also contacted 'Mr. Stead'.[36] Reading Herbert's account, one is struck by the intrusion of new communications technology into the unfolding of this major journalistic event. The contrast with the leaks on the Corn Laws in 1845 and the launch of the Tamworth Manifesto in 1834 are clear. The role of the news agencies and of the telegraph changed the pace of news dissemination dramatically. The ability to reach 170 papers simultaneously transformed political communication. As to the contents, Herbert fell back on the tried and tested trope of claiming he was misquoted, or that his words had at least been 'taken out of context':

> It was a complete distortion of what I had clearly said. But they were young, keen men – like myself then – and could not resist the temptation

to garnish what I said. My great blunder was not in giving the interview, but in not making the condition that I should see what they proposed to publish. It was a lesson I did not forget.[37]

Herbert had, of course, intended the story to run: but he was thrown off course by the extent of the coverage and the reaction, and clearly felt the need to fall back on what would become the standard excuse of his words having been 'taken out of context'. The extra element of confusion was that the story ended up in *The Standard*. The original and sole repository was supposed to have been the *Leeds Mercury*; but many suspected that Reid had shared the scoop with W.H. Mudford, editor of *The Standard*, and some claimed he had also shared it with some of the Scottish papers. This seems odd behaviour for a journalist with what was arguably one of the two or three biggest political scoops of the nineteenth century. Others thought he might simply have been overheard in conversation with Herbert at the National Liberal Club. Whatever the precise channel of information, the idea had been firmly planted in the public domain; and despite Gladstone's initial carefully qualified denials (and no one did careful qualification better than Gladstone), the Kite had served precisely the purpose such kites or trial balloons are meant to do: to plant the idea firmly in the public mind – to bring it within the sphere of practical politics.

THIRD TERM AND BEYOND

By early 1886, as the political class reassembled, and the minority Tory government was duly toppled, Gladstone was able to form his third administration and turn a famous leak into an official part of the new government's legislative programme. However, he did so without many of those who had previously served under him, who found themselves unable to follow him into his final crusade for Irish Home Rule. Hartington would not join the Cabinet; neither would Derby, the former prime minister's son (who had left Disraeli's Tories in disgust some years earlier and joined Gladstone's second government). John Bright, the veteran radical, was opposed. Chamberlain signed up initially, but soon resigned. (Dilke was embroiled in a personal scandal and was thus ineligible in any case). The party was irrevocably split, just as the Tory party had split over the Corn Laws 40 years earlier. The difference, however, was that Gladstone retained enough support to remain as leader of the critical mass of the Liberal Party: it was his opponents who would become Liberal Unionists, eventually becoming almost indistinguishable from the rest of the Conservatives with whom they would first cooperate, then govern and at last merge.

As Magnus, in his *Gladstone*, puts it: 'Unlike Sir Robert Peel, forty years earlier, Gladstone was not left in the position of a general without an army'.[38] He retained such crucial figures as Rosebery, Sir William Harcourt and Lord Spencer, while also holding onto less prominent politicians who would soon rise to greater importance such as Campbell-Bannerman and Henry Fowler: the sort of quiet, moderate-sounding Liberals who could reassure others that what was left was more than a group of Gladstone-worshippers and radical fanatics.

So what measure of press support could Gladstone expect for his new, and surely his last, major political campaign? When Morley left the *Pall Mall Gazette* to enter politics, and eventually the Cabinet, Gladstone must have assumed that Stead, as his editorial replacement, would be at least as congenial and supportive. However, Stead proved much less pliant. As well as campaigning for more help for the poor, he was fiercely anti-jingoistic, and felt that Gladstone, by launching the Egyptian campaign of 1882, was little better than Disraeli. To complicate matters further, Stead was a great admirer of General Gordon, who died in that campaign, thus ensuring difficulties with Gladstone in 1884–5. Moreover, as editor of what he regarded as the most important Liberal journal (the *Daily News* would have disagreed), he expected to be briefed regularly by Gladstone. Gladstone was happy for his private secretaries to keep Stead (and others) abreast of developments, but was not prepared to enter into regular Palmerston- or Aberdeen-esque intimacies. Herbert Gladstone, in rehearsal for his Hawarden Kite exploits, was the emissary sent to mend fences where possible. However, by the time of Gordon's death, Stead was in full cry against Gladstone. After Gordon's death, and Gladstone's parliamentary statement following its announcement, Stead thundered: '[Gladstone's] inability to see the simplest facts, or rather the unexampled ability of explaining them away, was never more strongly demonstrated...'.[39]

By the time Gladstone publicly espoused Home Rule, the passions of Gordon's death had subsided. At about the time the second Gladstone government fell, Stead was in the midst of the 'Maiden Tribute' child prostitution campaign; and when Gladstone was preparing to return to office at the end of 1885 (he did so early in 1886), Stead, still editor of the *Pall Mall Gazette*, was writing to Gladstone pledging cooperation over Home Rule, the now warier Gladstone replied: 'If convenience and conviction shall bring the 'P.M. Gazette' and myself upon the same lines at a critical moment, I am very glad'.[40]

At *The Times*, Chenery's successor Buckle was never likely to be an ardent, radical Gladstonian; but the transition from the 'Left Centre' to the 'Right Centre' was less abrupt than it might have been. There was a degree of personal contact between the young Buckle (who would remain in the post until 1912) and Gladstone, before the end of his second government. They met over dinner in Downing Street in July 1884, and had apparently already met once before. Buckle was also among the early personal callers on Salisbury once he assumed the premiership for the first time in 1885. Salisbury told Buckle: 'You are the first person who has... come to see me in the last few days who is not wanting something at my hands – place, or decoration, or peerage. YOU only want information!'.[41]

Despite Buckle's politeness and social ease, Gladstone would have known that, with Chenery's death and his replacement by the far from radical Buckle, *The Times* would not be numbered among his Home Rule cheerleaders. He must, however, have been rather perturbed to find that, as late as March 1886, several weeks into his third administration, the normally reliable *Daily News* was still talking of reserving its opinion until the full details of Gladstone's Home Rule plan had been unveiled. The influential *Scotsman* jumped ship immediately the legislation was announced in detail, leaving its readers in no doubt of its stand with the words: 'This will never do!'. The *Daily Chronicle* was not, at this stage, a reliable Gladstonian ally. In effect, the Gladstone Liberals' press support, among major national titles, had dwindled by 1886 to the *Daily News* and the *Pall Mall Gazette*. The defeat of the first Home Rule Bill in 1886 was promptly followed by the end of the third Gladstone government. Press support at the subsequent general election was thinner on the ground than in 1885, itself a campaign fought under difficult political conditions. As Gladstone prepared, in his 77th year, for what promised to be a lengthy spell of opposition, his support in the newspaper world was weaker than at any time since he had become party leader almost 20 years before.

NEW PRESS THINKING

As we have seen, Gladstone was in the vanguard of recognizing the potential influence of the expanding provincial press. Indeed, from his repeal of the newspaper duties, he was as much their 'father' as he was the parent of the *Telegraph* and other cheaper national papers.[42] But, just as the *Telegraph* had reluctantly abandoned him after Bulgaria, so now some of his provincial support deserted him after Home Rule. Loyalty was one thing, but for most papers and proprietors, being out of kilter with their own readers was quite another. The regional power bases of politicians also had a major effect. Thus, the Birmingham press was always likelier to stick with local MP Joseph Chamberlain than with Gladstone, and the *Birmingham Daily Post* duly did so when the Liberal split came. Likewise, the *Western Morning News* remained with Hartington. However, several other substantial titles kept the flag of Gladstonian Home Rule flying: the *Northern Weekly Leader* in Newcastle, and papers in Liverpool, Sheffield, Leeds and Bradford, stayed with Gladstone, as something of a North-South press divide threatened to polarize the country.

At the national level, despite the advent of H.W. Massingham as editor, the *Daily Chronicle* remained uncertain until 1890. The *Daily News* was far from being in tune with front-bench Liberal policy, and seemed rather too keen on keeping bridges open to Chamberlain and Lord Randolph Churchill (who had seemed the Tory likeliest to pursue a progressive line on Ireland during Salisbury's brief first government). Frontbenchers like Morley and John Bryce spoke of the *Chronicle* in the same despairing tones used by Derby and his colleagues of the *Herald* and the *Standard* in mid-century: as an officially supportive paper which often seemed to cause them more problems than their avowed opponents. The *Pall Mall Gazette* was in broadly the same position. A few years later, in 1888, *The Star* was founded, and was firmly in Gladstone's camp; and a sister weekly, *The Speaker*, followed in 1889. Others had turned Unionist: *The Spectator*, *The Observer*, *Lloyd's Weekly News* and the *Weekly Dispatch*. Labouchere's *Truth* remained Gladstonian; but with an idiosyncratic tone that made it as irritating on occasion as some of the other nominal supporters. The *Manchester Guardian* under Scott remained a valuable Gladstonian voice.

Gladstone himself was seen by quite a few journalists, including supportive ones, as rather autocratic in his attitude towards newspapers, with little of the easygoing bonhomie of Palmerston, or the sometimes almost obsequious ingratiation of Disraeli. Stead himself wrote:

Gladstone's admiration for the *Telegraph* dates from the time when Lawson used to begin & close every leading article by crying 'Hosanna to the People's William!' That kind of support Mr Gladstone always appreciates. When I did the same in the Bulgarian time, he thought there was no person like me, and said so. Contradiction is a thing which Mr Gladstone does not brook.[43]

Gladstone preferred the note of deference that was particularly likely to come from provincial editors and journalists; and was not a man to regularly spend hours gently cajoling a reluctant editor into acquiescence over brandy and cigars. In fact, he was more likely to be engaged in another form of journalistic activity: writing yet another in the almost lifelong series of offerings to one of the widening range of reviews to which he was always ready to contribute.

Loss and Gain

The most sensational press development of Gladstone's opposition spell, 1886–92, was undoubtedly the series of forged letters purporting to incriminate Gladstone's Irish collaborator Charles Stewart Parnell in terrorist activity. This story will be told in the next chapter as the consequences were arguably greater for Salisbury's government than for Gladstone's Liberals. The relationship between the Tories and Unionists and *The Times* was much closer by the later 1880s, as Buckle settled in, than they were with Gladstone. The Parnell affair ended in the discrediting of the forger Richard Pigott, of *The Times* itself and of the Salisbury government, seen as somehow inculpated in the whole murky business. Gladstone's prospects improved, only then to be dashed by the political fallout from Parnell's personal life.

Meanwhile, even the *Pall Mall Gazette* left Gladstone's camp. Stead was manoeuvred out of the de facto editorship, to be replaced for a while by Edward Cook. Cook's tenure, of less than two years, coincided with the crisis over Parnell's adultery; and when Gladstone finally felt constrained to write to Parnell explaining that by continuing in charge of his party, the Irish leader was jeopardizing Home Rule and rendering his own leadership 'almost a nullity', it was intended to be a *Pall Mall* exclusive. With Stead's departure, Gladstone could rely on Cook; and, although Morley pointed out that Gladstone's letter was too late for the *Pall Mall Gazette* deadlines, Gladstone was able to assume that it would produce a special edition. (In the event, it was too late, and the morning papers got the scoop).[44] However, less than two years later, as Gladstone won the 1892 election (albeit with a small overall majority), Cook found that his proprietor had sold the paper while he was away on holiday, with the eventual result that it switched political allegiance. For some weeks, there was mystery as to the identity of the new owner, and of his political intentions. By November 1892, three months into the fourth Gladstone government, but before the introduction of his second Home Rule Bill, the proprietor was revealed to be W.W. Astor, and the editorial voice now clearly announced its political colours in the ominous words 'we... who are Unionist'.

However, there was good news to compensate for the loss of the *Pall Mall Gazette*. Cook teamed up with the emerging proprietor George Newnes (who had already hired Stead on the *Review of Reviews*) to launch the *Westminster Gazette*, which was destined to become one of the most important Liberal periodicals of the coming decades. In early 1893, the paper was launched, wishing all power to Mr Gladstone's elbow as he embarked upon the final stage of his last great crusade. There were other encouragements for the Grand Old Man, as he was increasingly described by admiring Liberal supporters. The *Daily Chronicle* had returned to the fold in 1890, the *Morning Leader* came into existence in 1892 to balance *The Star* (its evening counterpart); and the *Pall Mall Gazette* was still onside up to the 1892 election, if not for long thereafter. (This was at the time of Gladstone's interview with Henry Norman from the *Pall Mall Gazette* referred to above).

FINAL TERM

Gladstone's fourth government contained a number of ministers with strong connections to the press. John Morley was the obvious example, with his former *Pall Mall Gazette* links; Arnold Morley was part owner of the *Daily News*; Sir William Harcourt was a veteran of many a *Times* leader column. Only Labouchere proved too bitter a pill to be swallowed by Queen Victoria. His attacks on the Royal Family in *Truth* cost him a Cabinet job. This time around, Gladstone was able to get Home Rule through the Commons: a major feat for a man of nearly 84, and marked by a mastery of legislative detail and parliamentary procedure only he could combine to such effect. However, the Lords were never likely to pass the Bill, and duly voted it down. Gladstone's last speech in the Commons in 1894 signalled the coming clashes between the two Houses of Parliament: clashes which, however, even the long-lived Gladstone would not survive to see.

Although the failure of Home Rule marked the end of Gladstone's final major campaign, he did not retire immediately. There was a slightly strange period in late 1893 and early 1894 when the political world waited to see whether the era of Gladstone really was over. There was also intense competition between papers as to who would be first with the story if and when his final retirement was confirmed. In the event, it was the apostate *Pall Mall Gazette* that was first with the news, albeit somewhat speculatively. Just over a month before it happened, the *Pall Mall Gazette* announced that Gladstone, currently resting in Biarritz, had decided to resign. That was at the end of January 1894. In the event, it was early March before he did so; but it was essentially correct. Understandably, prefiguring tensions between the *Daily Mirror* and *The Sun* in the Blair-Campbell era, the loyal *Westminster Gazette* was furious at being scooped. Gladstone's final private secretary Algernon West explained that the news had been given exclusively, but not to the *Pall Mall*, surmising for Cook's benefit that it must have been overheard by 'some servant'. It had actually been offered in advance to *The Times*. This must have been a great comfort to the *Westminster Gazette*!

Gladstone's political career might have been over by March 1894 (he formally retired from the Commons at the 1895 election); but he was still prepared to make the occasional press contribution. On two occasions, Gladstone proved ready to intervene to boost popular publications. As well as his famous 'interview' with the aristocratic correspondent of *Answers*, Gladstone was also prepared, in 1896, to send a message of welcome on the launch of Alfred Harmsworth's *Daily Mail*. Later in the same year, it was the eminent *Daily Chronicle* journalist H.W. Massingham who urged Gladstone to emerge from retirement and denounce Turkish atrocities in Armenia. Almost exactly 20 years after the Bulgarian campaign, Gladstone's successor as Liberal leader, Rosebery, chose to interpret this, together with attacks by the *Daily Chronicle*, as making his leadership untenable and resigned.

All the while, Gladstone continued his scholarly work, and his contributions to the reviews: a translation of Horace, an edition of Bishop Butler and, in the early days of 1898, his final publication – the interview with *The*

Daily Telegraph consisting of reminiscences of Arthur Hallam. Hallam was the close friend of both Gladstone and of Tennyson, before his premature death in the early 1830s. There was something appropriate and symmetrical in the fact that Gladstone's last public, press comment should come in the pages of the newspaper which, although it had long since abandoned his political colours, above all others symbolized the new generation of papers whose birth he had brought about by his reforms of the newspaper duties during the balmy days of his time as the greatest chancellor of the exchequer in British history.

THE VERDICT

There was always something of a paradox about Gladstone's relationship with the press. We in the twenty-first century should not, perhaps, be surprised that the press never created a scandal over his so-called 'rescue work'. His decades of encounters with London prostitutes, in which he endeavoured to turn them from their lives of vice to a more Christian way, were always liable to be misinterpreted and were the subject of gossip in the very highest circles, up to and including the Queen herself, especially after his conversion to Home Rule. However, there was never a serious danger of a mainstream newspaper running a negative story about it: or, indeed, a story of any sort. Gladstone would never have thought of calling in the editors for an off-the-record briefing about it; or even authorizing a friend or private secretary to do so. The press's self-censorship is not as surprising as it might be to a tabloid journalist today. It was both a testament to the political and journalistic mores – one might almost say the morals – of the day, and a tribute to the fact that Gladstone may on occasion have been seen as a political hypocrite by his opponents, but was unlikely to have been widely viewed as such in his personal life. In addition, there was still enough residual respect and deference towards Gladstone the individual, and socially towards the higher members of the ruling class collectively, to render such a disclosure unlikely. Despite one or two attempts at blackmail, his readiness to refer such rare occurrences straight to the police, and the involvement and support of his wife, rendered such attempts unsuccessful.

His engagement with the reviews, the 'higher journalism', was lifelong and intense: but this was undertaken for specific political purposes only relatively rarely, and in the interests of his own political career. The tension between perceptions of Gladstone's high moral purpose and his ability to make pragmatic decisions about how to engage with the newspapers has always made his success as a press manipulator difficult to gauge. We know that, in different ways, Palmerston and Disraeli had no qualms or scruples in this regard: they differed mainly in tactics and in the degree of success they attained. We have traced the evolutions in the thinking of Derby (in one direction, towards engagement) and Aberdeen (in the other, towards a degree of disillusionment). But, as in so many other ways, Gladstone is harder to categorize. Open-minded about new technologies such as the telegraph and even the phonograph, fully alive to the potential of the provincial press, prepared to embrace new methods of campaigning and political communication, he was undoubtedly an innovator in connecting with the public, and with public opinion. A recent Northcliffe biographer has claimed that Gladstone, towards the end of his career, charged £400 for press interviews, including the one conducted with Lord Mountmorres, 'Mr Answers', in 1892 for the young Northcliffe's *Answers* periodical. (The claim is Northcliffe's, and is not substantiated by any of Gladstone's own biographers).[45]

Gladstone showed an early awareness of the power of the visual image, and exercised a measure of control over the sale of photographs of himself, while also realizing the potential of papers such as the *Graphic* and the *Illustrated London News* to impress his distinctive face and appearance on the public at large. His photographic image was just as important as caricature representations of him: and he is perhaps the first prime minister of whom this is genuinely the case. Yet his personal approach to dealings with editors and journalists remained essentially traditional. Personally conservative in many of his views and attributes, he had a breadth of intellect and a curiosity which opened his mind to the possibilities of a new sort of relationship between politicians and their public, in which the national press was important, but no longer the sole channel of mediation. This, along with his many other achievements, helped to make him the most outstanding prime minister of the nineteenth century.

CHAPTER TEN

LORD SALISBURY AND LORD ROSEBERY

LORD SALISBURY WAS prime minister three times: 1885–6, 1886–92 and 1895–1902. He led the Conservatives jointly with Stafford Northcote from 1881 to 1885 and alone from 1885 to 1902. He was the longest-serving Tory leader since Derby, and the longest-serving prime minister since Liverpool. Lord Rosebery, by contrast, was prime minister for little over a year (1894–5), and party leader for only a little over a year more. Salisbury, the descendant of Lord Burghley and his son, ministers of Elizabeth I and James I, talked disparagingly of politics when it suited him, but only gave it up when he was close to death. Rosebery, who in earlier years might have appeared to some (like the Younger Pitt) as a 'heaven-born minister', found the actual experience of holding high office so wearing that he literally lost sleep over it on a regular basis, and was one of the few prime ministers who seemed genuinely keen to relinquish office. Even Goderich, with whom he is sometimes compared, was still fighting to stay in office when George IV dismissed him at the beginning of 1828. Rosebery never quite broke free of the shadow of Gladstone during his time at the top (rather as Eden struggled to break free of the shadow of Churchill, and Major from that of Thatcher).

Salisbury had a relatively short Commons career, Rosebery none at all, and they were thus insulated from some of the daily information-trading that characterized Commons-based career politicians. Yet both showed themselves, in different styles, as pragmatists and realists when it came to dealing with the press. Salisbury, indeed, considered himself a working journalist in the early part of his career, before he had full access to the Cecil money, title and estate. He wrote regularly for reviews rather than newspapers (like Gladstone); but showed a willingness to do what he had to in order to secure press support while in office. Rosebery, too, prided himself at times in his career on the

13. Robert Arthur Talbot Gascoyne-Cecil, 3rd Marquess of Salisbury, by Sir John Everett Millais, 1st Bt, 1883. © National Portrait Gallery, London.

14. Archibald Philip Primrose, 5th Earl of Rosebery, by Elliott & Fry.
© National Portrait Gallery, London.

quality of his press links, and was also one of the organizers of Gladstone's Midlothian campaign.

Although in different parties, there are elements of continuity between the two men's foreign policies; the area for which both are probably most often remembered and cited today. For much of his time as prime minister, Salisbury was also foreign secretary; and Rosebery held the same office under Gladstone, before becoming prime minister himself. Because Rosebery, by the 1890s, was a far from unquestioning follower of the Grand Old Man, some accounts stress these cross-party continuities, with Gladstone as the exception. Also, the brevity of Rosebery's premiership (and, indeed of the entire Gladstone-Rosebery period of office from 1892 to 1895, along with the even shorter third Gladstone government of 1886) has often tempted historians to consider 1885–1902 – or 1885–1905, if Salisbury's nephew and successor Balfour is added in – as a reasonably coherent section of political history.

Salisbury's career as a review-writer essentially came about because he married contrary to his father's choice and was partially 'cut off' for a period of several years. One should not exaggerate. He was not banished from elite circles: he was already an MP and was not formally disinherited. But he was left to shift for himself, as a son who was not initially expected to succeed to the Marquessate. So the writing was done for money, not, as in Gladstone's case, for intellectual exercise and peer respect. His chosen outlets were the *Saturday Review*, the *Quarterly Review* and *Bentley's Quarterly Review*, of which he was co-editor. He may also have been involved with *The Standard* newspaper. Throughout the late 1850s and early 1860s, he reviewed large quantities of material and covered much historical and political ground, though he strayed into many other fields as well. His range was wide within his chosen areas, but never as broad overall as Gladstone's; and, very much unlike Gladstone, when he no longer needed to continue writing regularly for money, he by and large stopped. In this respect, he was much more in the mould of a professional journalist or writer: ironically more like Disraeli (a comparison he would have abhorred) than Gladstone or Derby, the gifted intellectual amateurs. A recent Salisbury biographer predictably and rightly quotes Johnson's dictum about no man but a blockhead writing except for money.[1]

The conventional approach to Salisbury's journalism is to comb it for keys to his political ideology, either for flesh on the bones of his actions in later life, or for evidence of inconsistencies and changes of view. In another respect, he was the exact opposite of what we now generally understand a journalist to be: 'As a tireless propagandist for privilege, who used irony, paradox and epigram rather than any statistics, his writing inverts C.P. Scott's worthy dictum – for Cecil, comment was sacred, facts were free'.[2]

This distantly foreshadows modern critics of twenty-first century journalism, who now routinely accuse the papers and broadcast news outlets of shifting the balance of fact and comment away from Scott's ideal. The issue of anonymity was also important. Whereas Gladstone's much lengthier review career encompassed the writing of anonymous and of attributed articles, Salisbury's were all (at least nominally) anonymous. He believed that signed articles were three times more effective than unsigned ones but was happy to remain technically anonymous, and disliked discussing his career (for such it was between the end of 1856 and his brother's death in 1865, as a result of which he became heir to the title) in view of the relatively lowly social position occupied even by professional practitioners of the 'higher journalism', and its incongruity with status as a member, even a rather marginalized member, of an aristocratic family.

As well as contributing to reviews, Salisbury was able to use the review pages to attempt to influence current policy. He was never a supporter of the moderate reform proposals introduced by Derby and Disraeli in Derby's second government, let alone the much more radical measure carried in his third. Although they eventually worked together, Salisbury never really trusted Disraeli, and even Derby (to whom he was socially similar, but from whom there was a great divergence in personality and temperament) did not secure his unqualified admiration. Indeed, Salisbury, rather like Disraeli, seems to have been one of those political figures who only really found it easy to admire statesmen who were safely dead. His own heroes included Pitt the Younger and Castlereagh; just as Disraeli would wheel out Bolingbroke, Burke and even Shelburne, key elements of the evolving Conservative refashioning of the eighteenth-century legacy, when it suited him. Salisbury liked some aspects of Palmerston, but not the ones commonly admired: not Palmerston the robust exponent of a bullish foreign policy, but Palmerston the immobile opponent of all further parliamentary reform. He respected Gladstone for his intellect and his churchmanship, but cooled very quickly as Gladstone became the most eloquent spokesman for reform in the 1860s. He was also extremely negative on the subject of Abraham Lincoln and the Civil War, more or less openly siding with the Confederates, and referring to

Lincoln as a 'nullity' while at the same time accusing him of wishing to use the Civil War to establish a military dictatorship. 'What did Bomba do that Lincoln has not done?' he rather shrilly asked in one of his contemporary pieces, referring to the Bourbon monarch of Naples and Sicily, the subject of Gladstone's earlier condemnations: a question that even a sympathetic biographer finds rather absurd.[3] He also used the less formal atmosphere of the *Saturday Review* to compose shorter pieces, sometimes decided on at the editorial conferences he attended, to launch quite scathing personal attacks on figures such as Russell and Sir James Graham.[4]

The personal and sometimes rather anti-Semitic tone of his attacks on Disraeli over reform drew a protest even from his own father, a member of Derby's Cabinet. His father woundingly pointed out the contrast between his words in *Bentley's Quarterly Review* and other articles on the one side and his Commons voting record on the other. In an angry letter in reply to his father he wrote:

> It must be remembered that I write for money. Various concurring circumstances have left me with no other means of gaining money.... I must write in the style that is most likely to attract, and therefore to sell.[5]

According to taste, this was either rather shameless or painfully honest: and, of course, he is reminding his father that, had his father fully accepted his choice of wife, he would not be writing at all. The implied contempt for his journalistic activities is reinforced by comments he made about the new sorts of journalism unleashed by Gladstone's Paper Duty reforms. In the Commons, he said that he did not believe it 'could be maintained that a person of any education could learn anything worth knowing from a penny paper'.[6] This sits rather ill with a comment made decades later by the journalist T.H.S. Escott. Escott, possibly to win a wager, made Salisbury confirm, as he was about to become prime minister for the third time in 1895, their former association when Salisbury had 'lingered in the office' of *The Standard* (not a penny paper, of course; but not a review either) 30 years before.[7] This is surprising, although Salisbury, in later life, seems to have coyly confessed that he had 'eke[d] out his means by writing for newspapers'.[8] If Salisbury was reluctant to discuss his review work, how much more embarrassed would he have been to admit to such a connection with the despised newspapers. His daughter, in her biography of her father, recalled that even his review writing was a taboo topic within the family in later years.[9] His most recent academic biographer says:

> There was a persistent rumour that he had also written for the newspapers: the Tory *Standard* in the late 1850s and early 1860s, and the Peelite *Morning Chronicle* before 1855. The evidence that he was more than an occasional contributor, if that, is slight. The assertions to the contrary of T.H.S. Escott many years afterwards are suspect.[10]

Salisbury may have wished to keep his press management as secret as possible; in time, however, his connections with *The Standard*, and with other papers, were to become much more visible.

THE CECIL TOUCH

As Salisbury's career advanced, he was often suspected of having a secret influence over sections of the press, particularly *The Standard*. This was especially pertinent during his time as secretary of state for India and foreign secretary: he served twice as the former; under Derby from 1866 to 1867, before resigning over reform; and again under Disraeli from 1874 to 1878, before two years as foreign secretary up to 1880. During this time, he was often thought to have 'inspired' particular articles; and, as throughout his career, he displayed great ambivalence about the nature of his relationship with the press.

For a man who was rarely short of certainty on most issues, Salisbury oscillated alarmingly on the press: sometimes professing Olympian disregard, at others claiming ignorance of almost everything associated with it; but spending more on newspapers than on books, and at times displaying real energy in seeking to harness more press support for his party's and his own support. The certainty of his past review work, and the suspicion of covert involvement with *The Standard*, always imparted the whiff of sulphur – or at least newsprint – to Salisbury in the eyes of opponents and party rivals alike. When Salisbury faced the biggest internal political challenge of his premiership, from Lord Randolph Churchill, as well as a struggle for the party leadership and premiership, it also turned into something of a contest between two connoisseurs of press manipulation, at least to the extent that Salisbury claimed to be able to predict exactly how Churchill would use the papers against him. He also hastened the process of awarding honours to press barons, but professed disdain and contempt for the process, and indeed for the recipients, in a manner which suggests a rather distasteful wish both to possess his cake and to consume it. The man who professed extreme contempt for the new generation of agency reporters (telling W.T. Stead, of all people, that he had 'never had experience of a more imaginative body of men') nevertheless flouted the conventions of parliamentary debate to such an extent that he would turn his back on the Woolsack in the House of Lords in order to speak directly to the reporters in the Gallery.[11] The same Janus approach was adopted to press developments late in his career. The launch of the *Daily Mail* was privately greeted by the famously disparaging comment about it being 'a paper written by office boys for office boys', notwithstanding the telegram of good wishes sent to Harmsworth.[12] Gladstone also sent good wishes but, unlike Salisbury, he had nothing to gain or lose by this stage; and, even if he had still been in active politics, he would have been unlikely to receive much support from that quarter.

Just as Salisbury is often credited for giving a boost to 'villa Toryism', the growing support for the party in the new suburban areas of many of the larger towns and cities, while wishing to avoid contact with the inhabitants of those villas other than on rare mass occasions or via the ballot box, so he adopted an entirely pragmatic approach to press support and influence, while wishing to be seen to have no contact with or interest in it. The perception, noted earlier, that Gladstone sometimes seemed 'above' press manipulation was not a deliberate pose, though he probably realized that it did him no harm. With Salisbury, it does seem to have been much more consciously adopted. It is very rare to find Gladstone on record, even in private, as speaking with real contempt about the press as a whole, though he certainly railed against the alliance of the Tory metropolitan press and 'clubland' later in his career.

Salisbury, like Disraeli, though probably for different reasons, is easier to detect saying one thing in public and its opposite in private. The proprietors of *The Globe* and the *St James Gazette*, who were given honours by Salisbury, would clearly not have appreciated his private tone; and Lord Glenesk, the former Algernon Borthwick, of the *Morning Post* would have been horrified to discover that Salisbury had apologized to Hartington for his ennoblement, blaming it on Victoria's partiality for him. There was indeed a spate of newspaper honours in the 1890s: from Gladstone and Rosebery as well as from Salisbury. Gladstone rewarded prominent provincial figures from the *Liverpool Daily Post*, the *Dundee Advertiser* and the *Northern Daily Telegraph*; and Rosebery knighted W.H. Russell, four decades after his Crimean War reports. Many of the proprietorial honours were for men who had also served – albeit briefly in some cases – in parliament: they could thus be argued away as being officially awarded for political rather than for journalistic services. Indeed, it is easy for the cynic to assert that often it was precisely the political nature of those journalistic services that was being rewarded.[13]

THE PRESS MANAGER

Salisbury's press management activities started in earnest after the death of Disraeli in 1881, when he and Sir Stafford Northcote were joint leaders of the opposition. Northcote himself, who was eventually to be treated with real ruthlessness by his leadership rival, has suffered in the eyes of history from the ridicule poured on him by another ruthless, but less self-controlled figure; Lord Randolph Churchill. 'The Goat', as Northcote was nicknamed, was in fact a political leader of real substance. He had started out in politics working for Gladstone in his long-ago Tory days, had a distinguished Cabinet career and was himself both interested in, and effective at, using the press. As we have seen, he was active on behalf of his party and of Disraeli around the time of the 1874 election, attempting to bolster support both nationally and regionally.

In some of the internal party manoeuvring necessary to ensure that it was Salisbury, not Northcote, who would be sent for by the Queen when Gladstone's second government fell, Salisbury had an unlikely ally: one of Britain's worst poet laureates, perhaps the very worst; Alfred Austin. He penned the two most notorious lines in nineteenth-century poetry not written by William McGonagall, and was certainly a lamentable literary figure. ('Across the wires the electric message came: / "He is no better, he is much the same"', written about the then Prince of Wales's near-fatal illness of December 1871). He was also a *Standard* journalist with whom Salisbury formed a close working association. Salisbury is believed to have corrected his copy for the paper on occasions, with the knowledge of the editor W.H. Mudford. Northcote himself, like Salisbury, had been a press contributor in an earlier life, writing for the *Quarterly Review* and to *The Times*, as well as *The Globe*, on issues of the day.[14] He was also aware of the importance of the press, describing the 1880 change of ownership of the *Pall Mall Gazette* in his diary as 'the news of the day'[15] and cautioning Parliament against taking on the power of the press over the matter of leaks or 'premature disclosures': '... [G]reat caution is necessary', he warned in 1879, 'in any proceeding that brings the House of Commons (or either House) into direct collision with the press'.[16]

Ultimately, and despite the manoeuvrings of the candidates in the press, the choice as to who should be the next Tory prime minister was the Queen's. Even as late as 1957 ('Wab or Hawold?') and 1963 (Lord Home, soon to be Sir Alec Douglas-Home), Elizabeth II had a real role in the selection of a Tory leader, and thus a prime minister; so it should be no surprise that Victoria was the decisive factor in choosing Salisbury over Northcote in 1885. In the initial period after Disraeli's death, Northcote was probably the favourite; but he was the older man by 12 years, and Salisbury probably looked the likelier to give Gladstone a run for his money (an essential factor for the far from impartial and by now strongly pro-Tory queen).

Insofar as the press had a role, and Salisbury's recent biographer implies that its influence on the decision was the greatest of any party apart from the Queen, it would probably have tipped the balance towards Salisbury.[17] Certainly, Austin and Mudford at *The Standard* were working in that direction; and the early press influence of Randolph Churchill and his so-called 'Fourth Party' would also have been exercised against Northcote, whom they perceived and portrayed as insufficiently aggressive, and still a little in awe of his old boss Gladstone. In the event, the two men collaborated in office for a while. In the first Salisbury government, in an unorthodox arrangement, Salisbury was prime minister and Northcote, ennobled as Lord Iddesleigh, first lord of the Treasury. (The peerage was widely interpreted as a move to ensure he would not be Leader of the Commons). Early in the second ministry, Northcote was initially foreign secretary, before being summarily dispatched by his erstwhile rival, in a move which led directly to his death.

In a sad final irony for the man who had warned Parliament so gravely about the perilous power of the press, Northcote was to learn of his dismissal as foreign secretary by Salisbury from the newspapers.[18] Salisbury had told Alfred Austin of his intentions, Austin had informed Mudford, the editor, and he in turn had done what most self-respecting journalists would have done: printed it. Salisbury's anger that they had ignored his request to keep it secret was either uncharacteristically naive, or simply for show, to assuage the grief of Northcote.[19] At the subsequent meeting with Salisbury, when he was offered the lord presidency, Northcote collapsed and died.

POWER

The overall Tory press position had strengthened considerably by the time Salisbury became leader in 1885; and was to do so further as Gladstone came out for Home Rule. Papers such as *The Daily Telegraph* and the *Morning Post* were now safe for Toryism for the foreseeable future. The rapprochement with *The Times*, following Chenery's death and his replacement by Buckle, was unlikely to be seriously threatened while Gladstone was campaigning for Home Rule. Indeed, it was excessive zeal and credulity in its efforts to discredit Home Rule which led to what its own historians recognized as the most disastrous episode in the history of the paper up to that point: the series on 'Parnellism and Crime'. Moreover, the resignation of Randolph Churchill in late 1886, effectively designed to bring Salisbury down, was also in part played out in the pages of that newspaper.

When Salisbury formed his second administration after the failure of Gladstone's first Home Rule attempt, Lord Randolph Churchill was given the chancellorship of the exchequer, along with the Commons leadership, in which he succeeded Northcote's own replacement Michael Hicks Beach. Within five months, Churchill was threatening to resign over what was ostensibly an argument about Churchill's wish to reduce government – specifically defence – expenditure, but which most have since seen as a fairly naked power play. The story of Churchill's dramatic resignation has been often told, and mention is usually made of the leak to *The Times* and of Salisbury's prediction. It also marked a significant development in the way politics was reported in *The Times* (and, in due course, elsewhere) which has received less attention.

Once Churchill had decided to resign, just before Christmas 1886, following what he saw as an unsatisfactory correspondence with Salisbury, he left an evening theatre performance half way through, telling his wife that he was off to his club. In fact, he went to *The Times* and attempted to persuade Buckle to publish the entire correspondence. This, Buckle refused to do, but he nevertheless published the story the next morning, reported in a tone which clearly indicated the paper's support for the Prime Minister, not the resigning chancellor. The version from the Salisbury camp relates that Salisbury and his wife awoke that morning, 23 December, with Salisbury suggesting: 'Send for *The Times* ... Randolph resigned in the middle of the night and, if I know my man, it will be in *The Times* this morning.'[20]

The novelty in the way the news of the resignation was presented (as a story, not as a leader item) came from the fact that leader articles were beginning to be separated from the actual delivery of news. Under Barnes and Delane, major political stories would be broken within the leader column itself: facts and interpretation converging in one place. Under Buckle, less familiar with the innermost councils of politics, the presentation of news was separated and marked as a contribution from the 'Political Correspondent', and the leader written separately to deliver the paper's interpretation of and verdict on the event. This was an effective way of embodying C.P. Scott's dictum on the separation of fact and comment in a tangible, visual and very literal fashion. Although the phrase 'Political Correspondent' had not been adopted by 1886, it soon came into use, setting the scene for a format and template which still remains in use in print, broadcast and some online media. Whereas major stories such as the assassination of Perceval in 1812, or the Corn Laws exclusive, would previously have been broken in the leaders, now the news was delivered separately packaged and presented; while the leader delivered the first attempt to interpret or 'spin' it in the way the paper wished.[21]

Politically, Salisbury emerged on top. Randolph Churchill was out of the Cabinet aged 37, and would never hold office again. The death of Northcote early in January 1887, following rapidly upon the 'breaking' of Lord Randolph, left Salisbury as the pre-eminent Tory, and he would not face another serious internal leadership challenge before his retirement in 1902. There is evidence of a concerted press campaign that went beyond *The Times* to bolster Salisbury's position. Salisbury was probably behind a letter sent to *The Times* on the day of Churchill's resignation, urging the appointment of George Goschen to succeed him. (Goschen was the Unionist whom Churchill famously 'forgot' when making political calculations as to his own irreplaceability). The *Morning Post* also stayed 'on message', coming out on Christmas Day in Salisbury's support. Churchill, meanwhile, seems to have blamed Salisbury's wife for articles adverse to him which had appeared in

The Standard.[22] However, the next major press development of Salisbury's premiership unquestionably weakened both his political and his moral authority: and it, too, involved *The Times*.

FORGERY

Even the official *History of The Times* does not attempt to rewrite the general view that the affair of 'Parnellism and Crime' did serious damage to the paper's own authority and reputation, as well as to the standing of Salisbury and his government. A series of letters were published in *The Times* in early 1887, purporting to be from Charles Stewart Parnell, founder and leader of the Irish Parliamentary Party and a hugely significant figure in the turbulent arena of Irish politics, to Patrick Egan, a Fenian bomber. The letters – which were forgeries – implicated Parnell in the murders of English officials as well as more general organized criminal activities, and were a blatant attempt not only to discredit Charles Stewart Parnell and the Irish party, but to damage Gladstone and the Home Rule Liberals as well. The letters would be exposed in 1890 as forgeries, with Parnell taking *The Times* to court for libel and receiving £5,000 in damages, as well as a standing ovation – led by Gladstone – on his return to Parliament, but a link between Home Rule and Irish militancy, even terrorism, had been established in the popular consciousness as a result of the affair.

The letters were widely believed at the time. Their publication in *The Times*, coming when it did, does have the hallmarks of what we would call a sophisticated 'spin' operation. Salisbury was only just recovering from the Churchill challenge and the criticism of his treatment of Northcote. Moreover, he had just appointed his nephew Arthur Balfour to the Irish chief secretaryship. On the justified assumption of close collaboration between Salisbury's Tories and Buckle's *Times*, the letters would appear to serve the dual purpose of bolstering both uncle and nephew in their political roles. *The Times* had briefly wavered in 1886, when Gladstone's third government fell, seeming to favour the Unionist Hartington ahead of Salisbury as head of the next administration. Once Salisbury had weathered this minor storm, he seems to have been keen to ensure that there would be no further prevarication on the part of the paper.

Salisbury's real cynicism was arguably more on display in relation to the special commission set up to investigate the whole affair. Confident that the commission could be used as a way of giving the broad impression of Irish wrongdoing and terrorism, it appears that Salisbury did not much mind if the letters turned out to be forgeries, as they did, so long as the overall impression of Parnell and his supporters left more than a trace of negative feeling in the minds of voters in the rest of Britain. Even close supporters were wary of Salisbury's tactics, and his main supporter seems to have been the increasingly violent anti-Home Rule Joseph Chamberlain rather than Balfour.

Salisbury's collusion with *The Times* at this period extended to sending announcements to the paper ahead of similar releases to other papers and the news agencies (the Press Association and the Central News Agency). However, while that might have been within the framework of acceptable conduct for several other prime ministers, it was most unorthodox to share secret service information with the paper, in effect to aid its case at the commission. Still more unorthodox was the decision to allow the paper's solicitor access to the secret files held at Dublin Castle. Many of Salisbury's senior colleagues, including Balfour and also Hartington (not yet in government, but in *de facto* alliance with the Tories), urged him to keep his distance from the commission. He did not do so, and suffered for it politically.

Nevertheless, there was now no serious doubt that *The Times* and Salisbury were in close alliance and he would never be in real danger of losing its support for the rest of his career, even after Gladstone's final departure and the medium-term deferral of Home Rule. Buckle too survived. John Walter III, a stauncher Tory than ever, refused his resignation, despite the fact that the paper had gone into deficit, as a result of the fine imposed by the court for its libel, for the first time in its history.[23]

Meanwhile, Salisbury picked up on the parts of the special commission's report which did give some credence to the broader charge of violence, affecting to believe that the narrow matter of the authenticity of the actual letters was a relatively minor factor in the overall picture. When Parnell's personal life entered the public and political sphere, and his own position became untenable, much of the political gain for Gladstone and the Liberals was reversed. What might have been a large majority for Gladstone in 1892 became a much smaller one, ensuring that a relatively narrow Commons win on Home Rule in 1893 would lack the political momentum needed to overawe or challenge the adverse verdict of the Lords.

Towards the Third Term

As Salisbury consolidated his position as unchallenged Tory leader, he seems to have evolved a fairly consistent press management style. His was not the Palmerston or Disraeli approach, mingling flattery and intimacy as needed. Nor was it the more hands-off approach of Derby and Peel, intervening selectively on major occasions. In some ways, it was closer to Gladstone's *modus operandi*: not appearing to the public as an obvious manipulator (in the way Randolph Churchill and Joseph Chamberlain did); not wishing to spend party funds on starting new publications with no guarantee of success; but maintaining the level of contact necessary to gain his ends, while still contriving to appear rather above it all. Indeed, Salisbury was seen by some as 'the Prime Minister most accessible to the press. He is not prone to give information: but when he does, he gives it freely, & his information can always be relied on'.[24] This was written by Sir Edward Hamilton, Gladstone's private secretary, in 1887. As the 'Parnellism and Crime' controversy and the special commission unfolded, Salisbury, as we have seen, was all too 'prone to give information'.

Even at moments of uncertainty, such as the 'wobble' at *The Times* in favour of a Hartington government, Salisbury knew that he could also rely on other influential papers. Although he was not especially close to Lord Glenesk (whose peerage he begrudged), the *Morning Post* was onside, as was *The Daily Telegraph*; and *The Standard* could always be relied on to take his side in internal Tory matters as well as against the Liberals. The links with Austin and Mudford remained; and they could be used to talk down Hartington and talk up Salisbury in 1886. Austin as leader writer and Mudford as editor might themselves quarrel – as when Austin blamed Mudford for running the story on Northcote's removal from the Foreign Office – but neither fell out with Salisbury. The Prime Minister also leaked his version of the Randolph Churchill resignation to Cook of the *Pall Mall Gazette*, leaving Churchill feeling well and truly outmanoeuvred in the art of press management at which he had previously thought himself to excel.

Paradoxically, if understandably, the overall press picture began to change during Salisbury's third and final period in office, from 1895 to 1902. Gladstone had gone; Home Rule would not return to the agenda in the near future; the Liberals were divided and lost the elections of 1895 and 1900 heavily. The Conservatives were unlikely to lose office in the near future.

The immediate replacement of Gladstone by Rosebery narrowed the political gap between the party leaders considerably; and, even after he in turn had gone, and the party changed direction back towards a more recognizably Gladstonian feel under Harcourt and then Campbell-Bannerman, they did not yet look like a serious alternative government.

Harcourt, and Campbell-Bannerman before his premiership, were technically only Commons leaders; but they were the figures who gave the party its political tone, and the Liberals, in any event, were much less likely to choose another peer as prime minister after the experience of Rosebery. Indeed, Salisbury and Rosebery were the last peer prime ministers. For a period, as we shall see, some of the Tory-supporting papers were seriously tempted by Rosebery. A right-of-centre leader of a left-wing party is often attractive to the Tory press, especially if they look like winners. Palmerston had been the obvious example and, of course, in more recent times, Tony Blair also slipped easily into this mould. However, Rosebery did not endure long enough to reap the rewards, and such a welcoming tone was much less likely to be shown towards Harcourt or Campbell-Bannerman. The consequence of all this was that the acerbic and highly partisan tone of newspaper reporting of politics quietened to an extent after 1895. The Boer War of 1899–1902 was an exception: there was considerable stridency in the reporting of political divisions over that conflict; but for much of the rest of Salisbury's time, the Tory papers were not sufficiently convinced of the prospect of a change of government to wish to be seen as too close to Salisbury's government.

Because Salisbury's post-1895 government was now an official coalition between Conservatives and Liberal Unionists – formalizing what had been the political reality since the Home Rule split of 1886 – the Tory leadership had to take into account the different shades of the Tory and Unionist press. Joseph Chamberlain, a leading Unionist and now one of the most powerful men in the Cabinet, had a control of the regional press to match his control of the political machine in Birmingham and much of the rest of the West Midlands. The Liberal Unionists, still headed by Hartington, now Duke of Devonshire, had their own press support. There were tensions between the respective press factions; but, with the possible exception of the brief Rosebery period, there was never much chance of really major realignment across the party divide.

ROSEBERY

Lord Rosebery seemed from an early age the politician with the best chance of contradicting the motto '*Non palma sine pulvere*' ('there is no palm without dust', or, more idiomatically, 'success never comes without a struggle'). As a peer, he never had to electioneer on his own behalf, to worry about money or to struggle for notice. As T.H.S. Escott observed in 1898, after his premiership and party leadership had ended in failure: 'The one great misfortune which has dogged Rosebery through his life is the absence, at each successive stage, of difficulties at once bracing and chastening'.[25]

He is one of those figures in British political history to whom it has always seemed tempting to apply the famous verdict on the Emperor Galba, '*Capax imperii nisi imperasset*' ('He would have seemed an excellent ruler had he never succeeded to the throne'). Unlike others to whom it has been applied more recently, such as Neville Chamberlain, Anthony Eden and sometimes Gordon Brown, Rosebery did not have a particularly long official or Cabinet career behind him when he succeeded as prime minister. Neville Chamberlain was chancellor twice, the second time for nearly six years, and a considerable health secretary. Eden was foreign secretary three times, for a total of just over ten years, and was one of the most important and successful holders of the office in the twentieth century. Gordon Brown's ten years as chancellor are still controversial; but there were many occasions before the economic crisis on which he was variously described as the greatest chancellor since Lloyd George or even Gladstone without irony. Rosebery, by contrast, held the Foreign Office for two brief periods, along with a short spell as lord privy seal, along with the Office of Works. So his reputation for being '*capax imperii*' was based more on impression and persona than on substantive achievement.

Because his premiership was over by the age of 48, and his party leadership ended before he reached 50, Rosebery had one of the longest post-summit careers of all prime ministers. In that long 'retirement', he eventually came to acquire something of a reputation as a press manipulator. In the difficult years from 1896 to 1905, as the Liberals fragmented into what can broadly be termed imperial enthusiasts and imperial sceptics, Rosebery was still seen (and probably still saw himself) as potentially returning to the party's leadership; and, as a sometimes more than titular leader of the imperialist camp, had a significant press constituency. But what of the earlier part of his career?

The journalist and early newspaper historian H.R. Fox Bourne believed that, in 1873, the 26-year-old Rosebery had become the secret proprietor of the ailing *Examiner*. The paper had a great heritage, but a distinctly limited future: it closed ingloriously in 1880. Whether or not Rosebery was involved – and there is no evidence that he was – it certainly betokens an early perception in the journalistic community that here was a wealthy young peer with his eye on a political career who might be prepared to spend money on acquiring a paper or a journal to that end.[26]

Some years later, after his brief service in office at the end of Gladstone's second ministry, and some years after helping to stage-manage the Midlothian campaign, Rosebery was certainly involved in discussions about the future of the *Daily News*. From motives which are not entirely clear, Rosebery seems to have entered a phase where he enjoyed backstairs intrigue and gossip, both political and journalistic, without having to put himself out unduly to acquire it. He was able to rely on the likes of Labouchere to do the 'newsgathering', while he processed it; deciding what to pass on to Gladstone, and what to keep to himself.

Rosebery is also thought to have been Buckle's closest confidant in his early days as *Times* editor. The official *History of The Times* has nothing to say on this. Indeed, the third volume, dealing with Buckle's time as editor, takes an entirely different approach from its two predecessors, almost entirely avoiding the close analysis of the interaction between politicians and journalists which was such a distinctive feature of the preceding volumes. (The *History*, of course, is the work of multiple, and ostensibly anonymous, authors).

Early in his political career, Rosebery also took particular care to keep on good terms with *The Scotsman*, supplying it with inside and privileged information during the expiring days of the second Gladstone government. Rosebery regarded Scotland as his political base, especially early on: though he turned down Gladstone's offer of the Scotland portfolio, perhaps not wishing to be pigeonholed. In a similar way, his great rival Harcourt was keen not to be associated only with legal roles in government, serving instead as home secretary and chancellor under Gladstone and Rosebery. Charles Cooper of *The Scotsman* strongly urged Rosebery not to remain with Gladstone over Home Rule in 1886, as the paper itself prepared to abandon the Liberals.[27]

Rosebery did not follow Gladstone and Salisbury into prolific and regular writing and reviewing. He was, however, an effective author with biographies of Pitt the Younger and Randolph Churchill to his name, as well as studies of the early years of Pitt the Elder and the last years of Napoleon, and collections of 'Appreciations and Addresses' and 'Miscellanies' on literary and historical topics. (Balfour and Asquith followed the latter trend with similar collections). Typically, however, he played no role in the production of the first of these collections, claiming never even to have read it; and gave only limited help to John Buchan in collating and editing the second.[28]

His other great hobby was racing. The most prominent racing prime minister of the century had been Lord Derby who, ironically, never won his namesake race. Rosebery did win it, in 1894, as prime minister. Even here, though, the *Nineteenth Century* contributor St Loe Strachey found something a little odd:

> The Newmarket Lord Rosebery is an artificial creation. Lord Rosebery, it is whispered by those who know both him and the Turf, has none of the genuine love for racing that distinguished the great Earl of Derby... Lord Rosebery... wanted to create racing and horsey atmosphere round himself and so to obtain that mixture of the sportsman and the politician which has always been so warmly appreciated by the English people.[29]

One is inevitably reminded of more recent press comment and debate over the genuineness of Tony Blair's oft-proclaimed passion for and knowledge of football, repeated occasionally in the case of David Cameron. (Such charges were seldom if ever levelled against Harold Wilson, John Major or Gordon Brown. They were all often attacked on other grounds, but not over the genuineness of their sporting enthusiasm and knowledge).

THE PALM WITHOUT THE DUST?

By siding, albeit slightly reluctantly, with Gladstone over Home Rule, Rosebery certainly increased his chances of the premiership; and ensured a distinctive position for himself within Liberalism in the eyes of the Tory press as the most politically attractive figure in a party which it had otherwise written off. The politics of Rosebery's ascent to the premiership were relatively straightforward, but very acrimonious. By the time Gladstone's retirement neared, the potential candidates for the succession were Rosebery the foreign secretary and Harcourt the chancellor. Gladstone himself let it be known later that he would have favoured Lord Spencer, the first lord of the admiralty. Spencer, as Lords leader, was at least nominally a contender for the premiership as the Liberals approached their return to power in 1905, while Campbell-Bannerman led the Commons. (In the event, his health was too poor for him to be seriously considered by Edward VII when Balfour resigned). However, as a final mark of her dislike, Victoria did not seek Gladstone's advice either formally or informally. Of course, by 1894, those who Gladstone had formerly anticipated succeeding him were out of the picture. Granville had died in 1891, and Hartington was preparing to formalize the Unionists' alliance with the Tories by taking office in the next Salisbury Cabinet, along with Joseph Chamberlain, whom Gladstone had never envisaged as his successor, but who had certainly seen himself in that light.

Harcourt was 20 years Rosebery's senior, and had much more Cabinet experience. He also knew at least as much about the ways of the press as his younger rival. He had been a leader-writer from his youth, submitting articles to the *Morning Chronicle* while still a Cambridge undergraduate and joining as a leader-writer in 1849, when not yet 22. When the paper's editor, J.D. Cook, left to found the *Saturday Review*, Harcourt (who was also reading for the Bar) went with him, and was joined by occasional contributors including his future opponent Salisbury (at that time Lord Robert Cecil) and future Cabinet colleague John Morley. As 'Historicus', Harcourt went on to write regularly for *The Times*. Indeed, as Harcourt started on his political and ministerial careers, he was sometimes seen, like Lowe, as one of Delane's 'representatives' in government, although this does not do justice to his independence of mind and trenchancy of views. Indeed, it was his freedom in expressing his forceful views towards, and opinions of, just about everyone, not excluding Gladstone himself, which almost certainly did for his prime ministerial aspirations.

Rosebery was further removed from the views of many of the senior members of Gladstone's final Cabinet (Fowler and the young Asquith were exceptions); but, for all his enigmatic qualities and seeming ambivalence about political life, he probably looked a better bet as someone to serve under than Harcourt, who not only did not suffer fools gladly, but often seemed to find even intelligent men equally irritating. Koss's view is that Rosebery's support came primarily from the Court and the press, while Harcourt's position was much stronger in the parliamentary party.[30]

There is no question that Rosebery was one of the few senior Liberals to evoke any enthusiasm from the Queen – presumably on the grounds that he was the most like a Tory, especially – but not only – on foreign policy. The Tory papers preferred Rosebery for similar reasons; and even elements of the Liberal press will have remembered comments such as Harcourt's jibe that the Liberals and Gladstone had done well to win a majority of 40 in 1892 'in spite of the opposition of *The Times* and the support of the *Daily News*'.[31] (Ironically, when the time came, Harcourt's official biography was written by A.G. Gardiner, the great *Daily News* journalist. Like most contemporary tombstone biographies written by journalists, it surprises us by its comparative reticence on Harcourt's press activities).[32] Much of the parliamentary party would certainly have preferred Harcourt because he was politically more in tune with their views, and because Rosebery had never been in the Commons and seemed more than usually aloof from and mysterious to many of them.

When Salisbury became prime minister in 1885, Northcote (about to become Lord Iddesleigh) had hoped for something like a co-premiership: something never remotely likely with a man as quietly ruthless as Salisbury. Harcourt, too, hoped for something similar with Rosebery, once the decision had been taken: but, again, it was impracticable, not so much because Rosebery was equally ruthless but because of Harcourt's undisguised contempt for the younger man. Rosebery had served under Harcourt from 1881 to 1883. Harcourt was home secretary and Rosebery his under-secretary for an uneasy period of nearly two years: they cooperated reasonably effectively, but Rosebery's resignation in early 1883 certainly complicated matters further, although there was no direct falling out.[33] When Rosebery secured the premiership, his relationship with Harcourt, without whose cooperation as chancellor and Commons leader he could barely function, became worse than between almost any comparable pairing. Tony Blair and Gordon Brown, Harold Wilson and George Brown, Asquith and Lloyd George were models of harmonious collaboration in comparison.

In addition, it became clear that Rosebery was temperamentally ill-equipped to be prime minister at all, suffering from insomnia and looking unhealthy for much of his brief 15-month spell in office. He was the first prime minister since Goderich who was clearly personally unsuited to the role of chief minister. The Liberal newspapers, too, were caught up in the crossfire of a party fragmenting after the departure of Gladstone. There were machinations at the *Daily Chronicle* to turn it against the Harcourt-Morley wing of the Cabinet towards Rosebery. Harcourt's view of the paper was even more disdainful than of the *Daily News*. 'My dear chap', he remonstrated with Morley, who wished it was more supportive:

> you would surely not rather have the *Daily Chronicle* on your side. Why, bless my soul, our party has had more harm done it through the *Daily Chronicle* than anything else.[34]

Debacle

Rosebery's task was made no easier by Buckle of *The Times*. Buckle believed that Rosebery was an acceptable alternative to an unbroken series of Tory governments (much less likely to occur after the Reform Acts of 1832, 1867 and 1884). However, he was opposed to Rosebery taking office in 1894, at the tail end of Gladstone's administration. He thought that Rosebery and the Liberals needed another period of opposition to refresh themselves and to lessen the policy gap between the parties. For this reason, Buckle dedicated himself to dislodging the Rosebery government, allegedly in its own interest. A mere three months into Rosebery's administration, when Buckle was told that Rosebery was upset by his decision to act upon this notion, Buckle replied:

> I told Rosebery when he took office that I should do my best to overthrow his Government... He ought really to be pleased, for in spite of all attacks he has lasted longer than most people, myself included, expected.[35]

Nothing better illustrates the low expectations of Rosebery's premiership: low expectations which, with the exception of its slightly longer-than-predicted lifespan, were amply fulfilled. At a time when most new prime ministers, even in the 24-hour news cycle of the twenty-first century, are still basking in their political honeymoons, it was regarded as remarkable that Rosebery was still there! Liberal journalists like Cook and Massingham were also expressing their disappointment and discontent. On the surface, relations with the *Daily News* should have been close. Two of its leader-writers, Justin McCarthy and Herbert Paul (both also Gladstone biographers), were Liberal MPs, and one of the proprietors, Arnold Morley, a Cabinet minister. However, relations remained poor. Harcourt himself gave the sharpest insight into how senior ministers saw their situation when he described the government as hanging on by its eyelids.

The *Daily Chronicle*, meanwhile, after an internal coup engineered by Massingham and Henry Norman (another future Liberal MP), had been converted into a Roseberyite (rather than a Gladstonian) paper; but remorse soon set in, as Rosebery's star quickly dimmed. There was no solid base of press support for Rosebery's administration primarily, because the ministry itself was built on sand. Badly divided parties can be prolonged in office by skilful and dexterous tactical leadership of the sort displayed by Harold Macmillan (after Suez), Harold Wilson and John Major, not to mention Lord Liverpool; even Balfour had some success on the merely chronological level: but Rosebery lacked those particular strengths, and possibly even the will.

He had been an effective behind-the-scenes press manipulator on his way up; and was to be so again during his lengthy period as an ambivalent Liberal 'king over the water'. But as prime minister, and in the following 16 months as Leader of the Opposition, he showed little of the skill or interest required to succeed. Rosebery's disengagement was evidenced when, in 1896, by now in opposition, he asked the *Daily News* to focus on the Armenian atrocities, only to be told that the paper had been writing about little else for months! Rosebery was also an ineffective bystander when major changes occurred at both the *Daily News* and the *Westminster Gazette* in 1895–6. By the time Cook moved to the *Daily News*, his pro-Rosebery views were a real hindrance to his standing with the rest of the editorial staff. John Robinson, the long-serving *Daily News* journalist and memoirist, thought that Cook's appointment was part of an organized (if rather belated) plot to mould the Liberal press into a faithful echo of what was intended to be a long-term transformation of the party in the same direction.[36]

THE 'NEW JOURNALISM' AND THE NEW PRESS MANAGEMENT?

Among the other potential rewards available to party leaders by the later 1890s was the support of the future press baron Alfred Harmsworth and his growing stable of titles. With a very different perspective from Buckle's, Harmsworth, later Lord Northcliffe, was also attracted to Rosebery; and, had he lasted longer in the Liberal leadership, there would have been real scope for an overlap between the two men's views, for all that Rosebery was a long way from possessing Harmsworth's mastery of populism. Salisbury also lacked it; but the imperialist, even jingoistic, bent of large sections of late Victorian opinion could take many forms.

However, by the time there was a real chance of a Harmsworth-Rosebery alliance, the latter's career at the top was over. It was Rosebery's silence over the Armenian massacres by the Turks, with all their rich and tragic echoes of the Bulgarian atrocities of 20 years earlier, which ended Rosebery's leadership. His silence, and refusal to condemn, was a policy which not even normally close allies like Asquith could support. Just as Tony Blair's refusal to condemn the 2006 Israeli incursion into Lebanon marked the moment when many Labour MPs decided he had to step down as prime minister, so Rosebery's similar silence spelled the end for his party leadership. When Gladstone joined his voice with the likes of Asquith, the pressure mounted. But it was a carefully restrained speech by Harcourt, and the spin put on it by the *Daily Chronicle*, which triggered Rosebery's resignation announcement in October 1896. The *Daily Chronicle*, and Massingham in particular, had been among Rosebery's loudest cheerleaders only a year or two previously. Now, the paper was effectively orchestrating a manoeuvre with Harcourt, and with his influential son Lewis ('Lou-Lou'), to secure a public utterance which could be used to make Rosebery's position untenable.[37]

Rosebery had written privately to several close colleagues, including Asquith, to forewarn them of his decision to resign. Asquith, indeed, was on his way to see Rosebery to dissuade him when he was handed a copy of *The Scotsman* which made the announcement public. Other papers had the story too, almost certainly directly from Rosebery himself, but both Rosebery and Asquith were in Scotland at the time and saw the local papers first. By the time Asquith arrived at Rosebery's home, Dalmeny, among the other guests was Harmsworth, who had come to interview Rosebery: not about his resignation, but about a major pre-planned speech he was due to give the next day. With true journalistic luck, he was able to supply the *Daily Mail* with an exclusive interview and a profile.[38] The speech went ahead; but Rosebery's leadership did not. Harcourt succeeded as the pre-eminent figure, but not as titular overall leader: this he shared with Lord Kimberley, though he would almost certainly have gained the premiership if Salisbury had fallen, just as Campbell-Bannerman would have taken precedence over Lord Spencer in 1905 even before his illness.

THE VERDICT

With Rosebery's departure went the last chance of a major realignment of press support in the 1890s. Salisbury, already 16 months into his third and final premiership, could relax in the knowledge that neither Harcourt nor Campbell-Bannerman was attractive enough to Tory papers and proprietors to cause him serious worry; and, even if Kimberley and Spencer might have presented slightly more tempting figures, they did not have the dynamism or charisma that Rosebery had appeared to offer as an acceptable alternative to Salisbury. There were the sorts of press rows that assail any government, which could have spelled real danger for a weaker administration; plus, of course, the Boer War. But press coverage of the Boer War was predominantly pro-war, and posed far more difficulties for the divided Liberals than for the essentially united Tories and Liberal Unionists. Such press rivalries as there were in the later Salisbury era were often between the Chamberlain and Devonshire wings of the Tory-Unionist coalition family. Salisbury, for all his ruthlessness with colleagues, adopted a less personalized approach to the premiership than his immediate predecessors and, until he was pressured by colleagues to relinquish it in 1900, always spoke of the Foreign Office as if it were more important and more central to his preoccupations than the premiership itself.

Salisbury was also a wartime prime minister who was not personally identified with 'his' war to the extent that the truly great war leaders like the Elder Pitt, Lloyd George and Churchill were. Even some second-tier wartime premiers like Palmerston and Liverpool were more inextricably associated with 'their' conflicts than Salisbury. This was because the principal figure in the public's mind, as in the press's view, was Joseph Chamberlain, at that time secretary of state for the colonies. The more bellicose papers, disappointed with Salisbury's inability to 'speak for England' and to articulate robust war aims, even toyed with a press campaign to hasten Salisbury into an earlier retirement in favour of a Rosebery-Chamberlain coalition, seeking a more urgent approach to the Boer War.

However, the virtual rerun of the 1895 election result in the 'khaki' election of 1900 gave Salisbury the breathing space to prolong his premiership to the end of the war and secure the succession, not for a Chamberlain-Rosebery alliance, but for his nephew Arthur Balfour. New Tory titles like the *Sunday People*, firmly espousing the popular Toryism of the era of the Golden and Diamond Jubilees, came to seem like a symbol of Tory hegemony, although its tone was about as far removed from Salisbury's as could be imagined.[39]

With Victoria gone, Edward VII firmly established and the Boer War over, Salisbury could pick his moment and retire before he needed to be too obviously pushed. He had somehow contrived, like Gladstone, to be an effective user of the press without being seen as the type of politician who was likely to 'descend' to such tactics. Whereas Gladstone could be generally seen as 'above' that sort of thing, and more interested in higher morality, Salisbury traded off his aristocratic and personally eccentric 'absent-minded' style, and thus appeared to have his thoughts fixed resolutely on the higher realities of international strategy and diplomacy. His passing, and the arrival of the twentieth century, ushered in an era in which political press management would slowly move from the shadows into the harsher light of public exposure.

CONCLUSION

AFTER SALISBURY, THERE was no sudden leap into a new culture of press management. As discussed in chapter one, some historians speak of the 'long' nineteenth century, running from about 1780 to 1914. For press management purposes, perhaps a clearer demarcation point occurred in 1916: not only because of the transition from the relatively uninterested Asquith to the fascinated Lloyd George, but also due to a prime ministerial defenestration in which the role of the press itself took centre stage.

Political management of the press was framed by the big strategic decisions taken in the late seventeenth and eighteenth centuries to avoid a regime of outright censorship, favouring instead a multi-layered licensing regime. The era when 'a hundred flowers' bloomed and the press was unlicensed (1695–1712) gave politicians the chance to see what a free-for-all press climate would look like. Most were unimpressed. From Marlborough and Queen Anne downwards, the polemical press were a subject of dislike and mistrust. For at least one authority, it was Harley's great claim on the gratitude of posterity that he followed the licensing route with the Stamp Act rather than outright censorship. The same historian also credits his great adversary Walpole for sustaining this 'settlement'.[1]

While a study of public statements on the subject of the press is no guide to real attitudes (since a pose of contemptuous indifference remained *de rigueur* for a long time to come), it is clear that some prime ministers found this area of activity more attractive and interesting than others. Palmerston's interest was lifelong and genuine. Disraeli's was more varied. While Palmerston was always the practising politician enhancing his position, Disraeli had phases where press work was at or near the centre of his life. Some later prime ministers were interested and involved earlier in their careers, but less so while in office (Peel, and perhaps Aberdeen). Others, notably Derby and Wellington, publicly repented of their earlier indifference, and mastered the skills required when career-defining reforms were at stake (Catholic Emancipation with the Iron Duke, and Reform with Lord Derby). Still others worked at it without enthusiasm, but with application and professionalism where necessary – Liverpool pre-eminently springs to mind.

Prime ministers who were uneasy about their social origins perhaps took more pains to be seen as distant from the press: Canning, Peel and (occasionally) Disraeli are the obvious examples. Those on the highest levels of the social sphere, like Derby and Palmerston, on the other hand, could afford to 'condescend' to deal with the press without it affecting the way they were perceived.

Few prime ministers came to office with an overall and predetermined press policy: even Palmerston probably planned merely to follow the successfully improvisatory policy he had already followed in his long Cabinet career. Clearly, however, as *The Times* grew in dominance, most had at least an outline plan for keeping it onside, or winning it back. We have seen how much of a priority this was even for Derby, traditionally (if not entirely correctly) seen as indifferent to the press. His approaches to Delane in 1866–7 certainly did no harm to, and probably helped, the prospects of securing the Second Reform Act of 1867. Peel, too, was sophisticated in his approach to this vital task as he sought the premiership for the first time in 1834. On the rare occasions, however, when a detailed strategic approach to press management was entrusted to paper (as in the time of Perceval, and later by Croker), they remained largely unrealized blueprints.

Ironically, the moments in relations between press and government which traditionally attracted most historical attention – the wartime and postwar clampdowns under the Younger Pitt and Liverpool – had relatively little disruptive effect on the way more conventional press relations were practised. In essence, measures were aimed at what were seen as 'underground' attempts to circumvent the licensing regime, itself designed primarily to keep the papers out of the hands of the poorer, disenfranchised members of society. In that sense, they were not an attempt to replace the overall settlement, but rather to prevent its infringement. Their notoriety comes more, perhaps, from the other, non-press-related measures which they accompanied.

What finally ended that settlement was not repressive legislation, but the decision by Gladstone, as chancellor, to risk the wrath and all-but public opposition of his boss Palmerston to end the licensing regime: the Stamp

Act, the Paper Duties and the Advertisement Tax, in the later 1850s and early 1860s. This meant that, while the fundamentals of press management remained unaltered, there would be more papers with favours to be won, and more readers, in tandem with the expansion of the voting population between 1832 and 1884. Technology, too, ensured that a thriving regional press, with more editorial focus and potency than its somewhat pallid predecessors, was also available for wooing. Photographic images played their part in enhancing readers' and voters' familiarity with the appearances (and, perhaps, the characters) of their leaders. By the end of the nineteenth century, the development of phonograph technology (and its use by Gladstone) began to herald a world in which political communication would move beyond a voter's personal presence at a meeting or exclusive dependence on the power of printed text alone. From the early nineteenth century, in which newspaper circulations in the high hundreds were respectable, and in the low thousands excellent, to the end of the century, as the most successful papers headed for the million mark, their influence on public opinion increased as well, if not to quite the same extent. In 1800, public meetings as we know them barely existed (except in the rather disorganized milieu of an election campaign); and parliamentary reporting itself remained unsanctioned and necessarily inaccurate. By 1900, newspapers not only conveyed politicians' words but also their photographic images to the voters, whose own numbers, of course, had steadily increased throughout the century.

Amid all these changes, however, the deniability of press dealings remained. It was still largely taboo as a topic for public discourse; it was largely absent from near-contemporaneous biographical accounts of senior statesmen; and the nature of social stratification ensured that contacts had to remain largely private, even at proprietor and editor level. While the Gladstone reforms of the mid-nineteenth century initiated change in this area too, as the role of the press inched its way into the mainstream discourse of nineteenth-century politics, and a marginally greater degree of transparency in its workings became more prevalent, Gladstone was right to predict that the effects of his reforms would not have worked their way through within his (long) lifetime. The balance of real power moved more quickly than the more gradual earning of social 'respectability', marked most visibly by the acquisition of knighthoods and then peerages by a handful of powerful proprietors. Even those that did receive awards and honours tended to be offered them, at least ostensibly, on the basis of other public service, not of services to the newspaper industry. However, not many years remained before a new prime minister, David Lloyd George, would seek an urgent meeting with press baron Alfred Harmsworth (now himself ennobled as Lord Northcliffe), only to be rebuffed by a message that His Lordship did not see any useful purpose in such a meeting at this time. Not only was the power shifting, but the age of the press conference, the radio and open political struggles between politicians and press barons was beckoning.

LIST OF PRIME MINISTERS 1721 TO 1902

Robert Walpole 1721–42

Lord Wilmington 1742–3

Henry Pelham 1743–54

Duke of Newcastle 1754–6

Duke of Devonshire 1756–7

Duke of Newcastle 1757–62

Lord Bute 1762–3

George Grenville (father of Lord Grenville, see below) 1763–5

Lord Rockingham 1765–6

William Pitt the Elder, Lord Chatham (father of William Pitt the Younger, see below) 1766–8

Duke of Grafton 1768–70

Lord North 1770–82

Lord Rockingham 1782

Lord Shelburne 1782–3

Duke of Portland 1783

William Pitt the Younger 1783–1801

Henry Addington (later Lord Sidmouth) 1801–4

William Pitt the Younger 1804–6

Lord Grenville 1806–7

Duke of Portland 1807–9

Spencer Perceval 1809–12

Lord Liverpool 1812–27

George Canning 1827

Lord Goderich 1827–8

Duke of Wellington 1828–30

Lord Grey 1830–4

Lord Melbourne 1834

Robert Peel 1834–5
Lord Melbourne 1835–41
Robert Peel 1841–6
Lord John Russell 1846–52
Lord Derby 1852
Lord Aberdeen 1852–5
Lord Palmerston 1855–8
Lord Derby 1858–9
Lord Palmerston 1859–65
Lord [John] Russell (now a peer) 1865–6
Lord Derby 1866–8
Benjamin Disraeli 1868
William Gladstone 1868–74
Benjamin Disraeli (Earl of Beaconsfield from 1876) 1874–80
William Gladstone 1880–5
Lord Salisbury 1885–6
William Gladstone 1886
Lord Salisbury 1886–92
William Gladstone 1892–4
Lord Rosebery 1894–5
Lord Salisbury 1895–1902

ENDNOTES

INTRODUCTION

1   Gollin, A.M., *'The Observer' and J.L. Garvin* (Oxford University Press, Oxford: 1960), p.392.

2   See Seymour-Ure, C., *Prime Ministers and the Media* (Blackwell, Malden: 2003).

3   See Margach, J., *Abuse of Power* (W.H. Allen, London: 1978); and Price, Lance, *Where Power Lies* (Simon & Schuster, London: 2011).

4   Robinson, Sir J., *Fifty Years of Fleet Street*, edited by Thomas, F.M. (Macmillan, London: 1904), p.225.

5   Lehmann, J., *All Sir Garnet* (Jonathan Cape, London: 1964) p.307.

6   See Hunt, F.K., *The Fourth Estate* (Henry Vizetelly, London: 1850); Fox Bourne, H., *English Newspapers* Vol. 1 (Chatto and Windus, London: 1887); Andrews, A., *The History of British Journalism* (R. Bentley, London: 1859); Grant, J., *The Newspaper Press* (Vol. 2, Kessinger Legacy Reprints, printed on demand; originally published London: 1871).

7   For useful background, see Boyce, G. et al., *Newspaper History* (Constable, London: 1978).

8   Ibid., pp.120–3.

CHAPTER ONE

1   See especially Hanson, Lawrence, *The Government and the Press 1695–1763* (Oxford University Press, Oxford: 1936).

2   See especially Foot, Michael, *The Pen and the Sword* (MacGibbon & Kee, London: 1966).

3   Hanson: *The Government and the Press*.

4   Ibid.

5   Peters, M., *Pitt and Popularity* (Clarendon, Oxford: 1980) *passim.*

6   For Bute see Hannay, D., *Smollett* (Walter Scott, London: 1887), p.146. For North and Johnson see Smith, C.D., *The Early Career of Lord North* (Athlone Press, London: 1979), pp.172–5.

7   For the events leading up to Pitt the Younger's premiership, see, for example, Norris, J., *Shelburne and Reform* (Macmillan: St Martin's Press, London: 1963).

8   In Koss, S., *The Rise and Fall of the Political Press* Vol. 1 (Hamish Hamilton, London: 1981), p.36.

9   Quoted in Aspinall, Arthur, *Politics and the Press c.1780–1850* (Home and Van Thal, London: 1949), p.163.

10 Fox Bourne, H., *English Newspapers* Vol. 1 (Chatto and Windus, London: 1887), p.246.

11 *History of The Times* Vol.1 (Printing House Square, London: 1935), p.68.

12 Zamoyski, Adam, *The Last King of Poland* (Cape, London: 1992), pp.370–1.

13 William Cobbett quoted in Aspinall: *Politics and the Press*, p.75.

14 *History of The Times* Vol. 1, p.72.

15 Ibid., pp.73–4.

16 Aspinall: *Politics and the Press*, pp.284–5.

17 Wilkinson, D., *The Duke of Portland* (Palgrave Macmillan, Basingstoke: 2003), pp.21, 93.

18 Aspinall: *Politics and the Press*, pp.88 and note.

19 Gray, Denis, *Spencer Perceval* (Manchester University Press, Manchester: 1963), pp.86–8.

20 Ibid., p.132.

21 Ibid., p.134.

22 Quoted in Aspinall: *Politics and the Press*, p.91.

23 Gray: *Spencer Perceval*, p.287.

CHAPTER TWO

1   Rea, R.R., *The English Press in Politics 1760–74* (University of Nebraska Press, Lincoln: 1963), p.9.

2   *History of The Times* Vol. 1, p.128.

3   Ibid., pp.151–4.

4   Aspinall, Arthur, *Politics and the Press c.1780–1850* (Home and Van Thal, London: 1949), p.35.

5   *History of The Times* Vol. 1, p.128.

6   Ibid., pp.214–215.

7   Aspinall: *Politics and the Press*, pp.369–70.

8   See Brock, W.R., *Lord Liverpool and Liberal Toryism* (Frank Cass, London: 1967), *passim*.

9   *History of The Times* Vol. 1, p.226.

10 Aspinall: *Politics and the Press*, p.199.

11 Gash, N., *Lord Liverpool* (Weidenfeld & Nicolson, London: 1984), p.135; and Brock: *Lord Liverpool and Liberal Toryism*, pp.105–7.

12 Cookson, J.H., *Lord Liverpool's Administration 1815–1822* (Scottish Academic Press, Edinburgh: 1975), p.111.

13 Yonge, C.D., *Life and Administration of... Lord Liverpool* Vol. 1 (3 vols, Macmillan, London: 1868), pp.81–2.

14 Wickwar, W.H., *The Struggle for the Freedom of the Press* (Allen & Unwin, London: 1928), p.130.

15 Cookson: *Lord Liverpool's Administration*, p.113.

16 Downie, J.H., *Robert Harley and the Press* (Cambridge University Press, Cambridge: 1979), Conclusion *passim*.

17 *History of The Times* Vol. 1, p.144.

18 Gash: *Lord Liverpool*, p.168; *History of The Times* Vol. 1, p.215.

19 Lucas, Reginald, *Lord Glenesk and the Morning Post* (Rivers, London: 1910), pp.20–1.

20 Turner, E.S., *Unholy Pursuits* (Book Guild, London: 1998), p.109.

21 Quoted in Gash: *Lord Liverpool*, p.193.

22 Ibid., p.185.

23 Petrie, Sir Charles, *Lord Liverpool* (James Barrie, London: 1954), frontispiece.

24 *History of The Times* Vol. 1, p.153.

25 Aspinall: *Politics and the Press*, p.201.

26 *History of The Times* Vol. 1, p.218.

27 Ibid., p.244 and note.

28 Ibid.

29 Hinde, Wendy, *George Canning* (Collins, London: 1973), p.464.

30 *History of The Times* Vol. 1, p.255.

31 Aspinall: *Politics and the Press*, pp.218–19.

32 Ibid., p.371.

33 Jones, W.D., *Prosperity Robinson* (Macmillan, London: 1967), pp.198–9.

34 Longford, Elizabeth, *Wellington: Years of the Sword* (Weidenfeld and Nicolson, London: 1969), p.299; and Longford, Elizabeth, *Wellington: Pillar of State* (Weidenfeld and Nicolson, London: 1969), p.122.

35 Ibid.

36 Twiss, Horace, *Life of...Lord Eldon* Vol. 3 (3 vols, John Murray, London: 1844), p.32.

37 Aspinall: *Politics and the Press*, p.227.

38 *History of The Times* Vol. 1, p. 221.

39   Longford: *Wellington: Pillar of State*, p.180.
40   Ibid.; see also Inglis, B., 'Sir Arthur Wellesley and the Irish Press', *Hermathena* lxxxiii (1954), *passim*.
41   Longford: *Wellington: Pillar of State*, p.139.
42   Ibid., p.410.
43   Aspinall: *Politics and the Press*, pp.333–4.
44   Ibid., p.232.
45   Croker quoted in Aspinall: *Politics and the Press*, p.233.
46   See Gladstone, W.E., *Gleanings of Past Years* (7 vols, John Murray, London: 1879).
47   Pool, B. (ed.), *The Croker Papers* (Batsford, London: 1967), pp.257–8.
48   *History of The Times* Vol. 1, p. 264.
49   Ibid., p.268.
50   Ibid., p.270; and Aspinall: *Politics and the Press*, p.261.

CHAPTER THREE

1   Aspinall, Arthur, *Politics and the Press c.1780–1850* (Home and Van Thal, London: 1949), p.33.
2   Brougham.
3   *History of The Times* Vol. 1, pp. 271–2.
4   Aspinall: *Politics and the Press*, pp.174–5.
5   Ibid., p.236.
6   *History of The Times* Vol. 1, pp.276–7.
7   Ibid., p.278.
8   *The Times*, 22 December 1834.
9   Ibid.
10   *History of The Times* Vol. 1, p.232.
11   Aspinall: *Politics and the Press*, p.238.
12   *History of The Times* Vol. 1, pp.299–304.
13   Pool, B. (ed.), *The Croker Papers* (Batsford, London: 1967), pp.257–8.
14   Ibid., loc. cit.
15   Aspinall: *Politics and the Press*, p.246.
16   Ibid.
17   Ziegler, Philip, *Melbourne* (Fontana, London: 1978), p.37.
18   *Quarterly Review*, December 1839, p.302.
19   Aspinall: *Politics and the Press*, pp. 102; see also pp.239–41.
20   Koss, S., *The Rise and Fall of the Political Press* Vol. 1 (Hamish Hamilton, London: 1981), p.76.

21   Aspinall: *Politics and the Press*, pp.124, 418–20.

22   Ibid., pp.240–1.

23   *History of The Times* Vol. 1, pp.334–5.

24   Aspinall: *Politics and the Press*, p.235.

25   *The Times*, 25 June 1834.

26   *History of The Times* Vol. 1, p.356.

27   Ziegler: *Melbourne*. p.331.

28   Mitchell, L.G., *Lord Melbourne* (Oxford University Press, Oxford: 1997), pp.259–60.

Chapter Four

1   Gash, N., *Lord Liverpool* Vol. 2 (2 vols, Weidenfeld & Nicolson, London: 1984), pp.126–7.

2   Aspinall, Arthur, *Politics and the Press c.1780–1850* (Home and Van Thal, London: 1949), pp.117–121, 264–5.

3   Ibid., p.142.

4   Ibid., p.144.

5   Ibid., p.371.

6   *History of The Times* Vol. 1, p.337. Hudson, D., *Thomas Barnes of 'The Times'* (Cambridge University Press, Cambridge: 1944) is also useful on this period.

7   Ibid., p.338.

8   Ibid., p.341.

9   Ibid., pp.342–5; Aspinall: *Politics and the Press*, p.374.

10   Gash: *Lord Liverpool* Vol. 2, pp.94–5.

11   *History of The Times* Vol. 1, p.344.

12   Hudson: *Thomas Barnes of 'The Times'*, p. 83.

13   Ibid., p.348.

14   Ibid., p.350.

15   Aspinall: *Politics and the Press*, p.466.

16   Pool, B. (ed.), *The Croker Papers* (Batsford, London: 1967), pp.184–5.

17   *History of The Times* Vol. 2, p.6.

18   Koss, S., *The Rise and Fall of the Political Press* Vol. 1 (Hamish Hamilton, London: 1981), p.62.

19   *History of The Times* Vol. 2, p.12.

20   Ibid., pp.12–13.

21   Ibid.

22   Koss: *The Rise and Fall of the Political Press* Vol.1, p.64.

23   Scherer, P., *Lord John Russell* (Susquehanna University Press, Selinsgrove Pennsylvania: 1999), p.32.

24   Aspinall: *Politics and the Press*, p.247.

25   Russell's 'Recollections and Suggestions' quoted in Aspinall: *Politics and the Press*, p.383.

26   Koss: *The Rise and Fall of the Political Press* Vol. 1, p.118.

27   Ibid.

28   *History of The Times* Vol. 2, p. 192.

29   Koss: *The Rise and Fall of the Political Press* Vol. 1, p.77.

30   *History of The Times* Vol. 2, pp.109–10.

31   Ibid.

32   Greville's diary, 28 December 1852, quoted in *History of The Times* Vol. 2, p.110.

33   Ibid., p.202.

34   Ibid., pp.561–2.

35   Ibid., p.398.

36   Ibid., p.400.

CHAPTER FIVE

1   See Hawkins, A., *The Forgotten Prime Minister* (2 vols, Oxford University Press, Oxford: 2007 & 2008).

2   See, for instance, the journals of his son Lord Stanley (the 15th Earl; Vincent, J.R. ed., *Disraeli, Derby and the Conservative Party*, Harvester Press, Hassocks: 1978), and his foreign secretary Lord Malmesbury (Malmesbury, Lord, *Memoirs of an Ex-Minister*, Longmans Green & Co., London: 1884).

3   Ibid.

4   Aspinall, Arthur, *Politics and the Press c.1780–1850* (Home and Van Thal, London: 1949), p.125.

5   Hartley, J. (ed.) *Selected Letters of Charles Dickens* (Oxford University Press, Oxford: 2012), p.13 and note.

6   Aspinall: *Politics and the Press*, pp.158–9 and note.

7   Hawkins: *The Forgotten Prime Minister* Vol. 1, pp.157–8.

8   Jones, W.D., *Lord Derby and Victorian Conservatism* (Blackwell, Oxford: 1956), p.121.

9   Ed. Vincent: *Disraeli, Derby and the Conservative Party*, p.16.

10   Ibid., p.57.

11   Ibid.

12 Malmesbury: *Memoirs of an ex-Minister*, pp.400 & 213.

13 Hawkins: *The Forgotten Prime Minister* Vol. 1, p.390.

14 Stewart, R., *The Politics of Protectionism: Lord Derby and the Protectionist Party 1841–52* (Gregg Revivals, Aldershot: 1994), p.91.

15 Ibid.

16 Vincent: *Stanley Journals*, pp.60–1.

17 Ibid., p.61.

18 Jones: *Lord Derby and Victorian Conservatism*, p.180.

19 *History of The Times* Vol. 2, p.155.

20 Vincent: *Stanley Journals*, pp.72–3.

21 Stewart: *The Politics of Protectionism*, p.163.

22 Jones: *Lord Derby and Victorian Conservatism*, p.192.

23 Hawkins: *The Forgotten Prime Minister* Vol. 1, pp. 333–4.

24 Vincent: *Stanley Journals*, p.102.

25 Ibid., p.165.

26 *History of The Times* Vol. 2, p.328.

27 Greville quoted in Hawkins: *The Forgotten Prime Minister* Vol.2, p.165.

28 Hawkins: *The Forgotten Prime Minister* Vol. 2, p.183.

29 Ibid.

30 Ibid., pp.205–7.

31 Vincent: *Stanley Journals*, p.192.

32 Derby, Lord, *Translations of Poems Ancient and Modern* (John Murray, London: 1868), p.49.

33 Jones: *Lord Derby and Victorian Conservatism*, p.301.

34 Hawkins: *The Forgotten Prime Minister* Vol. 2, p.310.

35 Vincent: *Stanley Journals*, p.250.

36 Maxwell, Sir H., *Clarendon* Vol. 2 (2 vols, Edward Arnold, London: 1913), p.320.

37 *History of The Times* Vol. 2, p.405.

38 Hawkins: *The Forgotten Prime Minister* Vol. 2, p.419.

CHAPTER SIX

1 Brighton, P., 'The Shadow Behind the Throne? The Press Campaign against Prince Albert 1853–4', *European Royal History Journal* LXXXVI (Los Angeles: 2012).

2 Koss, S., *The Rise and Fall of the Political Press* Vol. 1 (Hamish Hamilton, London: 1981), p.125.

3 *Morning Journal*, 22 August 1829; *The Age*, 23 August 1829.

4   Laughton, J.K., *Memoirs of the Life of Henry Reeve* (Longman's, Green & Co., London: 1898), pp.175–6.

5   *History of The Times* Vol. 2, p. 93.

6   Ibid., p.93 and note.

7   Greville quoted in *History of The Times* Vol. 2, p.99.

8   Chamberlain, Muriel, *Lord Aberdeen* (Longmans, London: 1983), pp.300–1.

9   *History of The Times* Vol. 2, p.108.

10 Ibid., p.109.

11 Brighton: 'The Shadow Behind the Throne'.

12 Greville, 10 December 1853, quoted in *History of The Times* Vol. 2, p.115.

13 Ibid., p.116 and note.

14 Chamberlain: *Lord Aberdeen*, p.502.

15 *History of The Times* Vol. 2, p.118.

CHAPTER SEVEN

1   Koss, S., *The Rise and Fall of the Political Press* Vol. 1 (Hamish Hamilton, London: 1981), p.132; Fenton, L., *Palmerston and 'The Times'* (I.B.Tauris, London: 2012) covers some of the same ground as this book, and, although too late to be of detailed use, presents a view of Palmerston and the press with which I am in broad agreement

2   Bourne, K., *Palmerston: The Early Years* (Allen Lane, London: 1982), p.232.

3   Brown, D., *Palmerston* (Yale University Press, London: 2012), p.172.

4   Bourne: *Palmerston: The Early Years*, pp.157–8, 479ff.

5   Brown: *Palmerston*, p.185.

6   Grant, J., *The Newspaper Press* (Vol. 2, Kessinger Legacy Reprints, printed on demand, originally published London: 1871) Vol. 3, p.237.

7   Siebert quoted in Censer, J. & Popkin, J., *Press and Politics in Pre-Revolutionary France* (University of California Press, Berkeley: 1987), pp. vii–viii.

8   Bourne: *Palmerston: The Early Years*, p.483.

9   Ibid., p.481–2.

10 *History of The Times* Vol. 1, p.380.

11 Ibid., p.460.

12 Ibid., p.384.

13 Bourne: *Palmerston: The Early Years*, pp.485–6.

14 Brown: *Palmerston*, p.188.

15 Lucas, Reginald, *Lord Glenesk and the Morning Post* (Rivers, London: 1910), p.118.

16 Koss: *The Rise and Fall of the Political Press* Vol. 1, p.139.

17   Ibid., p.178.

18   Bourne: *Palmerston: The Early Years*, p.490.

19   Ibid.

20   Bell, H.C.F., *Palmerston* Vol. 1 (2 vols, Longmans, London: 1936), pp.335, 498.

21   Martin, Kingsley, *The Triumph of Lord Palmerston* (Hutchinson, London: 1963), p.83.

22   *History of The Times* Vol. 2, p.182.

23   Brighton, P., 'The Shadow Behind the Throne? The Press Campaign against Prince Albert 1853–4', *European Royal History Journal* lxxxvi (Los Angeles: 2012)

24   Ridley, Jasper, *Palmerston* (Panther, London: 1972), p.572.

25   Chambers, James, *Palmerston* (John Murray, London: 2004), p.378.

26   Ridley: *Palmerston*, p.708.

27   *History of The Times* Vol. 2, p.254.

28   Ibid., pp.257–8.

29   Laughton, J.K., *Memoirs of the Life of Henry Reeve* (Longman's, Green & Co., London: 1898), p.338.

30   *History of The Times* Vol. 2, p.262.

31   Ibid., p.264.

32   Ibid., loc. cit.

33   Ibid., loc. cit.

34   Ibid., p.267.

35   Ibid., p.202.

36   Robinson, Sir J.R., *Fifty Years of Fleet Street,* edited by Thomas, F. M. (Macmillan, London: 1904), p.225.

37   Grant, J., *The Newspaper Press* (Vol. 2, Kessinger Legacy Reprints, printed on demand, originally published London: 1871), pp.215–16.

38   *History of The Times* Vol. 2, pp.334–5.

39   Ibid., p.337.

40   Ibid., p.343.

41   Lucas: *Lord Glenesk and the Morning Post*, pp.152–3.

42   Ibid., p.153.

CHAPTER EIGHT

1   Blake, Robert, *Disraeli* (Eyre & Spottiswoode, London: 1967), p.26.

2   Gordon, Sir A., *Lord Aberdeen* (Sampson Low, Marston & Co., London: 1893).

3   Monypenny, W.F. & Buckle, G.E., *The Life of Benjamin Disraeli* Vol. 1 (2 vols, John Murray, London: 1929) , p.78.

4   Ibid., p.87.

5   Ridley, Jane, *The Young Disraeli* (Sinclair-Stevenson, London: 1995), p.47.

6   Blake: *Disraeli*, p.44.

7   Bradford, Sarah, *Disraeli* (Grafton, London: 1985), p.84.

8   Ridley: *The Young Disraeli*, pp.164–6.

9   Bradford: *Disraeli*, pp.127–8.

10 Ibid., p.128.

11 Weintraub, Stanley, *Disraeli* (Hamish Hamilton, London: 1993), p.163.

12 Monypenny and Buckle (hereafter M & B): *The Life of Benjamin Disraeli* Vol. 1, pp.336–7.

13 *History of The Times* Vol. 1, p.441.

14 Bradford: *Disraeli*, p.132.

15 Blake: *Disraeli*, p.162.

16 Ibid.

17 M & B: *The Life of Benjamin Disraeli* Vol. 1, pp.507–8.

18 Ibid., p.566.

19 Bradford: *Disraeli*, pp.190–1.

20 Ridley: *The Young Disraeli*, p.291.

21 Ibid., p.290.

22 Bradford: *Disraeli*, p.271.

23 Vincent, J.R. ed., *Disraeli, Derby and the Conservative Party*, Harvester Press, Hassocks: 1978, p.8.

24 Ibid., p.9.

25 Ibid., p.16.

26 Ibid., p.57.

27 Ibid., loc. cit.

28 Ibid., p.73.

29 Blake: *Disraeli*, pp.352–3.

30 Ibid., p.354.

31 Vincent: *Stanley Journals*, p.102.

32 Ibid., p.125.

33 M & B: *The Life of Benjamin Disraeli* Vol. 1, p.1312.

34 Ibid., p.1314.

35 Weintraub: *Disraeli*, p.331.

36 Ibid., loc. cit.

37 M & B: *The Life of Benjamin Disraeli* Vol. 1, p.1322.

38 Bradford: *Disraeli*, p.321.

39 Cook, Sir E., *Delane of The Times* (Constable & Co., London: 1915), p.182.

40   Blake: *Disraeli*, pp.163–4.

41   Cook: *Delane of The Times*, p.187.

42   Ibid., p.59.

43   Ibid., pp.96–7.

44   Vincent: *Stanley Journals*, pp.165, 168.

45   Koss, S., *The Rise and Fall of the Political Press* Vol. 1 (Hamish Hamilton, London: 1981), p.150.

46   Vincent: *Stanley Journals*, p.192.

47   Koss: *The Rise and Fall of the Political Press* Vol. 1, p.151.

48   Ibid., pp.152–5.

49   Vincent: *Stanley Journals*, p.241.

50   Cook: *Delane of The Times*, p.287.

51   *The Times*, 26 February 1868.

52   *History of The Times* Vol. 2, pp.406–7.

53   Ibid., p.407.

54   Koss: *The Rise and Fall of the Political Press* Vol. 1, p.199.

55   Ibid., pp.204–5.

56   Ibid., pp.205–6.

57   Cook: *Delane of The Times*, p.245.

58   Ibid., p.246.

59   Koss: *The Rise and Fall of the Political Press*, p.207.

60   Ibid., p.211.

61   Ibid., loc. cit.

62   Cook: *Delane of The Times*, pp.175–6; see also Dasent, A.I., *Delane* Vol. 2 (2 vols, John Murray, London: 1908).

63   *History of The Times* Vol. 2, p.521.

64   Ibid., loc. cit.

65   Koss: *The Rise and Fall of the Political Press*, p.215.

CHAPTER NINE

1   Matthew, H.C.G., *Gladstone* Vol. 1 (2 vols, Oxford University Press, Oxford: 1986–90), p.135.

2   Shannon, R., *Gladstone* Vol. 1 (2 vols, Hamish Hamilton, London: 1982; Allen Lane, London: 1999), p.12.

3   Koss, S., *The Rise and Fall of the Political Press* Vol. 1 (Hamish Hamilton, London: 1981), p.255; for Derby, see Kebbel, T.E., *Derby* (W.H. Allen & Co., London: 1890).

4   Morley, J., *Life of Gladstone* Vol. 1 (2 vols, Macmillan, London: 1905), p.32.

5   Matthew: *Gladstone* Vol. 1, p.55.
6   Morley: *Life of Gladstone* Vol.1, p.38.
7   Ibid., p.71.
8   Shannon: *Gladstone* Vol.1, p.430.
9   Cook, Sir E., *Delane of The Times* (Constable & Co., London: 1915), pp.150–1.
10   Ibid., loc. cit.
11   Shannon: *Gladstone* Vol.1, p.313.
12   Stansky, P., *Gladstone: A Progress in Politics* (Norton, New York: 1979).
13   Koss: *The Rise and Fall of the Political Press* Vol. 1, p.168.
14   Ibid., pp.114–15.
15   Ibid., loc.cit.
16   Ibid., pp.176–7.
17   *History of The Times* Vol. 2, pp.408–9.
18   Gladstone, William Ewart, *The Gladstone Diaries*, edited by Foot, M.R.D. and Matthew, C., Vol. 6 (13 vols, Oxford University Press, Oxford: 1968–94), pp.364–73.
19   Koss: *The Rise and Fall of the Political Press* Vol. 1, p.175.
20   Ibid., p.201.
21   Ibid., p.211.
22   Shannon: *Gladstone* Vol. 1, p.539.
23   Ibid., pp.511–12, 539–40.
24   Shannon: *Gladstone* Vol. 2, pp.89–90.
25   Ibid., p.169.
26   Ibid., loc. cit.
27   Matthew: *Gladstone* Vol. 2, pp.44–5.
28   Feuchtwanger, E.J., *Gladstone* (Allen Lane, London: 1975), p.192.
29   Shannon: *Gladstone* Vol. 2, pp.48–50.
30   Ibid., loc. cit.
31   Ibid., p.300.
32   Koss: *The Rise and Fall of the Political Press* Vol. 2, p.334.
33   Feuchtwanger: *Gladstone*, pp.232–3.
34   Ibid., pp.276–7.
35   Gladstone, Herbert, *After Thirty Years* (Macmillan, London: 1928), p.312.
36   Ibid., p.313.
37   Ibid., loc. cit.
38   Magnus, P., *Gladstone* (John Murray, London: 1954), p.344.
39   *Pall Mall Gazette*, 24 February 1885.
40   Koss: *The Rise and Fall of the Political Press* Vol. 1, p.262.
41   Ibid., pp.265–8.
42   Jenkins, R., *Gladstone* (Macmillan, Basingstoke: 1995), pp.225–6.

43   Koss: *The Rise and Fall of the Political Press* Vol. 1, p.293.

44   Ibid., p.321.

45   Thompson, J. Lee, *Northcliffe* (John Murray, London: 2000), pp.16–17 & 400.

CHAPTER TEN

1   Roberts, A., *Salisbury* (Weidenfeld & Nicolson, London: 1999), p. 37.

2   Ibid., p.38.

3   Ibid., p.49.

4   Steele, D., *Lord Salisbury* (Routledge, London: 2001), p.41.

5   Ibid., p.73.

6   Ibid., pp.35–6.

7   Ibid., loc. cit.

8   Ibid., loc. cit.

9   Koss, S., *The Rise and Fall of the Political Press* Vol. 1 (Hamish Hamilton, London: 1981), pp.9–10.

10   Steele: *Lord Salisbury*, p.35.

11   Roberts: *Salisbury*, pp.310–13.

12   Koss: *The Rise and Fall of the Political Press* Vol. 1, pp.368–9.

13   Ibid., pp.327–8.

14   Lang, A., *Sir Stafford Northcote, Lord Iddesleigh* (Blackwell, Edinburgh: 1891), pp.82, 127, 404.

15   Ibid., p.315.

16   Koss: *The Rise and Fall of the Political Press* Vol. 1, p.222.

17   Lang: *Sir Stafford Northcote*, p.394.

18   Roberts: *Salisbury*, p.426.

19   Ibid., p.315.

20   Ibid., p.411.

21   *History of The Times* Vol. 3, p.781.

22   Roberts: *Salisbury*, p.416.

23   Ibid., pp.452–5.

24   E. Hamilton, quoted in Koss: *The Rise and Fall of the Political Press* Vol. 1, p.287.

25   McKinstry, L., *Rosebery* (John Murray, London: 2005), p.36.

26   Koss: *The Rise and Fall of the Political Press* Vol. 1, p.191.

27   Ibid., pp.282–3.

28   McKinstry: *Rosebery*, p.210.

29   Ibid., p.183.

30   Koss: *The Rise and Fall of the Political Press* Vol.1, p.350.

31   Ibid., p.322.

32   See Gardiner, A.G., *Sir William Harcourt* (2 vols, Constable & Co., London: 1923) *passim*.

33   Jackson, P., *Harcourt and Son* (Fairleigh Dickinson University Press, Madison, New Jersey: 2004), p.95.

34   Koss: *The Rise and Fall of the Political Press* Vol.1, p.353.

35   Ibid., p.351.

36   Koss: *The Rise and Fall of the Political Press* Vol. 1, pp.365–6.

37   McKinstry: *Rosebery*, p.390.

38   Ibid., p.393.

39   Koss: *The Rise and Fall of the Political Press* Vol. 1, p.407.

CONCLUSION

1   Downie, J., *Robert Harley and the Press* (Cambridge University Press, Cambridge: 1979), Conclusion *passim*.

Select Bibliography

Among the MS sources consulted were the Liverpool Papers and Gladstone Papers in the British Library, and the Fowler Papers in Wolverhampton City Archives. All of the newspapers quoted from in the text were consulted, where available, online.

Aldous, Richard, *The Lion and the Unicorn* (Pimlico, London: 2007)

Andrews, A., *The History of British Journalism* (R. Bentley, London: 1859)

Aspinall, Arthur, *Politics and the Press, c. 1780–1850* (Home & Van Thal, London: 1949)

Ayling, Stanley, *The Elder Pitt* (Collins, London: 1976)

Bell, H.C.F., *Palmerston* (2 vols, Longmans, London: 1936)

Bew, J., *Castlereagh* (Quercus, London: 2011)

Black, Jeremy, *Pitt the Elder* (Cambridge University Press, Cambridge: 1992)

——, *The English Press 1621–1861* (Sutton, Stroud: 2001)

Blake, Robert, *Disraeli* (Eyre and Spottiswoode, London: 1967)

Bourne, K., *Palmerston: the Early Years* (Allen Lane, London: 1982)

Bourne, Richard, *Lords of Fleet Street* (Unwin Hyman, London: 1990)

Boyce, G. et al., *Newspaper History* (Constable, London: 1978)

Bradford, Sarah, *Disraeli* (Grafton, London: 1985)

Brett, M. (ed.), *Journals and Letters of Reginald Viscount Esher* (London: 1934–8)

Brighton, Paul D.J., 'The Shadow behind the Throne? The Press Campaign against Prince Albert 1853–4', *European Royal History Journal* LXXXVI (Los Angeles: 2012)

——, 'A Sign of "*The Times*": The Thunderer and the Marriage of Prince Frederick William and Princess Victoria', *European Royal History Journal* LXXXVIII (Los Angeles: 2012)

Brock, W.R., *Lord Liverpool and Liberal Toryism* (Frank Cass, London: 1967)

Brougham, H., *Life and Times Written by Himself* (3 vols, Blackwood, London: 1871)

Brown, D. A., *Palmerston* (Yale University Press, London: 2012)

Brown, P.D., *The Chathamites* (Macmillan, London: 1967)

——, *William Pitt Earl of Chatham* (Allen and Unwin, London: 1978)

Browning, Reed, *The Duke of Newcastle* (Yale University Press, London: 1979)

Cecil, David, *Melbourne* (The Reprint Society, London: 1955)

Censer, J. and Popkin, J., *Press and Politics in Pre-Revolutionary France* (University of California Press, Berkeley: 1987)

Chamberlain, Muriel, *Lord Aberdeen* (Longmans, London: 1983)

Chambers, James, *Palmerston* (John Murray, London: 2004)

Christie, Ian, *The End of North's Ministry* (Macmillan, London: 1958)

Clarke, Sir Edward, *The Story of My Life* (John Murray, London: 1918)

Clive, John, *Scotch Reviewers: the 'Edinburgh Review' 1802–15* (Faber, London: 1957)

——, *Thomas Babington Macaulay* (Secker and Warburg, London: 1973)

Conacher, J.B., *The Peelites and the Party System* (David and Charles, Newton Abbott: 1972)

Cook, Sir E., *Delane of The Times* (Constable & Co., London: 1915)

Cookson, J.E., *Lord Liverpool's Administration 1815–1822* (Scottish Academic Press, Edinburgh: 1975)

Crewe, Lord, *Lord Rosebery* (2 vols, John Murray, London: 1931)

Dasent, A.I., *Delane* (2 vols, John Murray, London: 1908)

Derby, Lord, *Translations of Poems: Ancient and Modern* (John Murray, London: 1868)

Disraeli, Benjamin, *Letters to Lady Bradford and Lady Chesterfield* (2 vols, Ernest Benn, London: 1929)

Downie, J.A., *Robert Harley and the Press* (Cambridge University Press, Cambridge: 1979)

——, 'The Development of the Political Press', in Jones, C. (ed.), *Britain in the First Age of Party 1680–1750* (Hambledon, London: 1987)

Earle, Peter, *Daniel Defoe* (Weidenfeld and Nicolson, London: 1976)

Egremont, Max, *Balfour* (Collins, London: 1980)

Ehrman, John, *The Younger Pitt* (3 vols, Constable, London: 1969, 1983, 1996)

Feiling, Keith, *The First Tory Party* (Clarendon, Oxford: 1950)

Fenton, L., *Palmerston and 'The Times'* (I.B. Tauris, London: 2012)

Ferris, P., *The House of Northcliffe* (Weidenfeld and Nicolson, London: 1971)

Feuchtwanger, E.J. *Gladstone* (Macmillan, Basingstoke: 1959)

Foot, Michael, *The Pen and the Sword* (MacGibbon and Kee, London: 1966)

Foster, R.F., *Lord Randolph Churchill* (Oxford University Press, Oxford: 1988)

Fox Bourne, Henry, *English Newspapers* (Vol.1, Chatto and Windus, London: 1887)

Fraser, P., *Lord Esher* (Hart-Davis, MacGibbon, London: 1973)

Gardiner, A.G., *Sir William Harcourt* (2 vols, Constable, London: 1923)

Garvin, J.L. and Amery, Leo, *Joseph Chamberlain* (6 vols, Macmillan, London: 1932–69)

Gash, Norman, *Mr Secretary Peel* (Longmans, London: 1961)

——, *Lord Liverpool* (Weidenfeld and Nicolson, London: 1984)

Gash, Norman, *Sir Robert Peel* (Longmans, London: 1986)

Gladstone, Herbert, *After Thirty Years* (Macmillan, London: 1928)

Gladstone, W.E., *Gleanings of Past Years* (7 vols, John Murray, London: 1879)

——, *Later Gleanings* (John Murray, London: 1897)

——, *The Gladstone Diaries*, edited by Foot, M.R.D. and Matthew, C. (13 vols, Oxford University Press, Oxford: 1968–94)

Gollin, A.M., *'The Observer' and J.L. Garvin* (Oxford University Press, Oxford: 1960)

Gordon, Sir A., *Lord Aberdeen* (Sampson Low, Marston & Co., London: 1893)

Gore, J. (ed.), *The Creevey Papers* (The Folio Society, London: 1970)

Grafton, Duke of, *Memoirs*, edited by Anson, Sir W. (John Murray, London: 1898)

Grant, James, *The Newspaper Press* (3 vols, Kessinger Legacy Reprints, printed on demand, originally London 1871)

Gray, Denis, *Spencer Perceval* (Manchester University Press, Manchester: 1963)

Guedalla, Philip, *The Duke* (Hodder and Stoughton, London: 1931)

Hague, William, *William Pitt the Younger* (Harper Collins, London: 2004)

Hamilton, E., *The Backstairs Dragon* (Taplinger, Michigan: 1969)

Hammond, J.L. LeB., *Charles James Fox* (Methuen, London: 1903)

Hannay, David, *Smollett* (Walter Scott, London: 1887)

Hanson, Lawrence, *Government and the Press 1695–1763* (Oxford University Press, Oxford: 1936)

Hardman, J., *Louis XVI* (Arnold, London: 2000)

Harris, Robert, *A Patriot Press* (Clarendon Press, Oxford: 1993)

——, *Politics and the Rise of the Press* (Routledge, London: 1996)

Hartley, Jenny (ed.), *Selected Letters of Charles Dickens* (Oxford University Press, Oxford: 2012)

Hawkins, Angus, *The Forgotten Prime Minister* (2 vols, Oxford University Press, Oxford: 2007 and 2008)

Healey, G.H. (ed.), *The Letters of Daniel Defoe* (Oxford University Press, Oxford: 1955)

Hibbert, Christopher, *The Destruction of Lord Raglan* (Penguin, Harmondsworth: 1965)

——, *Wellington* (Harper Collins, London: 1998)

Hill, B.W., *Sir Robert Walpole* (Hamilton, London: 1989)

Hinde, Wendy, *George Canning* (Collins, London: 1973)

History of The Times (Vols 1–3, Printing House Square, London: 1935, 1939 and 1947)

Hoffman, R.J.S., *The Marquis* (Fordham University Press, New York: 1973)

Holmes, Richard, *Marlborough* (Harper Press, London: 2008)

Hudson, D., *A Poet in Parliament* (John Murray, London: 1939)

——, *Thomas Barnes of 'The Times'* (Cambridge University Press, Cambridge: 1944)

Hunt, F.K., *The Fourth Estate* (2 vols, Henry Vizetelly, London: 1850)

Hurd, Douglas, *Robert Peel* (Weidenfeld and Nicolson, London: 2007)

Inglis, B., 'Sir Arthur Wellesley and the Irish Press', *Hermathena* LXXXIII (1954)

Jackson, P., *Harcourt and Son* (Fairleigh Dickinson University Press, Madison NJ: 2004)

James, Robert Rhodes, *Rosebery* (Weidenfeld and Nicolson, London: 1963)

——, *Lord Randolph Churchill* (Hamilton, London: 1988)

Jenkins, R., *Gladstone* (Macmillan, Basingstoke: 1995)

Jones, Kennedy, *Fleet Street and Downing Street* (Hutchinson & Co., London: 1920)

Jones, W.D., *Lord Derby and Victorian Conservatism* (Blackwell, Oxford: 1956)

——, *Prosperity Robinson* (Macmillan, London: 1967)

Judd, Denis, *Radical Joe* (Hamilton, London: 1977)

Jupp, Peter, *Lord Grenville* (Clarendon, Oxford: 1985)

Kebbel, T.E., *Life of the Earl of Derby* (W. H. Allen & Co., London: 1890)

Kelch, Roy, *A Duke without Money* (Routledge and Kegan Paul, London: 1974)

Kemp, Betty, *Walpole* (Weidenfeld and Nicolson, London: 1976)

Kennedy, A.L., *Salisbury* (John Murray, London: 1953)

Kitson Clark, G., *Peel and the Conservative Party* (Frank Cass, London: 1964)

Koss, Stephen, *The Rise and Fall of the Political Press in Britain* (2 vols, Hamish Hamilton, London: 1981 & 1984)

Lang, Andrew, *Sir Stafford Northcote, Lord Iddesleigh* (William Blackwood, Edinburgh: 1891)

Laughton, J.K., *Memoirs of the Life of Henry Reeve* (Longman's, Green and Co., London: 1898)

Lawson, P., *George Grenville* (Clarendon, Oxford: 1984)

Lehman, J., *All Sir Garnet* (Jonathan Cape, London: 1964)

Longford, Elizabeth, *Wellington: Years of the Sword* (Weidenfeld and Nicolson, London: 1969)

——, *Wellington: Pillar of State* (Weidenfeld and Nicolson, London: 1972)

Lever, Tresham, *Godolphin* (John Murray, London: 1955)

Lucas, Reginald, *Lord Glenesk and the Morning Post* (Rivers, London: 1910)

Mackay, Ruddock, *Fisher of Kilverstone* (Oxford University Press, Oxford: 1973)

Magnus, Philip, *Gladstone* (John Murray, London: 1954)

Malmesbury, Lord, *Memoirs of an Ex-Minister* (Longmans Green & Co., London: 1884)

Margach, J., *The Abuse of Power* (W.H. Allen, London: 1978)

Martelli, G., *Jemmy Twitcher* (Jonathan Cape, London: 1962)

Martin, Kingsley, *The Triumph of Lord Palmerston* (Hutchinson, London: 1963)

Matthew, H.C.G., *Gladstone* (2 vols, Oxford University Press, Oxford: 1986, 1990)

Maxwell, Sir H., *Clarendon* (2 vols, Edward Arnold, London: 1913)

McKinstry, Leo, *Rosebery* (John Murray, London: 2005)

Mitchell, L.G., *Lord Melbourne* (Oxford University Press, Oxford: 1997)

Monypenny, W.F. & Buckle, G.E., *The Life of Benjamin Disraeli* (2 vols, John Murray, London: 1929)

Morgan, K.O., *Keir Hardie* (Weidenfeld and Nicolson, London: 1975)

Morley, John, *Life of Gladstone* (2 vols, Macmillan, London: 1905)

Newman, Bertram, *Lord Melbourne* (Macmillan, London: 1930)

Nokes, David, *Jonathan Swift:A Hypocrite Reversed* (Oxford University Press, Oxford: 1987)

Norris, J., *Shelburne and Reform* (Macmillan: St Martin's Press, London: 1963)

Pearce, Edward, *The Great Man* (Jonathan Cape, London: 2007)

——, *Pitt the Elder* (Pimlico, London: 2011)

Pemberton, W.B., *Cobbett* (Penguin, London: 1949)

——, *Lord Palmerston* (Batchworth Press, London: 1954)

Peters, M., *Pitt and Popularity* (Clarendon, Oxford: 1980)

Petrie, Sir Charles, *Canning* (Eyre & Spottiswoode, London: 1946)

——, *Lord Liverpool* (James Barrie, London: 1954)

——, *George Canning* (Eyre and Spottiswoode, London: 1946)

Plumb, Jack, *Walpole* (2 vols, Cresset Press, London: 1956, 1960)

Pool, B. (ed.), *The Croker Papers* (Batsford, London: 1967)

Pound, R. and Harmsworth, G., *Northcliffe* (Cassell, London: 1959)

Prest, J., *Lord John Russell* (Macmillan, London: 1972)

Price, Lance, *Where Power Lies* (Simon & Schuster, London: 2011)

Rea, Robert R., *The English Press in Politics, 1760–1774* (University of Nebraska Press, Lincoln: 1963)

Reid, Stuart, *Lord John Russell* (Sampson Low, Marston & Co., London: 1895)

Ridley, Jane, *TheYoung Disraeli* (Sinclair-Stevenson, London: 1995)

Ridley, Jasper, *Palmerston* (Panther, London: 1972)

Robbins, K., *John Bright* (Routledge and Kegan Paul, London: 1979)

Roberts, Andrew, *Salisbury* (Weidenfeld and Nicolson, London: 1999)

Robinson, Sir J.R., *Fifty Years of Fleet Street*, edited by Thomas, F.M. (Macmillan, London: 1904)

Rodger, N.A.M., *The Insatiable Earl* (Harper Collins, London: 1993)

Roe, N., *Fiery Heart: The First Life of Leigh Hunt* (Pimlico, London: 2005)

Russell, Lord John, *Recollections and Suggestions 1813–73* (Longman's Green & Co., London: 1875)

Ryan, A.P., *Lord Northcliffe* (Collins, London: 1953)

Saintsbury, G., *The Earl of Derby* (Sampson Low, Marston & Co., London: 1892)

Scherer, P., *Lord John Russell* (Susquehanna University Press, Selinsgrove, Pennsylvania: 1999)

Schweizer, K.W., 'Lord Bute and the Press', in Schweizer, K.W. (ed.), *Lord Bute: Essays in Re-interpretation* (Leicester University Press, Leicester: 1988)

Seymour-Ure, C., *Prime Ministers and the Media* (Blackwell, Malden: 2003)

Shannon, Richard, *Gladstone* (2 vols, Hamilton, London: 1982; Allen Lane, London: 1999)

Sherrard, O.A., *Lord Chatham* (3 vols, Bodley Head, London: 1952, 1955, 1958)

Smeaton, Oliphant, *Tobias Smollett* (Oliphant Anderson & Ferrier, Edinburgh: 1897)

Smith, C.D., *The Early Career of Lord North* (Athlone Press, London: 1979)

Smith, E.A., *Lord Grey* (Alan Sutton, Stroud: 1996)

Somerset, Anne, *Queen Anne* (Harper, London: 2012)

Sommer, Dudley, *Haldane of Cloan* (George Allen & Unwin, London: 1960)

Spender, J.A., *Campbell-Bannerman* (2 vols, Hodder and Stoughton, London: 1923)

——, *Life, Journalism and Politics* (2 vols, Cassell and Co., London: 1927)

Stansky, Peter, *Gladstone: A Progress in Politics* (Norton, New York: 1979)

Steele, D., *Lord Salisbury* (Routledge, London: 2001)

Steinberg, Jonathan, *Bismarck* (Oxford University Press, Oxford: 2011)

Stevens, D.H., *Party Politics and English Journalism, 1702–1742* (Banton Menasha, Wisconsin, USA: 1916)

Stewart, R., *The Politics of Protection: Lord Derby and the Protectionist Party 1841–52* (Gregg Revivals, Aldershot: 1994)

Storey, Graham, *Reuters' Century* (Max Parrish, London: 1951)

Sweetman, J., *Raglan* (Arms and Armour, London: 1993)

Swift, Jonathan, *Journal to Stella* (George Routledge, London: 1906)

Thomas, P.D.G., *Lord North* (Allen Lane, London: 1976)

Thompson, J. Lee, *Northcliffe* (John Murray, London: 2000)

Trevelyan, George Otto, *The Early History of Charles James Fox* (Longmans, Green & Co., London: 1880)

Tunstall, Brian, *William Pitt, Earl of Chatham* (Hodder and Stoughton, London: 1938)

Turner, E.S., *Unholy Pursuits* (Book Guild, London: 1998)

Turner, M.J., *Pitt the Younger* (Hambledon, London: 2003)

Twiss, Horace, *Life of … Lord Eldon* (3 vols, John Murray, London: 1844)

Vincent, J.R. (ed.), *Disraeli, Derby and the Conservative Party: the Political Journals of Lord Stanley 1849 to 1869* (Harvester Press, Hassocks: 1978)

Walpole, S., *Lord John Russell* (2 vols, Longmans, Green & Co., London: 1891)

Weintraub, Stanley, *Disraeli* (Hamish Hamilton, London: 1993)

White, R.J., *Waterloo to Peterloo* (Penguin, Harmondsworth: 1968)

Wickwar, W.H., *The Struggle for the Freedom of the Press* (G. Allen & Unwin Ltd., London, 1928)

Wilkinson, D., *The Duke of Portland* (Palgrave Macmillan, Basingstoke: 2003)

Williams, Basil, *William Pitt* (2 vols, Longmans Green, London: 1913)

Wilson, John, *C. B.* (Constable, London: 1973)

Wilson, P.W. (ed.), *The Greville Diary* (William Heinemann, London: 1927)

Winstanley, D.A., *Chatham and the Whig Opposition* (Cambridge University Press, Cambridge: 1912)

Yonge, Charles Duke, *Life and Administration of ... Earl of Liverpool* (3 vols, Macmillan, London: 1868)

Young, Kenneth, *Arthur James Balfour* (G. Bell, London: 1963)

Zamoyski, Adam, *The Last King of Poland* (Cape, London: 1992)

Ziegler, Philip, *Addington* (Collins, London: 1965)

——, *Melbourne* (Fontana, London: 1978)

INDEX

Numbers in **bold** refer to specific chapters about the entry.